Washington Matthews

Ethnography and Philology of the Hidatsa Indians

Washington Matthews

Ethnography and Philology of the Hidatsa Indians

ISBN/EAN: 9783337061920

Printed in Europe, USA, Canada, Australia, Japan

Cover: Foto ©Thomas Meinert / pixelio.de

More available books at **www.hansebooks.com**

DEPARTMENT OF THE INTERIOR.

UNITED STATES GEOLOGICAL AND GEOGRAPHICAL SURVEY.

F. V. HAYDEN, U. S. GEOLOGIST-IN-CHARGE.

MISCELLANEOUS PUBLICATIONS.—No. 7.

ETHNOGRAPHY AND PHILOLOGY

OF THE

HIDATSA INDIANS.

BY

WASHINGTON MATTHEWS,
ASSISTANT SURGEON UNITED STATES ARMY.

WASHINGTON:
GOVERNMENT PRINTING OFFICE.
1877.

PREFATORY NOTE.

UNITED STATES GEOLOGICAL AND
GEOGRAPHICAL SURVEY OF THE TERRITORIES,
Washington, D. C., June 10, 1877.

During the year 1854, while engaged in exploring the then almost
unknown country along the Upper Missouri and its tributaries, the
writer of this note commenced the work of collecting vocabularies of the
languages and other ethnological data respecting the Indians of the
Northwest. He continued this work at intervals during a period of
about six years, and the materials thus accumulated were finally published
in 1862 in the "Transactions" of the American Philosophical Society
of Philadelphia, under the title of "Contributions to the Ethnography
and Philology of the Indian Tribes of the Missouri Valley". A brief
sketch of the Hidatsa Indians, and an incomplete vocabulary of their
language, was included in that work.

The author of the present volume, Dr. Washington Matthews, assistant surgeon United States Army, spent some years among these Indians while stationed at a military post in performance of his official duties as a medical officer of the Army. During this period he paid great
attention to the same subject, observing the manners, customs, and
other characteristics of these Indians, and making a close and careful
study of their language. In this way were secured the materials upon
which, elaborated with the utmost care and with conspicuous ability,
the present important memoir is based.

Dr. Matthews's earlier studies of the subject resulted in a Hidatsa-
English and English-Hidatsa vocabulary, prefaced by an essay on the
grammatical structure of the language. A small edition (100 copies) was
printed by Mr. J. G. Shea as one of his series of American Linguistics.
At the request of the writer,—who earnestly desired to push to comple-
tion the work he had long since undertaken, but was compelled by pressure of other engagements to suspend,—Dr. Matthews spent much time
in entirely remodeling and greatly enlarging the scope of his paper, to
include the ethnography as well as the philology of the tribe. His final
result is herewith presented.

Besides revising and adding much new matter to the vocabularies, Dr.
Matthews has here made those other important additions, without which
the article could hardly have been considered monographic. The whole
of the "ethnography" and "philology" are new. The manner in which
the work has been accomplished reflects great credit upon the author
and upon the Medical corps of the Army, whose capacity for scientific
work Dr. Matthews honorably illustrates in his own person. Of the
value of the work as a contribution to American Ethnology, little need

be said; I regard it as the most important memoir on our aboriginal Indian languages which has appeared since the Dakota grammar and dictionary, by Rev. S. R. Riggs, was published by the Smithsonian Institution.

It was originally intended to publish this treatise as a portion of a general work on Indian ethnography now in course of preparation by the undersigned. The delay in its appearance which such course would entail, and the great merit of the work here accomplished, render it desirable, in justice both to the author and to the subject, that it should appear as a separate publication.

As circumstances rendered it impossible for the author to attend personally to the work during its passage through the press, the duty of superintending its publication devolved upon Dr. Elliott Coues, U. S. A., to whom the thanks of the Survey are due for the careful manner in which he has accomplished the task.

F. V. HAYDEN,
United States Geologist.

TABLE OF CONTENTS.

ETHNOGRAPHY.

PHILOLOGY.

ETHNOGRAPHY.

ETHNOGRAPHY.

PART I.

THE VILLAGE AT FORT BERTHOLD, AND ITS INHABITANTS.

§ 1.—The Hidatsa, Minnetaree, or Grosventre Indians, are one of the three tribes which at present inhabit the permanent village at Fort Berthold, Dakota Territory, and hunt on the waters of the Upper Missouri and Yellowstone Rivers, in Northwestern Dakota and Eastern Montana.

The history of this tribe is so intimately connected with that of the politically-allied tribes of the Aricarees and Mandans that we cannot well give an account of one without making some mention of the others. In this first part of the Ethnography, all the tribes are included.

§ 2. LOCATION.—An arid prairie-terrace, some four miles wide, stretching southward to the Missouri from the base of bluffs which form the edge of a higher plain, becomes gradually narrower as it approaches the river, and terminates in a steep bluff of soft rock and lignite which overhangs the river. On the southern extremity of this terrace, near the brow of the bluff, stand the Indian village, and what remains, since a recent fire, of the old trading-post of Fort Berthold. This is on the left bank of the Missouri, in latitude 47° 34′ north, and longitude 101° 48′ west, nearly. About five years ago, a large reservation was declared for them in Dakota and Montana, along the Missouri and Yellowstone Rivers. Fort Berthold is in the northeast corner of this reservation.

§ 3. DWELLINGS.—The village consists of a number of

houses* built very closely together, without any attempt at
regularity of position. The doors face in every possible direction; and there is great uniformity in the appearance of the
lodges; so it is a very difficult matter to find one's way among
them.

Old-style lodges.—Most of the houses of the village were
in 1865 peculiar, large, earth-covered lodges, such as were
built by various tribes of Indians of the plains, in the valley
of the Missouri, and so often, with varying accuracy, described
by travelers.† Each one of these lodges consists of a wooden
frame, covered with willows, hay, and earth. A hole in the
top, which lets in the light and lets out the smoke, and a door-
way on one side, are the only apertures in the building. The
door is made of raw-hide stretched on a frame, or of puncheons,
and it is protected by a narrow shed or entry from six to ten feet
long. Over the smoke-holes of many of the lodges are placed
frames of wicker-work, on which skins are spread to the windward in stormy weather to keep the lodges from getting smoky.
Sometimes bull-boats are used for this purpose. On the site
of a proposed lodge, they often dig down a foot or more, in
order to find earth compact enough to form a good floor; so,
in some lodges, the floors are lower than the general surface of
the ground on which the village stands. The floor is of earth,

---

* In the fall of 1872, Dr. C. E. McChesney, then physician at the Berthold
agency, counted, with great care, the buildings in the village, and, in a letter, gave
me the following results:—

Old-style (round) lodges of Rees	43
Log-cabins of Rees	28
Total number of houses of Rees	71
Old-style lodges of Grosventres and Mandans	35
Log-cabins of Grosventres and Mandans	69
Total number of houses of Grosventres and Mandans	104
Total of houses in village	175

He remarks:—" I could not separate the Grosventres from the Mandans, owing to the
stupidity of the interpreter. If anything, this number is under, certainly not over ;
but it does not vary more than ten."—Some five or six houses, occupied by white men
with Indian families, were probably not included in this enumeration.

† Lewis and Clarke, pp. 73, 78.—Gass, pp. 72, 73.—Maximilian, p. **343.**—De
Smet, pp. 76-77, and others.—Compare with descriptions of Kanzas, Omaha, and
Pawnee lodges in *Long's expedition*, pp. 120, 200, 436.

and has in its center a circular depression, for a fire-place, about a foot deep, and three or four feet wide, with an edging of flat rocks. These dwellings, being from thirty to forty feet in diameter, from ten to fifteen feet high in the center, and from five to seven feet high at the eaves, are quite commodious. The labor of constructing them is performed mostly by the women; but, in lifting and setting the heavier beams, the men assist. If, with the aid of steel axes obtained from the whites, the task of building such a house is no easy one at this day, how difficult it must have been a century ago, when the stone ax was their best implement, and when the larger logs had to be burned through in order that pieces of suitable length might be obtained!

The frame of a lodge is thus made:—A number of stout posts, from ten to fifteen, according to the size of the lodge, and rising to the height of about five feet above the surface of the earth, are set about ten feet apart in a circle. On the tops of these posts, solid beams are laid, extending from one to another. Then, toward the center of the lodge, four more posts are erected, of much greater diameter than the outer posts, and rising to the height of ten or more feet above the ground. These four posts stand in the corners of a square of about fifteen feet, and their tops are connected with four heavy logs or beams laid horizontally. From the four central beams to the smaller external beams, long poles, as rafters, are stretched at an angle of about 30° with the horizon; and from the outer beams to the earth a number of shorter poles are laid at an angle of about 45°. Finally, a number of saplings or rails are laid horizontally to cover the space between the four central beams, leaving only a hole for the combined skylight and chimney. This frame is then covered with willows, hay, and earth, as before mentioned; the covering being of equal depth over all parts of the frame. Earlier writers speak of the supporting-posts of the lodge as being forked. Nowadays, they seldom take the trouble to obtain forked sticks for this purpose.

From the above description, it will be seen that the outline of a vertical section, or of the elevation of such a lodge, is necessarily an irregular hexagon, while that of its ground-plan is polygonal, the angles being equal in number to the shorter uprights. Prince Maximilian's artist usually sketches the lodge very correctly; but Mr. Catlin invariably gives an incorrect representation of its exterior. Wherever he depicts a Mandan, Arickaree, or Minnetaree lodge, he makes it appear as an almost exact hemisphere, and always omits the entry. It would seem that, in filling in his sketches, he adopted the hemisphere as a convenient symbol for a lodge. The authors referred to by name in the foot-note on page — speak of the entry or passage.*

A partition of puncheons, poles, or hurdles is often raised between the fire-place and the door, particularly in cold weather, to shelter the group around the fire-place when the door is opened. Mats, hurdles, hair-pillows, and buffalo-robes laid on the ground constitute the seats. Curtained bedsteads are arranged around the circumference of the lodge, between the shorter uprights. Arms, implements, household-utensils, medicine-bags, etc., are hung from pegs on the various supporting-posts of the lodge. A wooden mortar, wherein corn and meat are pounded, is set in the earthen floor. The space between the outer row of supporting-posts and the outer wall is called 'atuti', or *bottom of the lodge*, and in it stored bull-boats, skin-lodges, and various other articles; here, too, we usually find the sudatory. Valuable horses are often housed at night in these lodges, in a pen near the door; but the residents of the log-houses, to be described hereafter, keep horses in separate sheds outside.

Log-houses.—Every winter, until 1866, the Indians left their permanent village, and, moving some distance up the Missouri Valley, built temporary quarters, usually in the center of heavy forests and in the neighborhood of buffalo. The chief objects of this movement were that they might have fuel convenient, and not exhaust the supply of wood in the neighborhood of the permanent village. It was also advisable that, during a portion of the year at least, they should not harass the game near home. The houses of the winter-villages resem-

* Perhaps it would be well to illustrate this with a copy of plate 47, vol. 1, of Catlin, and a copy of the figure on p. 343 of Maximilian.

bled much the log-cabins of our own western pioneers. They were neatly built, very warm, had regular fire-places and chimneys built of sticks and mud, and square holes in the roofs for the admission of light. Ten years ago, there were some cabins of this description in the permanent village at Fort Berthold; every year since, they are becoming gradually more numerous and threaten to eventually supplant the original earth-covered lodges. By reference to the note on page 4, it will be seen that, in 187?, the former outnumbered the latter by about nineteen.

Skin-lodges.—The practice of building winter-quarters is now abandoned. As game has recently become very scarce in their country, they are obliged to travel immense distances, and almost constantly, when they go out on their winter-hunts. Requiring, therefore, movable habitations, they take with them, on their journeys, the ordinary skin-lodges, or "tepees", such as are used by the Dakotas, Assiniboines, and other nomadic tribes in this region. Such lodges, too, they have always used on their summer-hunts, and on all long journeys except with war-parties. The skin-lodges of the prairie Indians have been so often described and depicted that any further reference to them in this paper would be unnecessary. It is enough to say that the tribes here considered, construct them in the same manner as do their neighbors, often ornamenting them with paintings, quill-embroideries, and other decorations.

Hunting-lodges.—In one of his "Solitary Rambles", Palliser found, on the Turtle Mountain, four days journey from Fort Berthold, in the spring of 1858, a Minnetaree hunting-lodge of which he says:—"They had built a triangular lodge of long wooden poles, like hop-poles, piling them in the shape of a cone, and so closely as to render the hut bullet-proof, a necessary precaution, as they could never venture there save in fear of their lives, the position lying in the regular pass of the Sioux, when they go to war with either them or the Crows. We took possession of the hut, not sorry to feel ourselves in a bullet-proof shelter, in a place where, I must admit, we ran some risk of being surprised by an Indian war-party."[*]

------

* p. 266.

In the winter of 1871, while hunting with a party of Indians from the Berthold village, in the bad-lands of the Little Missouri, I spent three nights in a lodge of exactly the same kind, which was quite old, and had often served as the temporary shelter of Hidatsa hunting-parties. It stood in an excellent but dangerous game-region, some four or five days journey from Fort Berthold, and was built for the convenience of parties composed only of men who found it advisable to visit that neighborhood without tents or other incumbrances. There are probably other lodges of this kind in the country around Berthold, but I have seen only this one.

§ 4. DRYING-FRAMES, corn-scaffolds, or, as some call them, "gridirons", stand in various parts of the village, and are quite numerous. They must resemble much the drying-frames of the agricultural tribes of the far east and south, if we are to judge by the descriptions given. They seem to differ in shape from those of the Omahas—of which the writer has seen photographs, but not the originals—by having the supporting-posts longer, and rising above the floor. They are made by setting in the ground some six or eight saplings, which rise to the height of twelve or fifteen feet. To these, at the height of seven or eight feet, cross-pieces are lashed; and on the latter a floor of poles or willow hurdles is laid; smaller poles are lashed to the tops of the upright supports. Corn and other vegetables, meat, robes, etc., are dried on these frames; and the labor of preparing and cleaning corn is done on the hurdle-floor, or on the ground underneath.

§ 5. CACHES.—The numerous *caches*, or pits, for storing grain, are noteworthy objects in the village. In summer, when they are not in use, they are often left open, or are carelessly covered, and may entrap the unwary stroller When these Indians have harvested their crops, and before they start on their winter-hunt, they dig their *caches*, or clear out those dug in previous years. A *cache* is a cellar, usually round, with a small opening above, barely large enough to allow a person to descend; when finished, it looks much like an ordinary round cistern. Reserving a small portion of corn, dried squash, etc., for winter use, they deposit the remainder in these subterranean storehouses, along with household-utensils and other articles of value which they wish to leave behind. They then fill up the orifices with earth, which they trample down and rake over; thus obliterating every trace of the excavation. Some *caches* are made under the floors of the houses, others outside, in various parts of the village-grounds; in each case, the distance and direction from some door, post, bedstead, fire-place, or other object is noted, so that the stores may be found on the return of the owners in the spring. Should an enemy enter the village while it is temporarily deserted, the goods are safe from fire and theft. This method of secreting property has long been in use among many tribes, has been adopted by whites living on the plains, and is referred to in the works of many travelers.

§ 6. CEMETERY.—BURIALS.—On the prairie, a short distance behind the village, are scattered around the scaffolds and the graves whereon and wherein are deposited the dead. Formerly, all who died in the village were placed on scaffolds, as is the custom with most of the Missouri Valley tribes; but the practice of burying in the ground, after the manner of the Europeans and Arickarees, is gradually becoming more common; and every year the scaffolds decrease, and the graves increase in number. When at a distance from their village on their hunts, if encamped in the neighborhood of timber, they lay the corpses in the branches of the trees instead of building scaffolds.

§ 7. PLACES OF WORSHIP.—There are, in the village, two open spaces, which, although of irregular shape, may be called squares; one of these is in the Mandan, the other in the Arickaree quarter. Beside each square stands a large round "medicine-lodge", or temple, built as described in the second paragraph of § 3, which is used for purposes that, in a general way, are called religious.

In the center of the Mandan square is a small circular palisade, about six feet high and four feet in diameter, made of neatly-hewn puncheons set closely together. It has somewhat the appearance of a large barrel, and is emblematic of the ark in which, according to Mandan mythology, the sole survivor of the Deluge was saved. The square, the medicine-lodge, with its four poles in front, surmounted by sacrificial effigies, and the ark, as they may be seen at Fort Berthold to-day, seem to be the almost exact counterparts of those which were seen in the old Mandan village at Fort Clarke, in 1832 and 1833, by George Catlin and the Prince of New-Wied, if we are to judge by the drawings they have given us. Within the temple and around the ark, the Mandans still perform the ceremony of the *Okeepa*, which Catlin so accurately describes. The awful severities of the rite have, however, been somewhat mitigated since his day.

The medicine-lodge of the Arickarees is larger than that of the Mandans, and is used for a greater variety of ceremonies. Some of these performances, consisting of ingenious tricks of jugglery and dances, representative of various hunts, we might be inclined to call theatrical rather than religious. Probably these Indians consider them both worshipful and entertaining. It is often hard to tell how much of a religious ceremony is intended to propitiate the unknown powers, and how much to please the spectators.

The Grosventres, or Hidatsas, have no house especially devoted to their "medicine". Some of their minor rites are performed in ordinary dwellings, in temporary houses, or in the open air. Their most important ceremony is conducted in a structure of willows erected for the occasion around a tall forked log. After the ceremony (described in § 22), the log, or pole, is left standing until the forces of nature throw it down. Several of these logs, in various stages of decay, may be seen on the prairie between the village and the cemetery.

§ 8. FORTIFICATIONS.—Many travelers have described their towns as being fortified,* sometimes with walls, but usually with ditches and stockades, or with stockades alone. The latter system of defense was in use at the village of Fort Berthold until the winter of 1865, when they cut down the palisades for fire-wood; and they have never since restored them. The presence of United States troops in their neigh-

---

* Lewis and Clarke, pp. 69, 70, 72, 73, 74, 82, 84, etc.—Maximilian, p. 342.—Catlin, N. A. Indians, pp. 73, 204.

borhood, and the growing weakness of the Dakotas, were probably the causes which led them to discontinue their fortifications.

§ 9. FARMS AND FARMING.—From the base of the prairie-terrace described in § 2, the bottom lands of the Missouri extend to the east and to the west, up and down the river. In the neighborhood of the village, they are covered partly with forest-trees, willows, and low brush, but chiefly with the little fields or gardens of these tribes.

Five years ago, all the land cultivated around the village consisted of little patches, irregular in form and of various sizes, which were cleared out among the willows. The patches were sometimes separated from one another by trifling willow-fences; but the boundaries were more commonly made by leaving the weeds and willows uncut, or small strips of ground uncultivated, between the fields. Every woman in the village capable of working had her own piece of ground, which she cultivated with a hoe; but some of the more enterprising paid the traders in buffalo-robes to plow their land. They raised the plants which nearly all the agricultural tribes of the temperate regions cultivated at the time of the discovery of America—corn, squashes, beans, and tobacco. They also improved the growth of the wild sunflower, the seeds of which they eat. Their system of tillage was rude. They knew nothing of the value of manuring the soil, changing the seed, or alternating the crops. Perhaps they had little need of such knowledge; for when the soil was worn out, they abandoned it; and there was no stint of land in the wilderness. Sometimes, after a few years of rest, they would resume the cultivation of a worn field that was quite near the village, for proximity lent some value to the land; but they had no regular system of fallowing. They often planted a dozen grains of corn or more to the hill, and did not hoe very thoroughly.

Within the last few years, there has been an improvement in their farming. The bottom to the west of the village is still divided up and cultivated in the old way; but the bottom to the east and a part of the upland have been broken up by the Indian agency, fenced, and converted into a large field. A portion of this field is cultivated (chiefly by hired Indians) for the benefit of the agency, and the rest has been divided into small tracts, each to be cultivated by a separate family for its own benefit. Potatoes, turnips, and other vegetables have been introduced. The men apply themselves willingly to the labors of the field; and the number of working men is constantly increasing.

The Arickarees and Mandans have doubtlessly tilled the soil for many centuries. Their accounts of the origin of corn are mingled with their earliest myths and traditions. There are some reasons for believing that the Arickarees represent an older race of farmers than the Mandans; for their religious ceremonies connected with planting are the more numerous, and they honor the corn with a species of worship. In every Arickaree lodge, there is a large ear of corn, which has lasted for generations, sticking out of the mouth of a medicine-bag. At their feasts, they make offerings to the corn by rubbing a piece of meat on it, while they pray to it for plentiful harvests, and address it by the name of "mother". The Hidatsas claim to have had no knowledge of corn until they first ate it from the trenchers of the Mandans; and they have no important ceremonies connected with the harvesting, yet they cultivated it long before the advent of the white man.

In favorable years, they had good harvests, and were able to sell corn to other Indians and to their traders, besides keeping all they wanted for their own use. But they are not always thus fortunate, for the soil of their country, even that on the Missouri bottoms, is not very rich; the summer season is short, with early and late frosts; the climate is dry; long droughts often prevail, to guard against which they have no system of irrigation; and, lastly, the grasshoppers—the plague of the Missouri Valley farmer—have often devoured the crops that had escaped all other enemies, and left the Indian with little more than seed enough for the coming spring.

§ 10. INHABITANTS OF THE VILLAGE.—When Lewis and Clarke ascended the Missouri, in 1804, they found four tribes of agricultural Indians, numerous and prosperous, inhabiting the Upper Missouri Valley, west of the Dakota nation. They had eight permanently inhabited towns, others which they lived in only temporarily, and a number more which they had abandoned and allowed to go to ruin. They are spoken of in Lewis and Clarke's journal as the "Ricaras," "Mandans," "Minnetarees," and "Ahnahaways." All that are left of the four tribes are now gathered together in this one village, at Fort Berthold, which does not probably number 2,500 souls. The remains, now nearly obliterated, of their old towns, may be traced on nearly every prairie-terrace adjacent to the Missouri, along six hundred miles of its course, from the mouth of the Lower White-Earth to the mouth of the Little Missouri. The Indians at Fort Berthold are, however, now generally referred to as "the three tribes"; for one of the nations spoken of by Captain Lewis—that which he calls Ahnahaways—is no longer an organized tribe, but has been merged into the Minnetarees. (See § 11.)

Arickarees.—The first-mentioned tribe is known by the various names of Arikaras, Ricaras, Arickarees, and Rees, all of which are from their Mandan name, Aríkára. They are related to the Pawnees of the Platte Valley, from whom they separated more than a century ago. In 1804, they were found living farther down the Missouri than the Hidatsa and Mandan tribes, and were at war with the latter. They made peace in the course of time, and gradually followed the other tribes up the Missouri, building new villages and abandoning old ones as they went. In August, 1862, they moved to Fort Berthold, and began to erect houses there beside those of the Mandans and Minnetarees. These three tribes have ever since occupied the same permanent village. Descriptions of the Arickarees, as they were seen at different periods, may be found in the works of Lewis and Clarke, Catlin, Maximilian, and Hayden. Lewis and Clarke give accounts of many of their early migrations, and the last-named three authors furnish vocabularies of their language.

The *Mandans*, about a hundred years ago, lived in several villages near the mouth of Heart River. From this neighborhood, they moved up the Missouri, stopping and building villages at different localities.* In 1804, they were found

---

* For an account of these movements, see Lewis and Clarke, pp. 83–85.

dwelling in two towns about four miles below the mouth of Knife River. One of these towns was named Métutahanke, Mitutahankish, or, as Maximilian writes it, "Mih-tutta-hang-kusch," meaning *Lower Village*. The other was called Rùptari or Nuptadi. They were almost exterminated by the small-pox in 1837, after which, for a time, they occupied only one village. In 1845, when the Hidatsas moved away from Knife River, some of the Mandans went with them, and others fol-lowed at different times afterward. For a short time, it appears that a few Mandan families occupied the old Amahami village. We have an account of some moving up to the vil-lage at Fort Berthold as late as 1858, and of others still remaining at the mouth of Knife River at the same time.*

The word Mandan seems to be a corruption of the Dakota name Matani or Mawatani. Previous to 1837, they called themselves simply Numakaki, *i. e., People, Men*. They some-times spoke of themselves and the Minnetarees together as Núweta, *Ourselves*. A large band of their tribe was called Siposka-numakaki, *Prairie-hen People*, or Grouse Men.† This name, Mr. Catlin, in his first work, renders "People of the pheasants",‡ and, in his last work, presents in the shape of "Nu-mah-ká-kee (pheasants)",§ and then, from this translation, leaves us to draw the "important inference" that the Mandans once lived in the Ohio Valley. They now often call them-selves Metutahanke, after their old village below Knife River.

Captains Lewis and Clarke, Mr. Catlin, the Prince of Neu-wied, and Dr. Hayden have written very full accounts of this tribe, and all but the first-named explorers present vocabu-laries of their language. The work of Prince Maximilian contains the most accurate and extensive information regard-ing their customs and manners. Notwithstanding the great changes in the tribe since 1834, the majority of his notes might be used without alteration in describing the Mandans of

---

* Boller, pp. 35, 36.

† The Mandan name Siposka (Hidatsa, sitska or tsitska) is applied to the *Tetrao phasianellus* (Linn.) or Sharp-tailed Grouse, the prairie-hen of the Upper Missouri.

‡ N. A. Indians, vol. i, pp. 80, 178; vol. ii, p. 260.

§ O-kee-pa, pp. 5, 44.

to-day. In a few cases, however, I believe that the deductions which he drew from his observations were incorrect.*

Minnetarees.—Since the other one of the three tribes, the Hidatsas or Minnetarees, forms the principal subject of this essay, it is spoken of at length; the description forming the second part of this sketch.

§11. AMAḤAMI.—The people who, by Lewis and Clarke, are generally called Ahnahaways, and, in this dictionary, Ama-ami, were closely allied to the Hidatsa, and spoke a language differing but slightly from that of the latter; yet they occupied a separate village and long maintained a distinct tribal organization. Their village, in 1804, was at the mouth of Knife River, and was one of three villages which for many years stood on the banks of that stream. (See §19.) In 1804, they were estimated as numbering about fifty warriors.† In 1833–'34, their village was said to contain eighteen houses.‡ These estimates indicate that there was no material change in their numbers during the intervening thirty years. After the epidemic of 1837, the whole or the greater part of the survivors joined the Hidatsa, and, as before stated, merged into the latter. In what year this fusion took place, I was unable to determine; it may have been gradual. A few of the Amaḥamis perhaps identified themselves with the Mandans. In 1858, after the Hidatsa had left Knife River, Boller saw some persons occupying a few huts at the mouth of Knife River, probably the old Amaḥami village. He says, however, that the occupants were Mandans.§

Lewis and Clarke evidently regarded these people as distinct from the dwellers in the other two villages on Knife River; ‖ but Catlin seemed to think that the Amaḥami village was merely one of the Minnetaree villages, for he says that the Minnetarees occupied the three villages on Knife River;¶ and the Prince of Neuwied seems to agree with Mr. Catlin.** Perhaps in the

---

* Thus, in speaking of the custom of carrying small bundles of sticks (p. 356), which then existed, and still to some extent exists, among the young men of the Mandans and Minnetarees, he says, "They do not meet with many coy beauties." If such were the case, why should they display tokens of their success? Why boast of a deed which was no great achievement?

† Lewis and Clarke, p. 96.   ‡ Maximilian, p. 178.
§ p. 36.   ‖ p. p. 89, 95, 97.   ¶ p. 185.   ** p. 178.

days of these latter travelers, the Amahamis may have sub-
mitted to the authority of the Minnetaree chief.

In one instance, Lewis and Clarke spell the name of this
tribe "Arwacahwas".*   In 1834, their village stood on the
same ground that it occupied in 1804; at both of these dates it
bore the same Indian names,† and the people bore the same
French name; ‡ yet Maximilian, aided by his interpreter, failed
to recognize the resemblance between the name of the tribe as
written by Lewis and Clarke and "Awachawi", as he, according to German orthography, so correctly spells it.   Such, at
least, is the impression produced by the perusal of the foot-note
on page 335 of his work.   In this note, too, Maximilian, in
criticising Lewis and Clarke's spelling, does not make due allowance for the fact that the American travelers wrote in a language whose alphabet is less suited to express the Indian words
than that of the language in which he wrote.

The descendants of the Amahamis, among the Hidatsa, are
now known from the rest of this tribe by their preference for
certain words and dialectic forms, which are not in common use
among those of unmixed Hidatsa blood, and did not originally
belong to the language of the latter.

§ 12. POPULATION.—The population of the village is not
known.   It is said that the inhabitants of some of the old villages allowed a census to be taken immediately before the epidemic which proved so fatal to them.   They believed that their
calamity resulted from the census, and have since resisted all
efforts to ascertain their numbers.   Many ingenious plans have
been devised for counting them without their knowledge, but
they have suspected and thwarted them all.   In the *Reports of
the Commissioners of Indian Affairs*, various estimates of their
strength may be found, but they are all conjectural.   In the
Report of 1862, it is stated§ that the Grosventres and Mandans, in that year, numbered 1,120, and the Arickarees (then
in a separate but neighboring village) 1,000,—total 2,120.   In

---

* p. 89.
    † Lewis and Clarke, p. 89, " Mahawha".—Maximilian, p. 335, " Machacha".
    ‡ Lewis and Clarke, p. 96, " called by the French Soulier Noir, or Shoe Indians.'
—Maximilian, p. 178, " Le village des Souliers."
    § Pages 193 and 195, in Report of Agent S. N. Latta to the Commissioner.

the *Report* of 1866 are the following "approximate numbers":* Arickarees, 1,500; Mandans, 400; Grosventres, 400;—total **2,300**. In the *Report* of **1871**, the population is thus given:† Arickarees, 1,650; Grosventres, 600; Mandans, 450;—total "about" 2,700. In these estimates, which vary greatly, the first gives **the** population of the Grosventres and Mandans together as more than the Rees; while, in the second and third estimates, the Rees are represented as about twice as numerous as the other **two tribes** together. In this respect, **I believe the** first quoted **estimate** to be nearest **the** truth; for the houses occupied **by the** Grosventres and Mandans number more than those occupied by the Rees.‡ In the estimate of 1866, **it will be seen that the** Grosventres and Mandans **are** represented as equal to one another. I have many reasons for believing this representation to be incorrect. The conjecture of the writer, based upon all ascertainable data, is that, within the past **ten** years, the proper population of the village has never been more than 2,500, and that, at present, it is much less. It is **pretty** certain, too, that of the three tribes the Arickarees stand **first in** numerical strength, the Hidatsa second, and the Mandans third.

However, if a perfect census of the village was taken any day, when no hunting-parties were out, it would not show the strength of these tribes; for the scouts who are enlisted at distant posts, their families, and the Minnetarees, who, of late years, have gone to live with the Crows, constituting in **all a** large proportion of this people, could not be included.

§13. CONVERSATION.—To the philologist, it is an interesting fact that this trio of savage clans, although now living in the same village, and having been next-door neighbors to each other for more than a hundred years, on terms of peace and intimacy, **and to a** great extent intermarried, speak, nevertheless, totally distinct languages, which show no perceptible **in**clination to coalesce. The Mandan and Grosventre (or Minnetaree) languages are somewhat alike, and probably of a very distant common origin; but **no** resemblance has yet been discovered between either of these and the Arickaree ("Ricara").

* Page 175, in Report of the Northwestern Treaty Commissioners.
† Page 520, in Report of Agent J. E. Tappan.
‡ See note on **p. 4.**

2

Almost every member of each tribe understands the languages of the other tribes, yet he speaks his own most fluently; so it is not an uncommon thing to hear a dialogue carried on in two languages, one person, for instance, questioning in Mandan, and the other answering back in Grosventre, and *vice versa*. Many of them understand the Dakota tongue, and use it as a means of intercommunication, and all understand the sign-language. So, after all, they have no trouble in making themselves understood by one another. These Indians must have excellent memories and "good capacity for study"; for it is not uncommon to find persons among them, some even under twenty years of age, who can speak fluently four or five different languages.

§ 14. ARTS.—Besides their agriculture and architecture, which have been already alluded to, they had the knowledge of many other useful arts, still practiced by them, which were entirely of native origin. They manufactured pottery; built boats of buffalo-hide; made mats and baskets of various descriptions, and wooden bowls so durable that they last for many generations; and formed spoons and ladles out of the horns of the buffalo and Rocky Mountain sheep. Their hair-brushes they made sometimes out of porcupine-quills, but more commonly of grass—the long, tough awns of the *Stipa juncea*. They fashioned whistles of the bones of large birds, and fifes and other wind-instruments out of wood; some of these were for musical purposes; others were to imitate, for the hunter's benefit, the bleat of the antelope or the whistle of the elk. They garnished their clothing with porcupine-quills, which they colored brilliantly with dye-stuffs of Indian discovery. They had flint and horn arrow-heads, and horn wedges with which they split wood. They knew something of the manufacture of glass, and made rude beads and pendants out of it; they possessed various pigments, and with them recorded the events of their day in symbolic pictures; and, in the manufacture and use of the various appliances of war and the chase, they had no superiors on the plains. Their arms were the same as those of the Dakotas and other western tribes; and they have been so often described that I feel there is little left for me to say concerning them.

For cleaning the village-grounds, they had rakes made of a few osiers tied together—the ends curved and spreading. Their most important agricultural implement was the hoe. Before they obtained iron utensils of the white traders, their only hoes were made of the shoulder-blades of elk or buffalo, attached to wooden handles of suitable length. Maximilian, in 1833,* considered the bone hoe as a thing of the past only; yet, as late as 1867, I saw a great number in use at Fort Berthold, and purchased two or three, one of which was sent to Washington, and, I presume, is now on exhibition in the museum of the Smithsonian Institution.†

They now make saddle-trees in somewhat the same way as we do, of wood or of part wood and part horn, covered with raw-hide. They also make neat pad-saddles of tanned elk-skin, stuffed with antelope-hair, and often handsomely embroidered, as well as other horse-equipments. They probably learned the art of making these articles some time during the last century, from the Indians of the south, of whom they first obtained horses.

For their children, they make toys, which, as with us, indicate for each sex the occupations of adult years. When the children are old enough, they make some of their own toys. They have pop-guns, the art of making which, as far as I could discover, was not learned from the whites. The boys make representations of hunts by fashioning out of mud, with much skill, little figures of the horse, the mounted hunter, and the flying buffalo.

Glass.—The articles of glass spoken of above are chiefly of two kinds: first, large, globular, or ellipsoidal beads; and, second, flat, irregularly triangular plates or pendants, which are glazed only on one side, and have a hole at the apex. The art of making these deserves more than a mere mention, since it is commonly believed that the aboriginal Americans, even the most civilized races, knew nothing of the manufacture of glass at the time of the Columbian discovery. The very earliest ethnographical account we have of the Arickarees and Man-

---

* p. 347.

† See Smithsonian Report for 1869, p. 36, where the specimen is erroneously attributed to the Yanktonnais.

dans shows that they knew how to make glass beads; and there is no doubt that the process employed in 1804 was essentially the same as that employed to-day. The following is the account of this given by Lewis and Clarke:—"A Mr. Garrow, a Frenchman, who has resided a long time among the Ricaras and Mandans, explained to us the mode in which they make their large beads, an art which they are said to have derived from some prisoners of the Snake Indian nation, and the knowledge of which is a secret, even now confined to a few among the Mandans and Ricaras. The process is as follows: glass of different colors is first pounded fine, and washed, till each kind, which is kept separate, ceases to stain the water thrown over it; some well-seasoned clay, mixed with a sufficient quantity of sand to prevent it becoming very hard when exposed to the heat, and reduced by water to the consistency of dough, is then rolled on the palm of the hand till it becomes of the thickness wanted for the hole in the bead; these sticks of clay are placed upright, each on a little pedestal or ball of the same material, about an ounce in weight, and distributed over a small earthen platter, which is laid on the fire for a few minutes, when they are taken off to cool; with a little paddle or shovel, three or four inches long and sharpened at the end of the handle, the wet pounded glass is placed in the palm of the hand; the beads are made of an oblong form, wrapped in a cylindrical form round the stick of clay, which is laid crosswise over it, and gently rolled backward and forward until it becomes perfectly smooth. If it be desired to introduce any other color, the surface of the bead is perforated with the pointed end of the paddle, and the cavity filled with pounded glass of that color; the sticks, with the string of beads, are then placed on their pedestals, and the platter deposited on burning coals or hot embers; over the platter an earthen pot, containing about three gallons, with a mouth large enough to cover the platter, is reversed, being completely closed, except a small aperture in the top, through which are watched the beads; a quantity of old dried wood, formed into a sort of dough or paste, is placed round the pot so as almost to cover it, and afterward set on fire; the manufacturer then looks through the small hole in the pot till he sees the beads assume a deep-red color, to which succeeds a paler or whitish red, or they become pointed at the upper extremity, on which the fire is removed and the pot is suffered to cool gradually; at length it is removed, the beads taken out, the clay in the hollow of them picked out with an awl or needle, and it is then fit for use. The beads thus formed are in great demand among the Indians, and used as pendants to their ears and hair, and sometimes worn round the neck."* This art is now only occasionally practiced in the village, and is mostly confined to the making of the flat, triangular pendants. I have heard the process described in much the same way as in the above quotation. From this quotation, however, which is in part ambiguous, the inference might be drawn that the ornaments, when completed, consist entirely of glass. Such is not the case in those I have seen; on the contrary, they consist of a core of baked earth covered with a thin shell of glass; and they have the appearance of having been perforated before heat was applied. But, in the matter of making the holes, the process may have been changed, or there may have been two ways of doing it.

The existence of this art among the Indians evidently greatly astonished Catlin, who gives it as one of the reasons on which he founds his theory of the Cymric origin of the Mandans. He says, speaking of the Mandans:—"In addition to this art," [pottery,] "which I am sure belongs to no other tribe on the continent, these people have also, as a secret with themselves, the extraordinary art of manufacturing a very beautiful and lasting kind of blue glass beads, which they wear on their necks in great quantities, and decidedly value above all others that are brought among them by the fur-traders.' "This secret is not only one that the traders did not introduce among them, but one which they cannot learn from them; and at the same time, beyond a doubt, an art that has been introduced among them by some civilized people, as it is as yet unknown to other Indian tribes in that vicinity or elsewhere. Of this interesting fact, Lewis and Clarke gave

---

* pp. 125–126.

an account thirty-three years ago, at a time when no traders or other white people had been among the Mandans to have taught them so curious an art."* It is surprising that Mr. Catlin, after reading the above-cited passages from Lewis and Clarke (and he leaves us to infer that he has read them), could state that the art of making these beads was confined to the Mandans; that it was unknown to the traders; that it was beyond doubt introduced by civilized people; and that no traders or other whites had been among these Indians before the time of Lewis and Clarke's visit.

The art of making these ornaments would appear to be old; yet the process as it existed in 1804 was evidently in part recent, since the Indians obtained the glass which they used from the whites. I have been informed by the Indians that in old days the art flourished among the Arickarees as well as among the Mandans; and certainly at the present day the Arickaree women understand it. I had two of the triangular pendants made *to order* in 1870, by an Arickaree woman, to whom I furnished the blue glass necessary. When I gave instructions to have the articles made, I was invited to witness the process, but circumstances prevented me from doing so. One of these pendants was sent to the Smithsonian Institution. It is strange, if true, that these Indians should have obtained their knowledge of this art from the Snake Indians, a ruder and equally remote tribe. It is also strange, and undoubtedly true, that in 1804, as well as now, they did not make their glass, but obtained it ready-made, and merely fused it for their purposes, obtaining it, doubtlessly, from the whites. It is strange that within a few years after glass beads of European manufacture were first introduced among them, and when such beads must have commanded a high price, they should pulverize them and use the powder in making ruder and more unsightly articles after their own design. But it is not probable that they should have learned such an art from civilized people prior to 1804, when they had as yet seen but few whites, and when the whites they had seen were mostly rude Canadian frontiersmen, among whom it is not reasonable to suppose

* North American Indians, vol. ii, p. 201.

there were any persons versed in glass-making. I have heard
Indians say, with uncertainty, that in former times they found
glass in the hills, and pounded it for their beads; meaning
perhaps that they used natural glass, which may be found
where lignite beds have taken fire, and elsewhere on the Upper Missouri. In view of all these facts, I have conjectured
that they had the art of making glazed earthen ornaments
before the whites came among them; and that when they saw
the brilliantly-colored beads of the traders, they conceived the
idea of improving their art by using these beads. If they
ever possessed the art of making glass *de novo*, there is no
record, tradition, or other evidence of it that I have been able
to find.

One of many reasons, though perhaps an insufficient
reason, for believing the art to be of no recent origin among
them, is that they used the triangular pendants, not as ornaments only, but as evidences of betrothal, as long ago as the
oldest men can remember. When a girl was promised in
marriage in her infancy by her parents, as was not infre-
quently done, one of these pendants was tied to her forelock
so as to hang down over her forehead. When the promise was
fulfilled, the husband removed the pendant and threw it away.

§ 15. Food, etc.—Since the introduction of various articles
of European food, their diet has been somewhat changed, yet
they still largely adhere to their original dietary.

Their chief food, until within the last eight or ten years,
was the meat of the buffalo, or bison, which, when fresh, was
cooked by roasting before an open fire, by broiling on the
coals or on an extemporized wooden broiler, or by boiling.
Their meat was boiled in earthen pots before brass and iron
pots were introduced by the whites. They knew the different
effects produced by putting the meat down in hot and in cold
water, and employed the former method when they did not want
soup. On hunts, they sometimes boiled the meat in skins,
heating the water with hot stones, after the method employed
by the Assinniboines, which has given the latter tribe its
name of Stone-cookers. Sometimes they chopped the fresh
meat fine, put it in a piece of bowel, and thus made a sort of

sausage, which was usually boiled. For preservation, meat is cut into thin sheets or into long strips and dried in the sun. I have seen dried meat three years old perfectly sweet. Sometimes it becomes worm-eaten without becoming rancid. In rainy weather, they often hang meat up in the smoke of the lodge to preserve it. The dried meat is sometimes eaten raw, but more frequently it is boiled or broiled; or it is broiled, pounded fine, and mixed with fat to make pemmican. They sometimes add sugar and berries to small quantities of pemmican. The meat of the elk and the deer is cooked and prepared in the same way as buffalo-meat, and of late, since the buffalo have so greatly decreased in number, is more used than the latter.

When game is abundant, they only use choice parts of an animal; but, when it is scarce, they discard nothing. They then pound the bones into small fragments, and subject them to prolonged boiling to make soup. During one winter of great scarcity, I knew of some Arickarees, who, not having horses, could not go out on the winter-hunt, to cut up and boil their bull-boats and the raw-hide doors of their houses for food. When hungry hunters kill an animal, they often eat the liver, the kidneys, and the hoofs of the fœtus, should there be one, raw. Raw liver is said to have a saccharine taste which is not unpleasant. Occasionally they eat other parts raw, but this is only when the quarry is little, the mouths many, and the prospect of a fire distant or doubtful.

Fat porcupine, bear, and beaver meat are esteemed, particularly the tail of the latter. They are fond of marrow and fat. Birds of prey, foxes, and wolves are eaten, but only when food is scarce. Turtles and fish are used as food; but I have never heard of any such use being made of snakes. The Grosventres have but recently learned to eat dog-flesh, and they still eat horse-flesh only under pressing necessity; but the Arickarees seem to have less prejudice to such food. Among many belonging to these tribes, a young, fat pup is considered a great delicacy. Insects, with one exception, and worms are never eaten, and few can now be persuaded to eat oysters. When a gravid buffalo, elk, or deer is killed, the *liquor amnii* is generally preserved and boiled for soup, the fœtus being cooked in it.

Formerly, they lived largely upon meat. When out on their hunts and war-parties, they often lived exclusively on it. There were many nomadic tribes around them who seldom tasted vegetable matter, often living for seven or eight months in the year exclusively on meat, and preserving perfect health. I have seen white men who had lived for years among the Indians, and during such residence, for six months of every year, lived on nothing but meat (and water of course), "Buffalo straight," as they expressed it, and who, in the summers only, occasionally varied their diet with a mess of roots or berries—not seeking such vegetable food with any particular longing or avidity. In various books of western travel, these statements are corroborated; yet there are modern physiologists who would try to persuade us that an animal diet is inadequate to the sustaining of human life in a healthy condition. When subsisting for the most part on fresh meat, these Indians had the soundest gums and teeth; and no flesh when wounded healed more rapidly than theirs. Lately, however, since the increase in the consumption of bacon and flour among them, and the destruction of their game, there have been many cases of scurvy, a disease which was particularly fatal to them in the winter of 1868-'69; and a tendency to abscesses, to suppurative terminations of diseases, and to a sluggish condition of wounds, manifests itself. The quantities of fresh meat they are able to consume are enormous. Sometimes, after a day's hunt, the hunters will sit up all night cooking and eating.

Their principal vegetable diet was the corn they raised themselves. Flour, issued by the agency, is now, to a great extent, taking its place. They eat some of the corn when it is green, but the greater part they allow to ripen. When ripe, they prepare it in various ways. They pound it in a wooden mortar with water, and boil the moist meal thus made into a hasty pudding, or cook it in cakes. They frequently parch the corn, and then reduce it to powder, which is often eaten without preparation. A portion of their corn they boil when nearly ripe; they then dry and shell it, and lay it by for winter use; when boiled again, it tastes like green corn. (See Madaśkihe in Dictionary.) This is often boiled with dried beans to make a succotash. Their beans are not usually eaten until ripe. Squashes are cut in thin slices and dried; the dried squash is usually cooked by boiling. Sunflower-seeds are dried, slightly scorched in pots or pans over the fire, and then powdered. The meal is boiled or made into cakes with grease. The sunflower-cakes are often taken on war-parties, and are said, when eaten even sparingly, to sustain the consumer against fatigue more than any other food. They gather all manner of wild roots and berries that are eaten by the nomadic tribes of the same region; but they do not consume them to the extent that the wilder tribes do. The only nuts that grow in their hunting-grounds are the acorns. I have never known them to collect or eat these.

I believe that they have always understood the value of salt and knew where to procure it. (See Matamahota in Dictionary.) They used it sparingly, however, and to season their vegetable messes only. Lately, since they can obtain salt so cheaply and plentifully from the traders and agency, they rarely hunt for it, and use it to a greater extent than they formerly did. In 1820, Major Long's Expedition met an Arickaree returning from the distant valley of the Arkansas, with about thirty pounds of pure salt, which "had evidently been formed by the evaporation of water in some pond or basin."[*]

In the earliest accounts that we have of these Indians, we find they cultivated a species of tobacco[†] (*Nicotiana quadrivalvis*). Sergeant Gass, who tried it in 1804, and who, we may presume, was a good judge of the weed, says that "it answers for smoking but not for chewing";[‡] and, in my time, I have heard similar opinions passed concerning it by tobacco-users. Lately, the cultivation of this tobacco has been greatly neglected, as the Indians obtain an article from the whites which they prefer. It is but recently that any of them have

---

[*] Long, vol. i, p. 449.
[†] Lewis and Clarke say " two different species of tobacco ", p. 76.
[‡] p. 73.

learned to chew tobacco.   All the men smoke; but the use of the pipe is very rare among the women.   These Indians seldom use tobacco alone, but mix it with the dried inner bark of one or more species of dogwood, *Cornus stotonifera* and *C. sericea.* (See Ope and Opehaśa in Dictionary).   They also mix with it the leaves of the *Eleagnus argentea*, which grows in Northern Dakota, and the leaves of a variety of *Arctostaphylos uva-ursi.*   Sometimes they smoke the dogwood-bark alone, without any mixture of tobacco.   Often they put a fragment of castoreum on top of the tobacco before lighting the pipe. The various points of ceremony and etiquette connected with smoking are the same with these tribes as with other western Indians; and they have been described by many observers.

§ 16. INTER-TRIBAL TRADE.—In former days, there was a trade carried on between these tribes and their Indian neighbors.   Of late years, it has greatly diminished, but it still exists to some extent.

With the nomadic tribes around, they exchanged their agricultural produce for horses, and, recently, for robes.   When the Dakotas saw a certain flower (*Liatris punctata*) blooming on the prairie, they knew that the corn was ripe, and went to the villages of the farming Indians to trade.   From the time they came in sight of the village to the time they disappeared, there was a truce.   When they had passed beyond the bluffs, they might steal an unguarded pony or lift a scalp, and were in turn liable to be attacked.

The straight, slender spruce-poles, which form the frames of their skin-lodges, are not obtained in the immediate neighborhood of the Missouri, but are cut in and near the Black Hills, many days journey from Fort Berthold, and in the country of the inimical Teton-Dakotas.   The Berthold Indians, consequently, purchase them of the Dakotas, giving a good buffalo-horse, or its equivalent, for the number sufficient for a lodge, about a dozen.

To tribes less skilled than were they in catching war-eagles, they traded the tail-feathers of these birds; a single tail being worth a buffalo-horse.   Their principal standard of value was a buffalo-horse, *i. e.*, a horse swift enough to outrun a young adult buffalo in the fall.

It appears probable that they once carried on a trade indirectly with the tribes of the Pacific coast, for they had *Dentalium* shells similar to those obtained on the Pacific, and they prized them so highly that the white traders found it advisable to obtain them for the trade. As late as 1866, ten of these shells, of inferior size, costing the traders only a cent apiece, would buy a superior buffalo robe, and formerly only two or three of the same quality were paid for a robe. Modern traders, with whom the writer has conversed, obtain their shells from eastern importers, and know nothing of the original source of supply. They suppose them to come from the Atlantic coast or the Great Lakes, and call them "Iroquois shells", which is probably their corruption of the Chinook "hyakwa"; but it is possible the reverse is the case.

They also used, and still use, as ornaments, fragments of the *Abalone* shells (one or more species of *Haliotis*) of the Pacific. These are now supplied to the trade under the name of California shells. Ten years ago, one of these shells, unpolished, sold for a good robe. There is little doubt that they used *Abalone, Dentalium,* and other sea-shells before the traders brought them. Old traders and old Indians say so. Even as late as 1833, it would seem that they had not yet become a regular part of a trader's outfit; for Maximilian says of the Mandans:—"They do not disfigure the bodies; only they make some apertures in the outer rim of the ear, in which they hang strings of beads, brass, or iron rings of different sizes, or shells, the last of which they obtain from other Indian tribes. If they are questioned respecting these shells, they answer that they were brought from the sea."*

§ 17. INTERCOURSE WITH WHITES.—In a recent little work entitled O-kee-pa, George Catlin says:—"Two exploring parties had long before visited the Mandans, but without in any way affecting their manners. The first of these, in 1738, under the lead of the brothers Verendrye, Frenchmen, who afterward ascended the Missouri and Saskatchewan to the Rocky Mount-

---

* p. 337. See also p. 338, "White dentalium shells."

ains; and the other, under Lewis and Clarke, about sixty years afterward."* He does not tell us where the account of the expedition of 1738 is to be found; he gives us no further evidence on this point; and, as no other mention of the journey has ever been seen by me, it will receive no further consideration in this essay.

In a letter published in Schoolcraft's *Information respecting… the Indian Tribes*, the writer, D. D. Mitchell, says, speaking of the Mandans:—"The early portion of their history I gather from the narration of Mr. Mackintosh, who, it seems, belonged to, or was in some way connected with, the French trading company as far back as 1772. According to his narration, he set out from Montreal in the summer of 1773, crossed over the country to the Missouri River, and arrived at one of the Mandan villages on Christmas day."† I have never seen Mackintosh's account, nor have I seen any more extensive notice of it than the one given by Mr. Mitchell; and from this, it does not appear that Mackintosh visited any of these agricultural Indians except the Mandans.

There is. every probability that some of these tribes received occasional visits from white traders and adventurers a century or more ago. It may be safely stated that every one of the bands represented in the Berthold village were visited by whites at least eighty years ago, and that they have been in constant communication with representatives of civilized races ever since. In 1804, British traders and French or Canadian interpreters were found in their camps; and the travelers of that year speak of "those who visited them in 1796".‡ Prince Maximilian, writing in 1833, says of "Charbonneau, who was interpreter for the Manitari language", that he "had lived thirty-seven years in this part of the country";§ that, at his first arrival, the Knife River villages stood precisely where they were in 1833; and that Charbonneau "immediately took up his residence in the central one".‖ From these statements we must conclude that Charbonneau settled among the Hidatsas about seventy-nine years ago; and old men of the tribe say that he

---

* p. 4.   † Part third, p. 253.   ‡ Lewis and Clarke, p. 96.
§ p. 318.   ‖ p. 321.

was not the first white man to come to their towns, yet that few preceded him.

It is likely that all the Europeans who came to these tribes in the early days were from the Hudson Bay Territory, and that they were mostly traders; but, in 1804, it seems that there were some whites sojourning in their country as hunters and trappers. The British fur-companies held the trade of these Indians until 1807,* when Manuel Lisa, who afterward founded the Missouri Fur Company, ascended the river in keel-boats to the Mandan villages and beyond. Until 1832, goods were brought up the Missouri chiefly in keel-boats or Mackinaw-boats, which were cordeled or towed by men, with great labor, against the rapid current of the river. Two summers, at least, were always occupied in dragging a boat from Saint Louis to the head of navigation; the crew sustaining themselves chiefly by hunting. In 1832, the first steamer reached the Mandan villages, and after that, for about thirty years, but one or two steamers a year went thus far up the river.

Although these Indians have so long known the whites, it is only within the last twelve or thirteen years that our intercourse with them has been sufficiently extensive to materially modify their customs and ideas. Previously, excepting two or three small military expeditions and an occasional traveler, the only whites they saw were the few connected with the fur-trade; and these persons, as a rule, sought to produce no change in the Indian, but, on the other hand, learned the Indian languages, adopted Indian customs, and endeavored to assimilate themselves to the Indians as much as possible, often vying with one another in their efforts to become amateur savages. Before the period to which I refer, we had traded to them woven fabrics and many trinkets of little value, had taught them the use of fire-arms and iron tools, had given them an opportunity for acquiring a taste for coffee and ardent spirits, but, in other respects, had wrought little change in their minds or manners. Eight years ago, they knew nothing of the use of money, and nothing of the English language except a few oaths and vulgar expressions, which the

* "He set off in the spring following the return of Lewis and Clarke" (Brackenridge, p. 90).

more docile had learned. The conservatives were still much the same as their grandfathers were.

In 1863, and during the two following years, in consequence of the Sioux outbreak of 1862, large military expeditions visited Fort Berthold, passing through the country of these Indians, and strong garrisons were established in their neighborhood, which are still retained. About this time too (1863), the emigration to the Montana gold-mines by way of the Missouri River began; and, instead of one steamer a year ascending the river as in the old days, they came up by dozens, some making two and three trips during the season of navigation. The Indians were thus brought into more intimate contact with the Americans, the seclusion of their country was ended, and a change more general and rapid in their affairs initiated. Since then, their game has been killed off, they have grown weaker, poorer, and more dependent, and, in many other respects, they have altered for the worse. As yet, no sustained effort has been made to Christianize them; and but little has been done to advance them in civilization. On the other hand, they have, according to some standards of excellence, bettered in many respects. They have of necessity given increased attention to the cultivation of the soil. The men, as before stated, have learned to perform labor, which, in earlier days, they deemed degrading. Many of their savage customs and ideas have been abandoned; and many of their ceremonies have been simplified or have fallen into disuse. They are generally less superstitious than they were ten years ago, and more skeptical with regard to their old myths.

Since 1866, a large number of their men have enlisted as scouts in the military service of the United States, and have been improved by the discipline of the camp. They have learned the responsibilities, and have done splendidly in the capacity of soldiers; many of them having heroically laid down their lives in our service.

During a short period of their history, the Arickarees were at war with the Americans; but for many years they have strictly maintained peace, and have fought with us and against our enemies. The Mandans and Minnetarees claim never to have shed a white man's blood, although some of their number have been killed by whites. For their fidelity they have been repaid in starvation and neglect. Many of these friendly Indians, particularly among the Arickarees, have, during the past ten years, died of actual hunger or the diseases incident to a state of famine. Within the past three years there seem to be some evidences of increased legislative interest in them, but the benefits arising therefrom are by no means equal to their needs or their deserts.

THE HIDATSA TRIBE.

§18. NAMES OF THE TRIBE.—*Grosventre*.—The people whose language is discussed in the accompanying grammar are commonly called, on maps, in official reports, and by white men in the Indian country, Grosventres. This was a name given to them by the early French and Canadian adventurers. The same name was applied also to a tribe, totally distinct from these in language and origin, which lives some hundreds of miles west of Fort Berthold; and the two nations are now distinguished from one another as Grosventres of the Missouri and Grosventres of the Prairie, names which would lead a stranger to suppose that they were merely separate divisions of one tribe.

In the account of Edward Umfreville, who traded on the Saskatchewan River from 1784 to 1787, we find mention of a tribe of Indians who lived near the falls of the south branch of the Saskatchewan, and whom he calls " Fall Indians". But he remarks :—" In this people, another instance occurs of the impropriety with which the Canadian French name Indians. They call them Grosventres, or Big-Bellies; and without any reason, as they are as comely and as well made as any tribe whatever, and are very far from being remarkable for their corpulency."* The tribe to which he refers is doubtless that which is now known as the Atsinas, or Grosventres of the Prairie. The similarity of the Canadian misnomers in all probability led Captain Lewis, in 1804, to speak of the Minnetarees on the Missouri as " part of the great nation called Fall Indians". † Comparing our Hidatsa words with their synonymes in Umfreville's Fall Vocabulary, or Dr. Hayden's later Atsina Vocabulary, we can discover no affinity between the Fall and Hidatsa tongues.

Umfreville's remarks concerning the impropriety of the

---

* p. 197. † p. 97.

3

name Grosventre would apply as well to those "of the Missouri"
as to those "of the Prairie". Maximilian says of the Hidatsa :—
"The French give them the singular name of Grosventres,
which is no more appropriate to them than to any other of the
Indian tribes."* Palliser remarks :—"They are most absurdly
termed Grosventres by the French traders, there being not the
slightest foundation for branding them with that epithet."†
Various writers who have visited this tribe concur in these
opinions.

Minnetarees.—In the works of many travelers they are called
"Minnetarees", a name which is spelled in various ways ; thus
Captain Lewis writes it "Minnetarees"; Catlin, "Minatarees";
De Smet, "Minataries"; Palliser, "Minitarees"; while in the
accompanying Dictionary it is spelled Minitari, or Miditadi.
This, although a Hidatsa word, is the name applied to them,
not by themselves, but by the Mandans; it signifies *to cross
the water*, or *they crossed the water*. The name may allude to
the Hidatsa tradition of their own origin, or to their account
that they came originally from the northeast, and had to cross
the Missouri before reaching the old Mandan villages, which
were on the west bank of the river, or the name may have
originated from some other cause ; but the story, be it true or
false, which is now given by both tribes concerned, to account
for its origin, is this : When the wandering Minnetarees first
reached the Missouri and stood on the bank opposite to one of
the villages of the Mandans, the latter cried out, "Who are
you?" The strangers, not understanding what was said, but
supposing that the Mandans (who were provided with boats)
asked them what they wanted, shouted in return, "Minitari,"
to cross the water, or "Minitari mihats," *we will cross the water*.
The Mandans supposed that in this reply the visitors gave them
their name, and called them Minitari ever after.

The name, as above intimated, will be found in this dictionary written 'Miditadi' or 'Minitari,' and its component parts,
'midi,' *water*, and 'tadi,' *to cross over*. The reason for this
varying orthography will be discovered by consulting the
grammar, paragraphs 19 to 23 inclusive, where it is shown

---

that *d*, *l*, *n*, and *r*, are interchangeable consonants. Prince Maximilian writes the word Manitari (adding a plural ending), which represents a way in which the Mandans often pronounce it—the Mandan word for water being *mani.*

Hidatsa was the name of the village on Knife River farthest from the Missouri, the village of those whom Lewis and Clarke considered the Minnetarees proper.* It is probable that after the epidemic of 1837 the survivors of the other villages moved thither, or that the majority of all the survivors came from Hidatsa, which then lent its name to the whole tribe—a name now generally used by this people to designate themselves, and for which reason the one most frequently employed in this essay.

The origin of the word Hidatsa is obscure. It is said by some to mean *willows;* but I know of no species of willow that bears this name. By a few of the tribe it is pronounced Hidaátsa, and in this form bears a slight resemblance to the word midahádsa, the present Minnetaree generic name for all shrub willows. It may possibly be an old form of the latter word; but, according to my present knowledge of the formation and phonetic changes of this language, I have no reason for believing it to be so.

There is little doubt that the tribe, or a portion of it, was once called Willows; and this may be the reason why some suppose Hidatsa to mean *willows.* But it is evident that even in former days travelers or their interpreters were uncertain with regard to the application of the name Willows, and later inquiries on the part of the writer have done little toward clearing the difficulty. In Lewis and Clarke's journal (1804), we find the inhabitants of Amatiha, the first village on Knife River above its mouth, spoken of as "Minnetarees Metaharta, that is, Minnetarees of the Willows";† while Prince Maximilian (1834) says that Hidatsa, or the village on Knife River farthest from the Missouri (above Amatiha), was called "Eláh-sa (the village of the great willows)."‡ It is plain that "Eláh-sa" is but a form of Hidatsa, for the aspirate is often pronounced or heard indistinctly; *d* and *l* are interchangeable with one another in this language (see Grammar, ¶¶ 20, 22), and *s* is often used for *ls*, (see ¶ 17). "Metaharta" represents possibly an old or dialectic form of "midahadsa", *willow*, which was mispronounced by the interpreter, and spelled from his mispronunciation by Captains Lewis and Clarke in an ill-devised way.

Other names.—Hewaktokto, the name of this tribe in the Dakota language, I have heard translated *Dwellers on a Ridge;* but I think the correctness of this translation may be questioned. Some of the Hidatsa believe that the appellation belonged originally only to the Amahamis, whose name signifies *mountain.*

In the Arickaree language, the Hidatsa are called Witetsnán. I have heard this rendered in two ways, viz, *Welldressed People* and *People at the Water;* the latter said to refer to their old residence at the ford of Knife River.

By the Crows, they are called Amasì, signifying *earthen houses* or *"dirt lodges"*, as the Upper Missouri interpreters would say.

§ 19. HISTORY.—These Indians relate of themselves as follows: They originally dwelt beneath the surface of a great body of water, situated to the northeast of their present home. From this subaqueous residence some persons found their way out, and, discovering a country much better than that in which they resided, returned and gave to their people such glowing accounts of their discoveries that the whole people determined to come out. Owing to the breaking of a tree, on which they were climbing out of the lake, a great part of the tribe had to remain behind in the water, and are there yet. After coming from the water, they began to wander over the prairies, and sent out couriers to explore the country around. Those who were sent to the south returned after a time with tidings of a great river and a fertile valley, of a nation who dwelt in houses and tilled the soil. They brought back with them, too, corn and other products of the country. Toward this promised land the tribe now directed its steps, and, guided by the couriers, they reached in due time the Mandan villages on the Missouri. When they arrived, however, instead of putting to death the newly-found people, they encamped quietly beside them, learned of them the arts of peace, and have ever since dwelt near them.

From the descriptions of their life previous to rising from the lake, it would seem as if their tradition originally mentioned an insular home or a home beyond some great body of water. The story of their coming up out of the lake, and of the breaking of the tree by which they rose, resembles so much the Mandan tradition as to lead us to believe that one nation borrowed its legend of the other, or that the two legends sprung, at no very remote time, from a common source. Some of the modern story-tellers say that the Minnewakan, or Devil's Lake, in Northern Dakota is the natal lake of the tribe. The Hidatsa call it Midihopa, which, like the Dakota name, signifies *sacred*, or *mysterious water*.

This account of their origin they tell usually as one story; but they have, besides, a voluminous account of what happened to them during their long wanderings on the prairie, from the time they left the lake until they reached the Mandan village, which account is embodied in a separate tale—the almost interminable legend of Itamapísa, the proper recital whereof, by an old story-teller, occupies three or four long winter-evenings. In this tale, it is said that they were often on the eve of death by starvation, but were rescued by a miraculous supply of buffalo-meat. Stones, they say, were strewn upon the prairie obedient to a divine order, and from them sprang to life the buffalo which they slaughtered. It was during these years of wandering, as the legend relates, that the spirit of the sun took a woman of this tribe up into the sky. In the course of time, she had a son, who descended to the earth, and, under the name of Itamapísa, or *Grandchild*, became the great prophet of his mother's people.

It might be more proper to introduce such tales elsewhere than under the head of history, but, perhaps, a scrap of historical truth may be picked from them, which is, that the Hidatsa were once a tribe of nomadic hunters, alternately starving and feasting as game was scarce or abundant, and that, since a comparatively recent date, they have settled in the neighborhood of the Missouri and become farmers by intercourse with tribes who previously tilled the soil. There are many circumstances which seem to corroborate this. It may be remarked, too, that the stories from which the above items are taken are believed by these Indians to be true, while many other tales, just as plausible as these, they declare to be purely fictional.

There are two affluents of the Missouri, named Knife River. One of these enters from the north, above Fort Berthold; the other from the west, below Fort Berthold. It was upon the banks of the latter stream that the former homes of this people stood. At least as early as A. D. 1796, there were three villages on Knife River. The first and largest, named Hidatsa, was on the north bank, about three miles from the Missouri, and was the home of a people whom Captains Lewis and Clarke, for some reason, regarded as the Minnetarees proper. The second village, named Amatiha, half a mile above the mouth of Knife River, and on the south bank of the stream, was the home of a people very closely allied to the inhabitants of Hidatsa, who spoke a language nearly but not exactly the same as that of the former, and had a separate chief, who seemed to acknowledge to some extent the authority of the chief of the upper village. The third village, named Amahami or Mahaha, was at the mouth of Knife River, on the south side, and was occupied, as before mentioned, by the Amahamis (see §11), a people allied to those of Hidatsa, but more remotely than the dwellers in Amatiha. The present Hidatsa or Minnetaree tribe of Fort Berthold consists of the survivors of these three villages and their descendants, with, perhaps, representatives of some small wandering bands of allied Indians which no longer exist as organized tribes. Lewis and Clarke seem to speak very positively of wandering Minnetarees, hunting in the neighborhood of Knife River,* and not considered as part of the Crow nation. In 1796, the Mandans were near neighbors of the Minnetarees, living some four miles south of the latter, in three villages, which in 1804 were found reduced to two.

Some forty years before the coming of Lewis and Clarke,

* p. 110.

i. e., about the year 1764, the Amahamis and the people of Amatiha dwelt farther south, in the neighborhood of Heart River, along with the Rees and Mandans; and it is likely that the people of Hidatsa lived there at the same time, or at an earlier date.

At one time, the Crows and the Hidatsa (under which term I will now include all the bands represented in the present tribe) lived in close proximity to one another, and constituted one nation; not, probably, one consolidated tribe under a single chief, but independent and allied bands, making common cause against other races, and speaking slightly different dialects, like the various bands of the Dakota nation to-day. In the course of time, the Crows, in two bands, separated from the Hidatsa, and moved farther to the south and west, becoming estranged from the latter but not inimical to them. This separation took place, doubtlessly, more than one hundred, and probably not less than two hundred, years ago.

The Hidatsa and Crow legends agree closely concerning the secession of the Crows, and their story is essentially as follows: During a season of scarcity, while portions of both peoples were encamped together, a single buffalo came in the neighborhood of the camp and was killed by some of the Hidatsa, who offered the paunch to the Crows. The latter, considering the offer illiberal, refused it, and a misunderstanding ensued, which resulted in separation. The Hidatsa have ever since called the Crows by the name of Kihatsa, or *they (who) refused the paunch.* (See kihatsa in Dictionary.) It may reasonably be doubted that such an incident as this, of itself, and without previous disagreements, would have been sufficient to have alienated these bands from one another; yet it is not improbable, if, as some say, there was, among the party of slighted Crows, a very proud and powerful chief, who regarded the action of the Hidatsa hunters as a personal insult. It is more likely, however, that they parted in consequence of some general misunderstanding concerning the division of game (and other matters perhaps), which may have culminated in some particular quarrel. There is no good reason for supposing the legend to be without foundation in fact. Laws concerning the distribution of game are often unlike in different bands. Cases sometimes arise, too, which their laws do not cover, and grave disputes occur in consequence. The legend and the name Kihatsa seem to have some allusion to the Hidatsa manner of dividing game. When two members of this tribe kill a buffalo, one takes the hind quarters and hump, and is said to "take the back"; the other takes the rest of the forequarters and the entrails, and is said to "take the paunch".

During the years 1804, 1832, 1833, and 1834, we have the evidence of travelers that the three Knife River villages remained just where they stood in 1796, and it is said by the Indians that there was no change until some time after the epidemic of 1837, when the survivors of the three villages formed themselves in one on Knife River. There they remained until 1845, when the Hidatsa (and about the same time the Mandans—see § 10) moved up the Missouri, and established themselves where their permanent village now stands, some thirty miles by land and sixty by river from their old home. Here, as before stated, they were joined by the Arickarees in 1862.

It may be well here to give some account of the trading-post, which has lent its name to the village and the locality. In 1845, soon after the Hidatsa settled here, the American Fur Company began, with the assistance of the Indians, to build a stockaded post, which they called Fort Berthold, in honor of a Mr. Berthold of Saint Louis. In 1859, an opposition trading company erected in the village some inclosed buildings, which they named Fort Atkinson. In 1862, the opposition ceased, and the American Fur Company obtained possession of Fort Atkinson, which they then occupied, transferring to it the name of Fort Berthold. They abandoned the old stockade, which was afterward (December 24, 1862) burned by a war-party of Sioux, who attacked the village. One side of the newer fort still stands, and is occupied by the Indian agency; the other three sides having been burned down October 12, 1874.

§ 20. CHARACTER.—To illustrate the character of the Hidatsa, I present, first, a few extracts from the writings of other observers, placing them in chronological order of observation. Some of the quoted writers visited this tribe in the most prosperous period of their history, others in later and unhappy days; yet their opinions are not at variance with one another.

1832.—"There is no tribe in the western wilds, perhaps, who are better entitled to the style of warlike than the Minatarees; for they, unlike the Mandans, are continually carrying war into their enemies' country; oftentimes drawing the poor Mandans into unnecessary broils, and suffering so much themselves in their desperate war-excursions that I find the proportion of women to the number of men as two or three to one through the tribe."—*Catlin, N. A. Indians,* vol. I, p. 187.

"This day's ramble showed us all the inhabitants of this little tribe, except a portion of their warriors, who are out on a war-excursion against the Riccarees; and I have been exceedingly pleased with their general behavior and looks, as well as with their numerous games and amusements, in many of which I have given them great pleasure by taking a part."—*Ib.,* p. 199.

1834.—"The Mandans and Manitaries are proud and have a high sense of honor."—*Maximilian,* p. 353.

1848.—"The Minataries are a noble, interesting people."—*Palliser,* p. 198.

1851.—"Some days after, we stopped at Fort Berthold, to land some goods at the great village of the Minataries, or Osier tribe, nicknamed the *Grosventres* of the Missouri." * * * * "The great chief of the latter village, called Four Bears, is the most civil and affable Indian that I met on the Missouri."—*De Smet,* pp. 76–77.

1854.—"The Grosventres have a large village of mud houses, very unsightly outside, but within warm and comfortable. These Indians are fine specimens of the red man. They are industrious, and raise corn enough to supply many of their neighbors with bread. They are well disposed toward the whites."—*Report of Commissioner of Indian Affairs for* 1854.*

1858.—"I shall ever look back upon the years spent in

---

* Extract from report of Lieutenant Saxton to Gov. I. I. Stevens.

the Indian country as among the pleasantest of my life; and if in all my dealings with white men I had found the same sense of honor that characterized my 'savage' friends, my appreciation of human nature would be much higher."*—*Boller,* p. vii.

"During the whole time that I lived among the Grosventres, I never missed a single article, although I took no trouble to keep my things out of sight. My house would often be crowded with Indians; sometimes only one or two would be present; yet if called away I felt satisfied that on my return I would find everything just as I left it."—*Ib.,* pp. 239, 240.

1862.—"They [Grosventres and Mandans] are a good people; peaceable, reliable, and honest. They keep as far as is possible the treaty made at Laramie."—*Report of Commissioner of Indian Affairs for* 1862, p. 194.†

I can indorse the above opinions, and can say that the Hidatsa are to-day, for Indians, examples in industry, general morality, forethought, and thrift.

§ 21. APPEARANCE.—More than forty years ago we find the general appearance of these Indians thus described by a careful observer:—"The Manitaries are in fact the tallest and best-formed Indians on the Missouri, and, in this respect, as well as in the elegance of their costume, the Crows only approach them, whom they perhaps even surpass in the latter particular."‡ "The Manitaries do not differ much in personal appearance from the Mandans; but it strikes the stranger that they are in general taller. Most of the men are well-formed and stout; many of them are very tall, broad-shouldered, and muscular; the latter may, indeed, be said of the greater proportion of the men. Their noses are more or less arched and sometimes straight. * * * The women are much like the Mandans; many of them are tall and stout, but most of them short and corpulent. There are some pretty faces among them, which, according to the Indian standard of beauty, may be called handsome."§

---

* From preface. These remarks seem to refer more particularly to the Grosventres and Mandans, with whom the author spent the greater part of the time that he lived " among the Indians".

† Report of Agent S. N. Latta to the Commissioner.

‡ Maximilian, p. 179.   § *Ib.,* pp. 395, 396.

At the present day, it can hardly be said that they are of finer *physique* than the Tetons and other roving bands of the Upper Missouri, who have suffered less, of late, from epidemic disease and hunger, but they still take greater pride in their dress and personal appearance than most of their neighbors. The frequent intermarriages of the Mandans and Hidatsa tend constantly to assimilate them more and more to one another in appearance; yet those claiming pure Hidatsa blood are generally taller and of more prominent features than those who consider themselves pure Mandans. We do not see as many faces among the Minnetarees pitted with small-pox as among the Arickarees and Mandans. Among all the tribes in the village, there are many disfigured by goiter and opacities of the cornea. All of the Hidatsa men bear on their bodies unsightly cicatrices resulting from the tortures of the Nahpike.

Tattooing may be spoken of in this connection. A few only of the old men are tattooed. The marks consist of numerous parallel bands on one side, or over the entire of the chest and throat, and over one or both arms. I have never seen tattooed marks on any of this tribe elsewhere, or in any other shape. The middle-aged men, the young men, the women, and the children are not tattooed. I believe that these marks on the old men were put on for something more than mere ornament, and had some forgotten significance. In Arickaree picture-writings, Grosventres are sometimes represented by a rude symbol of a man having the upper part covered with parallel stripes. As far as I can learn, this particular style of tattooing is peculiar to the Minnetarees.

Complexion —The majority of the Hidatsa have the ordinary dusky Indian complexion, which is, however, not of a uniform shade, as far as I have seen, in any tribe. There are none of this nation that would be considered dark for Indians. Among various tribes of western Indians may be found individuals, claiming pure aboriginal blood, who possess complexions much fairer than the average Indian, with light-colored hair and eyes. Such individuals are more common among the Mandans and Minnetarees than they are among most of the neighboring tribes. A natural or inherited clearness of com-

plexion, too, is more easily discernible among members of the
village tribes than among members of roving bands who are
more exposed to the weather. The presence of pale Indians
in these tribes was noted by travelers in early days, before
intermarriages with whites were common enough to have
accounted for it.

Lewis and Clarke* and Gass† notice this fairness when
speaking of the Mandans only, but their remarks are general.
Catlin speaks of the fairness of the Mandans only, and supposes
this peculiarity to arise from some pre-Columbian infusion of
European blood.‡ The Prince of New Wied, who visited these
tribes but one year later than Mr. Catlin, denies that the Mandans
are of fairer complexion than their neighbors,§ while he asserts,
at the same time, that, "after a thorough ablution, the skin of
some of them appears almost white."‖ I have heard old Mandans say that when the Minnetarees, including the Crows, first
came among them, the strangers were a fairer race than they.
Of the Crows, who, as before shown, once formed one nation with
the Hidatsa, Colonel Raynolds, in his *Report of the Exploration
of the Yellowstone* (1859), p. 48, says:—"The Crows are fairer
than the Sioux, many of the mountain band being sallow and
hardly a shade darker than whites who undergo similar exposure. This fact was so marked that the first seen were supposed to be half-breeds, but we were assured that they were of
pure Indian descent."

It is not necessary to suppose an intermixture of European
blood in order to account for lightness of color in an Indian.
There is no reason why marked varieties of color should not
arise in the Red Race as it has done in other races of men, and
as it has so often done, under cultivation, within specific limits
in the lower animals. I have seen full-blooded Indians who
were whiter than some half-breeds and whiter than the darkest
representatives of the Aryan Race. An increase of hairiness is
a more reliable sign of Caucasian blood in an Indian than a
diminution of color in the skin; and I never could discover
that those fair Indians, claiming pure blood, were more hairy
than others. The fairness of which I speak is not albinism,

---

* p. 89.   † p. 83.   ‡ Okeepa, pp. 5, 42.   § p. 314.   ‖ p. 337.

for the eyesight of the fair Indians is as perfect as that of the dark; they have no unusual appearance of the pupil, and exposure to sunlight darkens their skins. I have never seen an albino Indian.

Among various western tribes, individuals may be found who are characterized, even in childhood, by having coarse gray hair. From all I could see and learn, I should think that such persons are more numerous among the Minnetarees and Mandans than in any other tribe; and they are perhaps the most numerous among the Mandans.

§22. CEREMONIES.—Their most important ceremony is that of the Dahpike or Nahpike, which formerly took place regularly once a year, but is now celebrated every second or third year only. On the day when it is determined to commence this ceremony, some men of the Hidatsa tribe, dressed and mounted as for a war-party, proceed to the woods. Here they select a tall, forked cottonwood, which they fell, trim, and bark; to this they tie their lariats, and, by the aid of their horses, drag it toward the village. In the procession, the man who has most distinguished himself in battle, mounted on the horse on whose back he has done his bravest deeds, takes the lead; others follow in the order of their military distinction; as they drag the log along, they fire their guns at it, strike it with their sticks, and shout and sing songs of victory. The log, they say, is symbolical of a conquered enemy, whose body they are bringing into the camp in triumph. When the log is set up, they again go to the woods to procure a quantity of willows. A temporary lodge of green willows is then built around the log, as the medicine-lodge, wherein the ceremony is performed. The participants fast four days with food in sight, and, on the fourth day, submit to tortures which vary according to the whim of the sufferer or the advice of the medicine-men. Some have long strips of skin separated from different parts of their bodies, but not completely detached. Others have large pieces of the integument entirely removed, leaving the muscles exposed. Others have incisions made in their flesh, in which raw-hide strings are inserted; they then attach buffalo skulls to the strings and run round with these until the strings become disengaged by tearing their way out of the flesh. Others, again, have skewers inserted in their breasts, which skewers are secured by raw-hide cords to the central pole, as in the Dakota sun-dance; the sufferer then throws himself back until he is released by the skewers tearing out of the flesh. Many other ingenious tortures are devised. In the narrative of Long's Expedition to the Rocky Mountains, we find an account of the latter part of this ceremony,* prepared probably from the statements of Mr. Dougherty or Mr. Lisa, as the expedition did not go near the Minnetaree. country. All of the torments there described, and more, are inflicted to this day. Among them is the following:—"Another Minnetaree, in compliance with a vow he had made, caused a hole to be perforated through the muscles of each shoulder; through these holes cords were passed, which were, at the opposite ends, attached by way of a bridle to a horse, that had been penned up three or four days without food or water. In this manner he led the horse to the margin of the river. The horse, of course, endeavored to drink, but it was the province of the Indian to prevent him, and that only by straining at the cords with the muscles of the shoulder, without resorting to the assistance of his hands. And notwithstanding all the exertions of the horse to drink, his master succeeded in preventing him, and returned with him to his lodge, having accomplished his painful task."†

In describing the Minnetarees, Prince Maximilian says that they have the Mandan ceremony of the Okipa or O-kee-pa, with some modifications, and call it Akupehi. At this time, the Hidatsa call the Mandan ceremony Akupi (of which word probably Akupehi is an old form); but they apply no such term to their own festival. Maximilian did not spend a summer among those Indians, and, therefore, knew of both ceremonies only from description. If the Minnetaree festival to which he referred was, as is most likely, the Nahpike, he is, to some extent, in error. The rites resemble one another only in their appalling fasts and tortures. In allegory, they seem to be radically different.

The minor ceremonies are chiefly those connected with their

---

* pp. 276, 277, 278.   † pp. 277, 278.

bands, of which the men and women have separate organizations and separate ceremonies.* Rites connected with the eagle-trapping will be noticed hereafter. In one of his letters descriptive of the Minnetarees, Catlin gives an account of a green-corn dance,† and devotes a plate to illustrating the same.‡ He does not directly say that this is a Minnetaree festivity, but introduces the description in a way calculated to lead the casual reader to suppose that it is such. I have shown the plate to several of these Indians, and have given them the description of the dance, but have been invariably informed that they never had such a ceremony. In the same letter, he speaks of an improvident waste of the harvest in gluttonous eating of the green corn. His remarks on this point certainly do not apply to the Hidatsa. In Chapter XIII of his work, Boller gives a brief description of a dance or paduididi performed by the Goose Band, an organization of the old women of this tribe; and, in Chapter XIX, he describes certain ceremonies of the White Cow Band. The latter band, originally, I believe, belongs to the Mandan women, but Hidatsa women are now admitted to its mysteries.

§ 23. MYTHOLOGY AND SUPERSTITIONS.—*Objects of veneration.*—The object of their greatest reverence is, perhaps, Itsikamahidiš, the *First Made*, or First in Existence. They sometimes designate him as Itakatétaš, or *Old Man Immortal*. Some Indians say that itsikamahidiš means *he who first made*, but such a rendering is not in accordance with the present etymology of the language. They assert that he made all things, the stars, the sun, the earth, and the first representatives of each species of animals and plants, but that no one made him. He also, they say, instructed the forefathers of the tribes in all the ceremonies and mysteries now known to them.

Mahopa, or Mahopa-ietiaš, is the equivalent in the Hidatsa language for those terms in other Indian tongues which are usually translated "The Great Spirit". In this language, it may be (figuratively, perhaps) applied to the Itakatetaš, or any-

---

* See icke, iñokaicke, iñokamiaicke, masukaicke, masukakâdista, masukamadaki, midaicke, and paduididi, in the Dictionary.

† p. 189.   ‡ Plate 75.

thing else of a very wonderful or sacred nature. Much diversity of opinion exists among observers of Indian character concerning the ideas which the savages attach to this term; and the subject deserves more consideration than it has yet received. The ideas of all the tribes within our borders have undoubtedly been greatly modified by intercourse with the whites; and, recognizing this fact, many claim that the **Great Spirit,** or, more properly, **Great Mystery,** is a deity of the modern Indian only. I have certainly heard some old and very conservative Minnetarees speak of Mahopa as if they meant thereby an influence or power above all other things, but not attaching to it any ideas of personality. It would now be perhaps impossible to make a just analysis of their original conceptions in this matter. But the Old Man Immortal has no vague existence in their minds.

If we use the term *worship* in its most extended sense, it may be said that, besides this being, they worship everything in nature. Not man alone, but the sun, the moon, the stars, all the lower animals, all trees and plants, rivers and lakes, many bowlders and other separated rocks, even some hills and buttes which stand alone—in short, everything not made by human hands, which has an independent being, or can be individualized, possesses a spirit, or, more properly, a *shade.* (See idahi in Dictionary.)

To these shades some respect or consideration is due, but not equally to all. For instance, the shade of the cottonwood, the greatest tree of the Upper Missouri Valley, is supposed to possess an intelligence which may, if properly approached, assist them in certain undertakings; but the shades of shrubs and grasses are of little importance. When the Missouri, in its spring-time freshets, cuts down its banks and sweeps some tall tree into its current, it is said that the spirit of the tree cries while the roots yet cling to the land and until the tree falls into the water. Formerly it was considered wrong to cut down one of these great trees, and, when large logs were needed, only such as were found fallen were used; and to-day some of the more credulous old men declare that many of the misfortunes of the people are the result of their modern disregard for the rights of the living cottonwood. The sun is held in great veneration, and many valuable sacrifices are made to it.

Future state.—They believe neither in a hell nor in a devil, but believe that there are one or more evil genii, in female shape (see mahopamiiś in Dictionary), who inhabit this earth, and may harm the Indian in this life, but possess no power beyond the grave. Their faith concerning a future life is this: When a Hidatsa dies, his shade lingers four nights around the camp or village in which he died, and then goes to the lodge of his departed kindred in the Village of the Dead. When he has arrived there, he is rewarded for his valor, self-denial, and ambition on earth by receiving the same regard in the one place as in the other; for there, as here, the brave man is honored and the coward despised. Some say that the ghosts of those who commit suicide occupy a separate part of the village, but that their condition differs in no wise from that of the others. In the next world, human shades hunt and live on the shades of buffalo and other animals that have here died. There too there are four seasons, but they come in an inverse order to the terrestrial seasons. During the four nights that the ghost is supposed to linger near his former dwelling, those who disliked or feared the deceased, and do not wish a visit from the shade, scorch with red coals a pair of moccasins, which they leave at the door of the lodge. The smell of the burning leather, they claim, keeps the ghost out; but the true friends of the dead man take no such precautions.

Various superstitions.—They have a great many superstitious notions, yet I believe their superstitions are neither more numerous nor more absurd than those of the peasantry of some European nations to-day. There is, too, among them every degree of faith in these fancies, from almost perfect skepticism to the most humble credulity. I will not describe all of their superstitions known to me, but will refer, for illustration, to a few of them. They believe in the existence and visibility of human and other ghosts, yet they seem to have no terror of graveyards and but little of mortuary remains. You may frighten children after nightfall by shouting nohidahi (*ghost*), but will not scare the aged. They have much faith in dreams,

4

but usually regard as oracular those only which come after prayer, sacrifice, and fasting. They have queer notions respecting the effects of different articles of diet, thus: An expectant mother believes that if she eats a part of a mole or shrew, her child will have small eyes; that if she eats a piece of porcupine her child will be inclined to sleep too much when it grows up; that if she partakes of the flesh of the turtle, her offspring will be slow or lazy, etc.; but they do not suppose that such articles of food affect the immediate consumer. They have faith in witchcraft, and think that a sorcerer may injure any person, no matter how far distant, by acts upon an effigy or upon a lock of the victim's hair.

It is believed by some of the Hidatsa that every human being has four souls in one. They account for the phenomena of gradual death, where the extremities are apparently dead while consciousness remains, by supposing the four souls to depart, one after another, at different times. When dissolution is complete, they say that all the souls are gone, and have joined together again outside of the body. I have heard a Minnetaree quietly discussing this doctrine with an Assinneboine, who believed in only one soul to each body.

Amulets.—Every man in this tribe, as in all other neighboring tribes, has his personal medicine, which is usually some animal. On all war-parties, and often on hunts and other excursions, he carries the head, claws, stuffed skin, or other representative of his medicine with him, and seems to regard it in much the same light that Europeans in former days regarded—and in some cases still regard—protective charms. To insure the future fleetness of some promising young colt, they tie to the colt's neck a small piece of deer or antelope horn. The rodent teeth of the beaver are regarded as potent charms, and are worn by little girls on their necks to make them industrious.

Oracles.—Since their removal to their present village, they do not seem to have any very important local oracles to consult; but when they lived on Knife River, they had at least two such holy places. One of these was a famous holy stone, or "Medicine rock" (Mihopaś, or, Mandan, Mihopiniś), which is described by Long and by Maximilian. It was some two or three days' journey from their residence. The Hidatsa now seldom refer to it, and I do not think they ever visit it.

The other famous oracle, to which they now often refer, as they have still some fancies connected with it, was the Maka-dístati, or *House of the Infants*, a cavern, near the Knife River, which they supposed extended far into the earth, but whose entrance was only a span wide. This cave, they say, was inhabited by pigmies, or mysterious infants, who came out only at night, and then with great caution, lest they should be observed, and who followed a wise and watchful leader that knew the scent of man and snuffed the air as he advanced, like the leader of a band of antelope. They suppose that if he detected the presence of a human being, he gave the alarm and all retreated. After rainy nights, they saw tracks of some animals going from and returning to the cave, which tracks they said were those of the infants. The oracle was thus consulted: The childless husband, after a long fast, would repair to the neighborhood of the cave at night, and secrete himself behind a bowlder, to the leeward, to watch; if, in his hunger-weakened brain, he had a vision of the infants, he returned home, confident that he would be a father within a year. The barren wife who desired children would, at sunset, lay at the mouth of the cave a tiny play-ball and a little bow and arrow. If the ball was missing in the morning, she believed that within a year she would be the mother of a girl; while if the bow and arrow were missing, she supposed she would be the mother of a boy. If neither were "taken", she went back with little hope, and could not consult the oracle again until a year had elapsed. There are those among them who imagine that, in some way or other, their children come from the Makadistati; and marks of contusion on an infant, arising from tight swaddling or other causes, are gravely attributed to kicks received from his former comrades when he was ejected from his subterranean home.

An account, given in Long's travels, of a certain hill, which "was supposed to impart a prolific virtue to such squaws as resorted to it", etc.,* seems to refer to this oracle;

* Long, vol. i, pp. 274–275.

but, if such is the case, I believe the account to be incorrect in some respects.

§ 24. MARRIAGE, ETC.—Marriage is usually made formal by the distribution of gifts on the part of the man to the woman's relations. Afterward, presents of equal value are commonly returned by the woman's relations, if they have the means of returning them and are satisfied with the conduct of the husband. After the marriage, if the husband is a young man taking his first wife, he becomes an inmate of his father-in-law's lodge, and helps, by his hunting, to support his wife's parents. Some travelers have represented that the "marriage by purchase" among the Indians is a mere sale of the woman to the highest bidder, whose slave she becomes; but I feel that they misrepresent the custom, unless where their remarks may apply to some modern irregularities among the least reputable persons. Certainly, they misrepresent the custom as it exists in this tribe. The presenting of the wedding-gift is a form. The gift itself is a pledge to the parents for the proper treatment of their daughter, as well as an evidence of the wealth of the suitor and his relations. The larger the marriage-gift the more flattering it is to the bride and her relations; hence, the value of the presents offered has something to do in favoring a suitor's cause; but girls are left much to their own choice in selecting husbands for themselves. Parents sometimes, by persuasion, but rarely by any harsh coercion, endeavor to influence a daughter in the reception or rejection of an offer. I have known many cases where large marriage-presents have been refused from one party, and gifts of much less value accepted from another, simply because the girl showed a preference for the poorer lover. The fame of a man as a warrior, his influence and position in the tribe, do more to secure him a good wife than the presents he may offer. Skill in hunting is a high recommendation; parents commonly advise their daughters to marry the men who will never leave the lodge unprovided with meat. I knew a case of a poor young Mandan, who had a sickly and worthless wife of another tribe, to whom, however, he was very kind; when she died, a well-to-do Grosventre, who had three fine daughters, gave them all to the young widower in marriage, and with them a valuable present in horses and other property, saying, "The young man has a good heart, and will be kind to my children when I am dead." Sometimes when a girl is crossed in her love, she elopes with her favorite. The pair remain out on the prairie for a week or so, and then return to the village. Usually this ends the trouble. They are then considered married, but such marriages are looked upon as undignified, and different terms are applied to a marriage by elopement and a marriage by parental consent. (See kidake and uahe in Dictionary.)

Polygamy is practiced, but usually with certain restrictions. A man who marries the eldest of several sisters has a claim to the others as they grow up; and in most cases marries them, unless they, in the mean time, form other attachments and refuse to live with him. As certain female cousins are regarded as younger sisters, a man has often much latitude in selecting wives under this law. A man usually takes to wife the widow of a brother, unless she expresses an unwillingness to the arrangement, and he may adopt the orphans as his own children. When a Grosventre takes a second wife who is no relation to the first wife the results are generally unhappy. Sometimes the first wife leaves him and returns to her relations; sometimes she succeeds in chasing the second wife away. Occasionally, if the husband is well off, he provides them with separate establishments; sometimes, again, but rarely, the two wives agree.

Divorce is easily effected; yet, among the better class of people in the tribe, it is rare. A young man who possesses sufficient recommendations to secure a comely and industrious girl of good reputation and well connected is usually in no hurry to part with her, nor is she willing to leave him for trifling causes. The unions of such people often last for life. Among persons of different character, divorces are common. The Minnetaree woman is, as a rule, faithful to her husband, particularly when she is married to the man of her choice. It sometimes happens, however, that a married woman elopes. The injured husband may then satisfy himself by seizing all the property of the seducer and of the seducer's friends that he can lay his hands on, and the latter often give him opportunities of doing so, or voluntarily come forward with presents to appease him. If the husband should at first slay his faithless wife, which is rarely done, no one would call him to account for it; but if he or any of his relations have made seizures or accepted presents on account of the elopement, he does not dare to touch her when she returns. But the most praiseworthy course for the husband to pursue is to send for the runaways, request their return to the village, and, when they come back, invite them to his lodge and formally present the woman to her seducer, giving him a horse or some other valuable gift into the bargain. In short, if he would show that "his heart is strong", he must treat the whole affair as if he had had a good riddance. If a man discards a wife for infidelity, or if she elopes from him, he hopelessly disgraces himself if he takes her back.

Notwithstanding that such are their customs, it must be remembered that their social discipline is not very severe. Punishments by law, administered by their soldier band, they have, but only for serious offenses against the regulations of the camp. He who simply violates social customs of the tribe often subjects himself to no worse punishment than an occasional sneer or taunting remark; but for grave transgressions he may lose the favor and regard of his friends.

With the Minnetarees, as with other western tribes, it is improper for a man to hold a direct conversation with his mother-in-law; but this custom seems to be falling into disuse.

§25. NAMES.—Children are named when a few days old. Sometimes to males four names are given, all of which will have the same noun, but each one a different adjective. Only one of these names will be commonly used. In after years, the names of the males are changed once, or oftener, or rather new names are given; for they will be called as often by the old names as by the new. The first new name is usually given to a youth after he has first struck an enemy in battle. The names of women are rarely changed. Sometimes, if a name is long, a part of it only is used in ordinary conversation. Nicknames are often given on account of some absurd saying,

ludicrous circumstance, or personal peculiarity; and it sometimes happens that a person is called by his nickname almost
to the exclusion of his proper name. Boys are sometimes
named in honor of distinguished warriors deceased. Horses
are rarely named; but names are often given to dogs, particularly to such as children keep for pets. White men known to
the tribe are ordinarily named by these Indians from personal
peculiarities; thus, we have for whites names which translated
signify Long Neck, Fish-Eyes, Antelope-Eye, Old Crane, etc.
A white man who has been for many years employed at Fort
Berthold as an ox-driver, and who has, in consequence of his
employment, frequently occasion to say "wo, wo-haw!" is
known among the Grosventres as momohaš (Englished, Mómo-
haush or Bobohaush). Whites are sometimes called by the
translations of their regular Christian-names or surnames.
Thus, an old interpreter named Pierre Garreau is called miš
(Englished, Meesh or Beesh), from mi', *a rock;* and a Mr. Pease,
who formerly traded at Fort Berthold, is known to the tribe as
amaziš (Englished, Amaúzhish), from amazi, *beans.* It is probable that some of these translations are made by the whites
and then employed by the Indians.

I have seen some members of this and of other tribes who
are ashamed to tell their names, and when asked for their
names will answer reluctantly and with apologies, or seek a
third party to give the information; while other Indians, apparently as conservative, exhibit no such hesitancy. I think
that sensitiveness on this point is not so common among the
Indians at Fort Berthold as among other tribes; nor is it as
common among them now as it was ten years ago.

§ 26. RELATIONSHIP.—To illustrate their system of relationship, some of the Hidatsa names for relations are here synop-
tically given, although they may be found also in the Dictionary, each in its alphabetical order.

adutáka,—grandfather or great-grandfather, or grandfather's brothers.

ikú,—grandmother, great-grandmother, grandmother's
sisters.

áté,—father, father's brothers, uncles in the male line.

áté-ka'ti,—a true father.

tatíš,—another term for father, **never used** with the pronouns.

íka' or íkąš,—mother, **mother's** sisters, aunts in the female line.

hidú,—**a true mother** (same word as for bone).

hu,—**another term for** mother, said to **be of amahami** origin.

itídu,—a mother's brothers, **uncles in the female line.**

išámi,—a father's sisters, aunts in the male line.

itakíša,—**a general name for sisters and** female cousins, also the only name for a man's younger sister.

itamě'tsa,—a general name for brother or male cousin, also used in the sense of companion as in **English.** The only term for a woman's elder brother.

itáku,—a **woman's** younger sister.

idú,—**a woman's elder** sister.

itamía,—**a man's elder** sister.

itsúka,—a man's or woman's younger brother.

íaka,—a man's elder brother.

idíši,—**a** son, said by both parents.

iká,—a daughter, a brother's daughter.

kidá,—a husband.

itádamia,—a wife, a wife's sisters, particularly her younger sisters.

úa,—a true wife.

išikíši,—a husband's brother.

idá'ti,—a wife's brother, a brother's husband.

The above terms are for relations of the third person; many of them having the possessive pronoun of the third person 'i' inseparably prefixed, or to be removed only when pronouns of the first and second persons are used. To make the forms of the first and second persons 'ma' and 'di' are respectively substituted for 'i', or the fragmentary pronouns 'm' and 'd' used. We have thus, máte, *my father;* matsuka, *my younger brother;* dúa, *your wife;* díaka, *your elder brother,* etc. The words tatiš, ika', and hidu do not ordinarily take possessive pronouns, but are the same for all persons. All these may end with š. (See ¶ 90 in Grammar.)

In the above definitions, male cousins and adopted brothers are included under the term *brother*, and female cousins and adopted sisters under the term *sister*. Hence it is evident that their words expressive of relationship are often applied to the most distant and indefinite connections.

On examination of the foregoing list, the following facts may be noted : Of the terms for brother and sister, certain ones are used only for relatives of the male, others only for those of the female ; some are applied only to elder, others only to younger relatives; while two of the terms are general. There is a separate term for a maternal uncle, but none for a paternal uncle ; he is called by the same name as a father. When they wish to distinguish between an actual father and a father's brothers, they use the adjective ka'ti, *true, real*, in speaking of the former. While there is a name for paternal aunt, there is none to distinguish maternal aunt from mother ; yet there is a special word to designate the real mother, although she is commonly called by the terms which apply as well to her sisters. There are two names for wife ; one for a wife by actual marriage, the other for an actual wife as well as what might be called a potential wife, *i. e.*, a wife's sisters. There are two terms for brother-in-law, but no general term, as with us.

It must not be supposed, from the wide significance of some of their terms, that they do not discriminate between all grades and conditions of kinship. When they have no single word to define the relationship, they employ two or more words.

§ 27. Hunting.—Their methods of hunting are much the same as those of all the other plain Indians. In former days they made antelope-parks;* they stampeded herds of buffalo over bluffs; they approached animals carefully until within close arrow-range, or decoyed them to approach the hunter by imitative sounds, or, as in the case of antelope, by displaying attractive objects. When they obtained horses, the chasing of the buffalo became common; and when they came into the possession of fire-arms, they began to hunt much as white

---

* See Lewis and Clarke, p. 92 ; De Smet, p. 143 *et seq.* ; Maximilian, p. 385. Other authors describe this mode of hunting.

men do. They still often employ the primitive methods; thus, when they find antelope abundant, they make the oft-described antelope-park. The bow and arrow are still largely employed by the hunters; and fall-traps and snare-traps are made to catch foxes and other small animals. The boys practice themselves in the use of the bow by shooting at marmots and small birds, and in winter they set horse-hair snares for snow-buntings. The majority of their modes of capturing and killing the lower animals have been so extensively described by other observers* that I will make no further reference to them here. But I will give an account of their eagle-hunt, which, as far as I know, has never been fully described in any book of travels, although Maximilian and Hayden both speak of it.

Eagle-hunting.—Late in the autumn or early in the winter, when they go out on their winter-hunt, a few families seek some quiet spot in the timber, and make a camp with a view to catching eagles. After pitching their tents, they first build a small medicine-lodge, where the ceremonies, supposed to be indispensable, are performed, and then make several traps on high places among the neighboring hills. Each trap consists of a hole dug in the earth, and covered with sticks, sods, etc.; a small opening is left in the covering; a dead rabbit, grouse, or other animal is tied on top; and an Indian is secreted in the excavation below. The eagle, seeing the bait, sweeps down and fastens his claws in it; but, the bait being secured, he is unable to remove it. When the eagle's claws are stuck, the Indian puts his hand out through the opening, and, catching the bird by both legs, draws him into the hole and ties him firmly. The trapper then re-arranges the top of his trap, and waits for another eagle. In this way many eagles are caught; they are then brought alive into camp, the tails are plucked out, and the bird is set at liberty, to suffer, perhaps, a similar imprisonment and mutilation at some future time.

The covered hole or trap is called amaśi'. When the trapping-season is over, they break up the camp; and, if the locality is not already provided with a name, they call it the

* Particularly the exciting "buffalo-surround". See Catlin, N A. Indians, vol. I, p. 199 *et seq.*—Buller, p. 224 *et seq.*

amasĭ of whoever was master of ceremonies during the season. Two instances of this manner of naming are given in the list of Local Names.

The medicine-lodge is built after the manner of their ordinary earth-covered dwelling-houses, but is much smaller. The door-way is low and small; and the door, consisting of a skin stretched on a frame, is suspended from the top by a string. On the inside of the lodge, opposite to the door, is a sort of altar, on which various charms and relics are placed; around the edge, to the right and left of the door, hay is spread to serve as seats; and, in the center, is the fire-place. At night, after the trappers return, they sit to the left; their visitors sit to the right, as they enter. The latter enter and leave the lodge only by opening the door on the side corresponding with their seats. No person is allowed to spit on the floor, but he may spit behind him in the hay. Women are not allowed to enter the lodge, but may come to the door and hand in food and water.

When some of the men wish to take part in the trapping, they go, during the day, after a preliminary fast, to the medicine-lodge. There they continue without food until about midnight, when they partake of a little nourishment, and go to sleep. They arise just before dawn, or when the morning-star rises; go to their traps; sit there all day without food or drink, watching for their prey, and return about sunset. As they approach the camp, every one there rushes into his lodge, for the hunter must see, or be seen by, none but his fellow-hunters until he enters the medicine-lodge. On entering the lodge, they stay there for the night. About midnight they eat and drink for the first time since the previous midnight, and then lie down to sleep, to arise again before the dawn and go to their traps. If there be one among them who has caught nothing during the day, he must not sleep at night, but must spend his time in loud lamentation and in prayer. The routine described must be continued by each hunter four days and four nights, after which he returns to his own lodge hungry, thirsty, and tired, and follows his ordinary pursuits until he feels able to go again to the eagle-traps. During the four days of the trapping, the hunter sees none of his family, and speaks to none of his friends except those who are engaged in the trapping at the same time. They believe that, if any eagle-hunter does not properly perform all these rites, the eagle, when caught, will get one of his claws loose and tear the captor's hands. There are men in the tribe who have had their hands crippled for life in this way.

The chief objects of pursuit in this hunt are the tail-feathers and largest wing-feathers of the war-eagle, *Aquila chrysætus*, which are in such great requisition as emblems of valor. Of course, other birds of prey besides the war-eagle often seize the bait; of such three species are considered worthy of capture; but these inferior birds are often slain at the trap instead of being brought home alive.

§.28. WARFARE.—The tales which some of the old men of this tribe tell of the warlike expeditions of their fathers and grandfathers seem scarcely credible, although from the descriptions of distant countries that they contain they bear internal evidence of truth. The journeys performed by the Hidatsa war-parties of the last century were very long, but those undertaken by single individuals were more extraordinary. I have heard it related (with many descriptive embellishments and minute particulars) of an old warrior that he traveled directly to the south on foot until he reached the Platte River; there he built himself a bull-boat, and floated far down the Lower Missouri, where he found the land all forest, and where he plucked fruits and shot birds such as he had never seen before; and there, from the head of some unknown Indian, he raised a scalp, and returned to his people after an absence of twenty lunar months. Another story is told of one who traveled toward the north-star until he came to a land where the summer was but three moons long. Here he raised the scalp of some poor Tinneh, and came back to his native village in about seventeen moons from the day he started.

The Minnetarees now rarely meet the Shoshonees, or Snake Indians of the Rocky Mountains, either in war or in peace; yet, in 1804, as appears from the account of Lewis and Clarke, an almost constant warfare was carried on between these two tribes. There are old men now among the Hidatsa who speak of battles that they fought in their youth on the banks of streams that flow to the west. There are middle-aged men in this tribe who have, on mounted war-parties, passed through the Dakota hunting-grounds to strike the Chippeways in Minnesota. When the Chippeways would see the tracks of the scalp-hunters pointing toward the western prairies, they would perhaps blame the Dakotas, and revenge themselves on the latter. Of late years, their military operations have become more restricted since the Dakotas have given them all they could attend to near home.

Occasionally they have pitched battles with their enemies, but most of their hostilities consist in the raids of small war-parties, whose great object is not to take many scalps at any hazard but to inflict some injury without loss to themselves. The popularity of a partisan leader depends much on the small cause for mourning which his excursions entail on the tribe. When, however, they fight to resist a war-party, or meet an enemy by accident when they are not out on a regular war-excursion, they fight with little regard for life.* Many of their war-parties start out on foot, expecting to return with stolen horses.

Prisoners of war.---Young children are often taken prisoners of war. They are neither ill-treated nor compelled to perform unusual labors. Sometimes they are adopted by people who have lost children, and are then treated with parental kindness. When they have grown to maturity, they sometimes return to the tribe whence they came, but more often remain with their captors. I have never seen or heard of these Indians taking adult prisoners, for the purpose of torturing them to death, as was so common among the eastern tribes. The Hidatsa kills his enemy outright.

The *bodies of the slain*, however, they mutilate in every conceivable shape. Sometimes they burn them whole, on large pyres; sometimes they hack them in pieces and burn

---

* See account of a battle near Fort Berthold between Minnetarees and Sioux, given by Boller, p. 145.

the fragments as offerings to the sun. Palliser gives an account of a fight between the Minnetarees and the Sioux at Fort Berthold, which he closes with the following remarks:— "The skirmish now terminated; the Sioux retired and the Minnetarees returned to their village in triumph, dragging the body of their unfortunate victim along with them. Then commenced a truly disgusting sight; the boys shot arrows into the carcass of their fallen enemy, while the women, with their knives, cut out pieces of the flesh, which they broiled and ate. I turned away chilled with horror, and the whole scene haunted me for hours, and frequently afterward."* I first read this after I had known these Indians for some years, and was much surprised, for I had never heard of cannibalism among them, and had known of cases where some had died of hunger without resorting to this practice, which, among starving Europeans, is not uncommon. I had also heard Mr. Palliser's former hunting-companions and acquaintances on the Upper Missouri speak of him in terms of high praise as a man of veracity; and I have heard the adventures related in his book corroborated by eye-witnesses; therefore I took particular pains to inform myself on this point; and I was assured by the oldest white residents, as well as by the oldest Indians, that none of this tribe had ever, under any circumstances, devoured human flesh. They say that the neighboring tribe of Crees do sometimes eat parts of the bodies of enemies slain in battle; and they account for his assertion either by supposing that there were Crees visiting the camp at the time, or that the horrified Palliser "turned away chilled" upon witnessing the cutting and broiling, and without waiting to see if the flesh was eaten, but taking the latter for granted.

§ 29. STORIES.—Long winter-evenings are often passed in reciting and listening to stories of various kinds. Some of these are simply the accounts given by the men of their own deeds of valor, their hunts and journeys; some are narrations of the wonderful adventures of departed heroes; while many are fictions, full of impossible incident, of witchcraft and magic. The latter class of stories are very numerous. Some of them

---

* p. 286.

have been handed down through many generations; some are of recent origin, while a few are borrowed from other tribes. Of course, the interest of a tale depends much on the way it is told; although the plot remains the same with different narrators, the accessories and embellishments are added by each one to suit himself. Thus, some old men acquire great reputations as story-tellers, and are invited to houses and feasted by those who are desirous of listening to them. Good storytellers often originate tales, and do not disclaim the authorship. When people of different tribes meet, they often exchange tales with one another.

As an example of their tales of fiction, I have selected a story, said to belong originally to this tribe, and to have been known to it from time immemorial. An old Indian will occupy several hours in telling it, with much elegant and minute description, which I omit. On the other hand, I add nothing, and give the following as a simple abridgment of the tale as I have heard it told.

Tale of fiction.—Near the mouth of Burnt Creek, on the east bank of the Missouri, are the vestiges of some large round lodges, which stood there before the Indians came into the land. They were inhabited by various mysterious beings of great power in sorcery. In one of the lodges lived the two great demi-gods Long Tail and Spotted Body; a woman lived with them, who took care of their lodge, and who was their wife and sister; and these three were at first the only beings of their kind in the world. In a neighboring lodge lived an evil monster named Big Mouth, "who had a great mouth and no head". He hated the members of Long Tail's lodge, and when he discovered that the woman was about to become a mother he determined to attempt the destruction of her offspring.

When Long Tail and Spotted Body were absent on a hunt one day, Big Mouth entered their lodge, and, addressing the woman, said that he was hungry. The woman was greatly frightened, but did not wish to deny him her hospitality; so she proceeded to broil him some meat on the coals. When the meat was cooked, she offered it to him in a wooden dish

He told her that, from the way his mouth was made, he could not eat out of a dish, and that the only way she could serve him the food so that he could eat it was by lying down and placing it on her side. She did as he intimated, when he immediately devoured the meat, and in doing so tore her in pieces. She died, or seemed to die; but the children thus rudely brought into the world were immortal. One of these he seized, and throwing him into the bottom of the lodge, said: "Stay there forever among the rubbish and let your name be Atùtish."* The other he took out and threw into a neighboring spring, saying to him: "Your name is Máhash;† stay there forever, where you will love the mud and learn to eat nothing but the worms and reptiles of the spring."

When Long Tail and Spotted Body came home, they were horrified to find their sister slaughtered; they mourned her duly, and then placed her body on a scaffold, as these Indians do. After the funeral, they returned hungry to the lodge, and put some meat on the fire to cook. As the pleasant odor of the cooking arose, they heard an infantile voice crying and calling for food. They sought and listened, and sought again, until they at length found Atutish, whom they dragged forth into the light, and knew to be the child which they supposed was devoured or lost forever. Long Tail then placed Atutish on the ground, and, holding his hand some distance above the child's head, made a wish that "he would grow so high"; and instantly the child attained the stature, mind, and knowledge of a boy about eight years old. Then Long Tail made many inquiries concerning what had happened to him and the whereabouts of his brother; but the child could give no information of what took place during the visit of Big Mouth.

In a day or two after this transaction, the elders made for the child a little stick and wheel (such as Indian children use in the game called by the Canadians of the Upper Missouri *roulette*), and bade him play round in the neighborhood of the lodge, while they went out to hunt again. While he was play-

---

* Or atutiŝ. See 'atuti' in Dictionary.
† Or mahaŝ. See 'maha' in Dictionary.
I have given above these two names in an English form for the convenience of the reader.

ing near the spring, he heard a voice calling to him and saying
"miakas" (*my elder brother*). He looked in the direction from
which the voice proceeded, and saw little Mahash looking out
of the spring. Wanting a playmate, Atutish invited him to
come out and play. So Mahash came out, and the two brothers
began to amuse themselves. But when Long Tail and his
brother approached the lodge, on their return from the hunt,
Mahash smelled them far off, rushed away like a frightened
beast, and hid himself in the spring. When the elders returned,
Atutish told them all that had happened while they were gone.
They concluded that he of the spring must be their lost child,
and devised a plan to rescue him, which they communicated to
Atutish.

Next morning they made another and smaller roulette-
stick, for the enchanted child to play with. Then they divested
themselves of their odor as much as possible, and hid themselves near the spring and to the leeward of it. When all was
ready, Atutish went to the edge of the spring, and cried aloud
"Mahash! Do you want to come out?" Soon the latter lifted
his head cautiously out of the spring, raised his upper lip,
showing his long white fangs, snuffed the air keenly, looked
wildly around him, and drew back again into the water. Atutish
then went near where he had seen his brother rise, and called
again to him; but the child answered from the water that he
feared to come out, as he thought he smelt the hunters. "Have
no fear," said Atutish; "the old men are gone out hunting
and will not be back till night. I am here alone. Come out
to the warm sunlight. We will have a good time playing; and
I will give you something nice to eat." Thus coaxed and re-
assured, the other ventured out, still looking mistrustfully
around him. Atutish then gave him a piece of boiled buffalo-
tongue to eat, which the little boy said was the best thing he
had ever tasted. "Very well," said Atutish, "let us play,
and I will stake the rest of this tongue against some of your
frogs and slugs on the game." Mahash agreed; and soon, in
the excitement of the play, he forgot his fears. They played
along with the roulette some time without much advantage on
either side, until, at length, they threw their sticks so evenly

5

that it was impossible to tell which was farthest from the wheel. They disputed warmly, until Atutish said, "Stoop down and look close and you will see that I have made the best throw." The other stooped over to observe; and, while his attention was thus engaged, his brother came behind the little fellow, seized him, and held him fast. Atutish then called to the concealed hunters, who ran up, threw a lariat around the struggling captive and bound him firmly. Having secured the wild boy, their next task was to break the spell by which his tastes and habits were made so unnatural. To accomplish this, Long Tail and Spotted Body put him in the sweat-house and there steamed him until he was almost exhausted. They then took him out and began to whip him severely. As they plied the lash, they made wishes, that the keen scent would leave his nose, that the taste for reptiles would leave his mouth, that the fear of his own kind would leave his heart, etc. As they progressed with this performance, he suddenly cried out to Atutish, "Brother, I remember myself now. I know who I am." When he said this he was released; and his first impulse was to run to the spring. He ran there; but when he reached the edge, he stopped, for he found that he no longer loved the black mud and the slimy water; and he returned to the lodge.

Long Tail then placed the twins side by side, and holding his extended hand, palm downward, above their heads, a little farther from the ground than on the previous occasion, wished that they would both be "so high"; when, at once, they grew to the size of boys about fourteen years old, and they grew in wisdom correspondingly. Then Long Tail made bows and hunting-arrows for the boys, and a pair of medicine-arrows for their protection and for use on extraordinary occasions; and he addressed them saying, "You are now big enough to protect yourselves. Go out on the prairie and hunt, and we will see which one of you will be the best hunter." After that time they went out every day, and became expert hunters.

Once, as they were looking for game among the hills, they came to a scaffold on which a corpse was laid. "There," said Atutish, "is the body of our mother. She was murdered, no one knows how." "Let us try the strength of our medicine-arrows on her," said Mahash; "perhaps we can bring her back to life." So saying he stepped close to the scaffold and shot straight up. As the arrow turned to fall, he cried out, "Take care, mother, or you will get hurt;" and, as it descended near the body, the scaffold shook and a low groan was heard. Then Atutish stepped nearly under the scaffold and shot up in the air. As his arrow turned to fall, he cried out, "Mother! Mother! Jump quick, or the arrow will strike you." At once she arose, jumped down from the scaffold, and, recognizing her children, embraced them. The boys then asked her who was the author of their calamities, and how it all happened. She pointed to the lodge of Big Mouth, and related all the circumstances of her death. Upon hearing this, the boys swore they would be revenged. Their mother endeavored to dissuade them, describing Big Mouth to them, assuring them that his medicine was potent, and that he would certainly destroy them if they went near him. They paid no attention to her remonstrances, but proceeded to plot the destruction of the monster.

Now, this Big Mouth had a very easy way of making a living. He neither trapped nor hunted, nor took pains to cook his food. He simply lay on his back, and when a herd of deer came within sight from his lodge, or a flock of birds flew overhead, no matter how far distant, he turned toward them, opened his great mouth, and drew in a big breath, when instantly they fell into his mouth and were swallowed. In a little while, the boys had their plans arranged. They built a large fire, and heated some small bowlders in it. Then they carried the stones to the top of his lodge, put them near the smoke-hole, and began to imitate a flock of blackbirds. "Go away, little birds," said Big Mouth; "you are not fit to eat, and I am not hungry; but go away and let me sleep, or I will swallow you." "We are not afraid of you," said the boys; and they began to chirp again. At length Big Mouth got angry. He turned up his mouth, opened it wide, and just as he began to draw his breath to suck them in, the boys stepped aside, and hurled the stones down into the lodge. "Oh, what sharp claws those birds have! They are tearing my throat," exclaimed the monster, as he swallowed the red-hot rocks. The next moment he roared with pain and rushed for his water-jars, drinking immense draughts; but the steam made by the water on the rocks swelled him up; and the more he drank the worse he swelled until he burst and died.

The boys brought the body home, and, after they had danced sufficiently around it, their mother praised them for what they had done, but she said, "You must not be too venturesome. All these lodges around are inhabited by beings whose powers in sorcery are great. You cannot always do as well as you have done this time. You should keep away from the rest of them. There is one old woman in particular whom you must avoid. She is as powerful as Big Mouth; but you cannot kill her in the same way that you killed him, for she catches her food, not in her mouth, but in a basket. Whenever she sees anything that she wants to eat she turns her basket toward it and it drops in dead. If she sees a flock of wild geese among the clouds, no matter how high they fly, she can bring them down." When the boys heard this, they said nothing in reply to their mother, but set off secretly to compass the death of the witch. They went to the lodge of the latter, and, standing near the door, cried, "Grandmother, we have come to see you." "Go away, children, and don't annoy me," she replied. "Grandmother, you are very nice and good, and we like you. Won't you let us in?" continued the boys. "Oh, no," said she, "I don't want to hurt you; but begone, or I will kill you." Despite this threat, they remained, and again spoke to her, saying, "Grandmother, we have heard that you are very strong medicine, and that you have a wonderful basket that can kill anything. We can scarcely believe this. Won't you lend us the basket a little while until we see if we can catch some birds with it?" She refused the basket at first, but, after much coaxing and flattering, she handed it to them. No sooner were they in possession of the basket than they turned it upon the witch herself, and she dropped into it dead.

After this exploit, the mother again praised her boys, but again warned them to beware of other evil genii of the place, which she described. One of these was a man with a pair of wonderful moccasins, with which he had only to walk round anything that he wanted to kill. Another was a man with a magic knife, with which he could instantly cut or kill anything that he threw the knife at. These individuals they destroyed in the same manner that they overcame the basket-woman, by coaxing them to lend their magic property, and then slaying the owners with their own weapons. On each occasion, the boys retained the charmed articles for their future use.

When all this was done, the old mother called her boys and told them there was but one more dangerous being that they had to guard themselves against. She said, " He lives in the sky, where you can not get at him; but he can hurt you, for his arm is so long that it reaches from the heavens to the earth. His name is Long Arm." "Very well," said the boys, " we will beware of him." One morning, soon after receiving this advice, they went out very early to hunt, but could find nothing to kill. They walked and ran many miles, until late in the day, when they became very tired and lay down to sleep on the prairie. As was their custom, they stuck their medicine-arrows in the ground, close beside them. The arrows possessed such a charm that if any danger threatened the boys they would fall to waken them. While the brothers lay asleep, Long Arm looked down from the clouds, and, beholding them, stretched his great arm down toward them. As the arm descended, the arrows fell hard upon the boys, but the latter were so tired and sleepy that they did not waken, and Long Arm grasped Atutish and bore him to the sky. In a little while, Mahash woke up and discovered, to his horror, that the warning arrows had fallen and that his brother was gone. He looked round carefully on the prairie for the departing tracks of his brother or for the tracks of the man or beast that had captured him, but in vain. When at his wit's end, and almost in despair, he chanced to glance toward the sky, and there, on the face of a high, white summer cloud, he saw the doubled track of Long Arm, where he came near the earth and went back. Mahash laid down his bow and arrow and other accouterments, retaining only his medicine-knife, which he concealed in his shirt. He next stuck his magic arrows into the ground and got on top of them, and then he crouched low, strained every muscle, and sprung upward with all his might. He jumped high enough to catch hold of the ragged edge of the cloud. From that he scrambled higher until he at last got on Long Arm's trail, which he followed. For fear of recognition, he wished himself smaller, and, becoming a little, toddling child, moved on until he came to a great crowd, moving in one direction, with much talk and excitement. He ran up to an old woman who walked a little apart, and asked her what was the matter. She informed him that they had just captured one of the children of the new race which was growing on the earth—a boy who had destroyed many favored genii, and that they were about to kill and burn him. "Grandmother," said Mahash, "I would like to see this, but I am too little to walk there. Will you carry me?" She took him on her back and brought him to the place where the crowd had gathered. There he saw his brother tied to a stake, and a number of people dancing around him. He thought that if he could only reach the post unobserved and touch the cords with his medicine-knife, he could release his brother; but for some time he was puzzled how to do it. At length he slid down from the old woman's back, and wished that for a little while he might turn to an ant. He became one, and, as such, crawled through the feet of the crowd and up to the post, where he cut the cords that bound Atutish. When the latter was free, Mahash resumed his proper shape, and they both ran as hard as they could for the edge of the clouds. The crowd pursued them; but, as each foremost runner approached, Mahash threw his knife and disabled him. At last, Long Arm started after the brothers, running very fast. As he came within his arm's length of them, he reached out to grasp one of them. As he did so, Mahash again threw his knife, and severed the great arm from the shoulder. The boys got back safely to the earth. Then, having ridded themselves of all their enemies, they lived in peace, and in time they moved away from that locality.

§30. DIVISIONS OF TIME.—Many writers represent that savage Indian tribes divide the year into twelve periods corresponding to our months, and that each month is named from some meteorological occurrence or phase of organic creation observable at the time. Among others, Maximilian presents us with a list of twelve months,*—"The month of the seven cold days", "The pairing month", "The month of weak eyes", etc. He introduces this list in one of his chapters descriptive of the Mandans. He does not say it is their list of months. He publishes it without comment; and yet it is presented in such a way as to lead the reader to suppose that it is the regular and original Mandan calendar. Other authors present lists of Indian months in much the same way. As the results of my own observations, I should say that the Mandans and Minnetarees are generally aware that there are more than twelve lunations in a year, that they as yet know nothing of our manner of dividing the year, and that, although when speaking of "moons", they often connect them with natural phenomena, they have no formal names for the lunar periods. I think the same might be said of other tribes who are equally wild.

The Hidatsa recognize the lapse of time by days, by lunar periods, and by years. They also recognize it by the regular recurrence of various natural phenomena, such as the first formation of ice in the fall, the breaking up of the Missouri in the spring, the melting of the snow-drifts, the coming of the wild geese from the south, the ripening of various fruits, etc. A common way of noting time, a few years ago, was by the development of the buffalo calf in utero. A period thus marked by a natural occurrence, be it long or short, is called by them the kadu, season, time, of such an occurrence. Some long seasons include shorter seasons; thus they speak of the season of strawberries, the season of service-berries, etc., as occurring within the season of warm weather. They speak of the seasons of cold weather, or of snow (tsidie, mada), of warm weather (ade), and of death, or decay (mata), which we consider as agreeing with our seasons of winter, summer, and fall; but they do not regularly allot a certain number of moons to each of these seasons. Should you ask an interpreter who knew the European calendar what the "Indian names of the

* p. 354.

months" were, he would probably give you names of a dozen
of these periods, or natural seasons, as we might call them,
corresponding in time to our months.   In a few years, when
these Indians shall know more of our system of noting time
than they now do, they will devise and adopt regular Hidatsa
names for the months of our calendar.

Other facts concerning their cognizance of time may be
learned from Paragraphs 256 and 257 of the Grammar, and by
referring in the Dictionary to the following words, which are
names of different parts of the astronomical day :—atade, ata,
kiduhakute, midiatede, midiate, midiatedu, midiate-odakšipe,
midimapedupahide, midimapedupahi, midimapedupahi-daka-
midi, midiimahpide, midiimahpi, opade, opa, oktside oktsi,
oktsidu, mape and maku.

PHILOLOGY.

PHILOLOGY.

§I. Classification of the Hidatsa language.—The language of the Minnetarees has been classified as belonging to the linguistic group called the Dakota group, and very properly so called, not because there is any evidence that the present Dakota tongue is the parent language of the group or the most direct representative of an archaic parent language, but because it is the most extensively spoken, and the most thoroughly and intelligently studied language of the group.

§II. Relations of Dakota to Hidatsa.—The Hidatsa language resembles the Dakota in many respects; and a large list might be made of words which are the same in both languages, if we allow for the interchangeability of certain lingual and labial sounds in the Hidatsa, to be described hereafter. The following are examples:—hota, *gray;* i, *mouth;* ista, *eye;* itopa, *fourth;* ma, *I;* mini or midi, *water;* nita or dita, *thine;* nopa or dopa, *two;* te, *die;* topa, *four;* besides particles, such as i, denoting the instrument, to, interrogative, etc.

There are many more words in each language which very closely resemble their synonymes, or approximate synonymes, in the other; and several which in both languages are perfect homonymes and imperfect synonymes. These statements are illustrated in the following list:—

(DAKOTA.*)	(HIDATSA.)
dote,	doti, *throat ;*
hi,	hi, *tooth, edge, point ;*
hiŋ,	hi', *feathers, fur, hair ;*
ħa,	ħa, *rough ;*
inkpa,	icpu, *point ;*
inoŋpa,	inopa, *second ;*
ité,	íte, *face ;*
mita,	mata, *my, mine ;*
mitawa,	matawae, *mine ;*

* The Dakota words used throughout this essay are from Rev. S. R. Riggs's *Dakota Grammar and Dictionary.* Where the Dakota definitions differ from the Hidatsa, they are given separately.

(DAKOTA.)	(HIDATSA.)
nagi,	dahi or nahi, *ghost ;*
ɔ, *to shoot and hit,*	u, *to wound ;*
oti, ti, tipi,	ati, *house ;*
ożu,	oze, *to plant ;*
po,	pue, *foggy ;*
pte,	mité, *cow ;*
pute,	apute, *upper lip ;*
śupe,	śipe, *bowels ;*
to,	tohi, *blue ;*
u,	hu, *to come ;*
wa,	ma' or wa', *snow ;*
wasićuŋ,	maśi or waśi, *white man ;*
wata,	mati or wati, *boat ;*
wiŋ,	mia or wia, *woman.*

In a number of words which are nearly or quite synonymous in both languages, we find little difference in sound, except that the Dakota ć (English *ch* in *chain*) stands in place of the Hidatsa d; as in these examples : —

(DAKOTA.)	(HIDATSA.)
ćaġu,	daho, *lungs ;*
ćaŋcaŋ,	dada, *to tremble ;*
ćaŋte,	da'ta, *heart ;*
ćaże,	dazi, *name ;*
ćekpa,	dehpa, *navel ;*
ćeżi,	dezi, *tongue ;*
ćute, *side ;*	duta, *ribs ;*
ćahahake, *vertebræ ;*	dahaha, *vertebral processes ;*
mićuŋ,	madu, *my elder sister ;*
nićuŋ,	didu, or nidú, *thy elder sister.*

More commonly, however, we find the difference to consist chiefly in the Dakota words having y, where the Hidatsa words have d. As the Dakota causative prefixes ya and yu are represented in the Hidatsa by da and du, many verbs may be placed under this head. In the following words, and in many others, we have instances of this difference :—

(DAKOTA.)	(HIDATSA.)
ya,	da, *thou ;*
ya, *to go,*	da, *go thou ;*
yaġa, *to peel with the teeth,*	dahade, *to shell with the teeth ;*
yahdeća, *to tear with the mouth,*	daheśa, *to tear with the teeth ;*
yahepa, *to drink up,* as *water,*	dahupi, *to drink dry ;*
yamni,	dami, *three ;*

(DAKOTA.)	(HIDATSA.)
yuha, *to lift*,	duhe, **to lift**, *duha, lift thou ;*
yuhdeća, *to tear in pieces, etc.*,	duheśa, **to tear in** *any way ;*
yuhpa, *to throw down, etc.*,	duhpi, *to take down* **off** *of ;*
yuhuga, *to break a hole in, etc.*,	duhohi, **to** *break across ;*
yuksa, *to break off, etc.*.	dutsaki, **to pull** *apart ;*
yuśka, **to** *loosen,* **to untie,**	duśka, **to** *open, as a box ;*
yuśkića, *to press,* **squeeze,**	dutsikti, *to strangle ;*
yuta,	duti, **to** *eat ;*
yuza,	dutsi, *take hold* **of.**

In some of the above verbs it will be seen that the roots
are much alike in both languages. Many of the quoted definitions embody similar ideas, although they are differently worded.
It is well to remind the reader that even in the Dakota, in
verbs beginning with ya and yu, the y is changed to d in the
conjugation. (See Riggs's *Dakota Grammar*, § 50.)

In some cases, we find that the Dakotas use s where the
Hidatsa usually use ts; but on this point usage is somewhat
divided in the Hidatsa. (See Grammar, ¶ 17.)

(DAKOTA.)	(HIDATSA.)	(ENGLISH.)
haska,	hatski,	*long ;*
sihe,	tsi (itsi),	*foot ;*
sinte,	tsite,	*tail ;*
sni,	tsidin,	*cold ;*
nisunka,	ditsuka, nitsuka,	*your younger brother.*

And some other words might be quoted to exemplify this
difference.

In the words nagi and dahi, ćagu and daho, yaga and
dahada, quoted above, and in others, the g of Dakota takes the
place of h in Hidatsa.

Although, as has been shown, there are many words alike
or nearly alike in these two languages, allowance being made
for certain uniform sound-changes, it must be remembered
that a large majority of the Dakota words have no resemblance
to anything in the Hidatsa. Reduplication in verbs, which is
a prominent feature of the Dakota tongue, I have not observed
to occur in the Hidatsa except in one word, ikaka.

§ III. RELATIONS OF CROW TO HIDATSA.—The Hidatsa
bears a greater resemblance to the Crow than to any other
language. Some speak of one as being but a dialect of the

other; and so they might be regarded if we use the word dialect in a very wide sense. The Crow has its own dialects, differing to no great extent from one another. My opportunities for studying this language, particularly the dialects of the Mountain Crows, have been very limited. A vocabulary which I prepared of the language as spoken by the River Crows has been destroyed. I cannot, therefore, give a very full comparison of the Crow and Hidatsa. The Crow words presented below are from Dr. Hayden's *Ethnography and Philology*, which contains the most complete and accurate Crow vocabulary extant.

A comparison of Hayden's Crow vocabulary with this Dictionary shows that many words of similar meaning are spelled alike in both, as adaka, *you see*; amaka, *I see*; apaka, *a mosquito*; da, *go*; di, *you*; ika, *he sees*; maha, *a spring*; mape, *day*; ope, *tobacco*; ua, *a wife*, etc.; and that many other synonyms are nearly alike in spelling, as in the following examples, in each of which the Crow word precedes the Hidatsa:— ame, ama, *earth*; apahe, apahi, *cloud*; ape, apa, *leaf*; aze, azi, *river*; daho, daho, *lungs*; dahpitse, dahpitsi, *bear*; deze, dezi, *tongue*; due, duhi, *lift*; ho, hu, *come*; hoće, hutsi, *wind*; ide, idi, *blood*; mia, mi', *stone*; mie, mia, *woman*; mihahe, mihaka, *duck*; oki, uki, *clay*; pohe, puhi, *foam*.

The oft-quoted consonants (Grammar, ¶¶ 19–23), which are interchangeable in the Hidatsa, are also interchangeable in the Crow, but perhaps in a less degree in the latter than in the former. Of the labial series, the Crows seem to prefer *b* more than the Hidatsa; and of the linguodental series they use *r* and *n* to a greater extent than we find it used by the latter tribe. By taking this permutation of consonants into consideration, we find many words alike or nearly alike, both in Crow and Hidatsa, which would otherwise seem different. Examples:—

(CROW.)	(HIDATSA.)	(ENGLISH.)
amahabe,	amahami,	*mountain*;
are,	ade,	*warm*;
are, arek,	ade, adets,	*ache, it aches*;
apana,	apadi,	*to grow*;
apani,	apadi,	*porcupine*;

(CROW.)	(HIDATSA.)	(ENGLISH.)
atsimina,	atsimidi,	*milk;*
barue,	maduhi,	*I lift;*
batse, watsi,	matse, watse,	*man;*
batsikua,	matsikoa,	*sugar;*
batsua,	matsu,	*cherry;*
batsua,	matsua,	*sinew;*
batebue,	maitamua,	*bell;*
bi,	mi, bi,	*I, me;*
bidia,	mide, bide,	*door;*
bide,	mida,	*fire;*
birake,	midaha,	*kettle;*
bitskipe,	mitskapa,	*rose;*
bua,	mua, bua,	*fish;*
ibek,	imia,	*to cry;*
iruke,	iduka or iruka,	*meat;*
kana,	kada, kára,	*run away;.*
mana,	mada,	*winter;*
mina,	mida,	*goose;*
mine,	midi,	*water;*
nake,	daka,	*child;*
nam,	dami, nawi,	*three;*
namo,	damu, namu,	*deep;*
nomina,	dumidi,	*twist, wind;*
nop,	dopa, nopa,	*two.*

The Crows commonly use a sibilant, as *s*, *sh*, or *z*, where the Hidatsa use some other dental, as *t*. There are many Crow words which, except in this respect, differ but slightly or not at all from their Hidatsa synonymes, as the subjoined list will show:—

(CROW.)	(HIDATSA.)	(ENGLISH.)
ashe,	ati,	*house;*
ashu,	atu,	*head;*
bas,	máta,	*mine;*
base,	matá,	*autumn;*
basape,	matapa,	*my moccasin;*
baze,	mati,	*boat:*
bishe,	mite, bite,	*buffalo;*
dusa,	duta,	*rib;*
isa,	ictia,	*large;*
ise,	ite,	*face;*
same,	tami, tuami,	*how many;*
sapa,	tapa,	*what;*
sape,	tape,	*who;*
sheëk,	tets,	*dead;*
shipie,	tipia,	*mud;*

(CROW.)	(HIDATSA.)	(ENGLISH.)
sho,	to,	*where ;*
shorak,	todu,	*where, etc. ;*
shop,	topa,	*four.*

In a few cases, the above rule seems to be reversed, as in buata, motsa, *coyote, wolf;* dakaka, tsakaka, *bird;* tameh, tsame, *hot;* azkate, azikaza, *little river;* miekate, miakaza, *young woman;* tsecte, tŝeŝa, *wolf;* atanua, aŝadi, *to steal.* In these examples, the Crow words stand first.

The Crow has an oral period as well as the Hidatsa; in the former it is k, in the latter ts. (See Grammar, ¶¶ 33, 168.) As these oral periods are much used, they constitute an important element in the difference in tone of the two languages.

The Crows sometimes use s where the Hidatsa use ŝ or ts, and ć (English *ch* in *chain*) where the Hidatsa use k. There are many other instances of changes of sound in these languages which I have not now the means of illustrating sufficiently.

§ IV. SOME DIFFICULTIES IN THE STUDY OF THE HIDATSA.— The interchangeable labial and linguo-dental sounds are very perplexing features of this language. The sounds of *m, b,* and *w* are interchangeable; so also are those of *d, l, n,* and *r.* These permutations exist in other Indian tongues, though in few, I presume, to the extent to which they exist in this tongue. In the Dakota language, for instance, changes in these sounds are said to mark difference in dialect, while within each dialect the labials and linguals are not interchanged to an extent sufficient to excite remark.

The present Hidatsa tribe represents several bands formerly distinct; and the present language of this people, no doubt, represents nearly as many ancient dialects, the distinctive features of which cannot easily be determined at this day. The consolidation of these diverse dialects has had, perhaps, some share in producing this confusion of sounds; but, at most, it has had a very limited share. I believe that these Indians do not well appreciate the differences between these allied sounds as they fall on their ears, and consequently make no effort to distinguish them with their tongues. I have often, for experiment, taken a word which contained two or more of these sounds, and pronounced it, in the course of conversation, with every possible change, and without being once misunderstood. Thus, the word madakoe, *my friend, my comrade,* which contains but one labial and one dental sound, may be pronounced in at least twelve different ways,—which we have characters to represent, as, madakoe, marakoe, manakoe, malakoe, badakoe, barakoe, banakoe, balakoe, wadakoe, warakoe, wanakoe, and walakoe,—without fear of misapprehension, although they usually pronounce it malakoe or barakoe. Furthermore, when you hear an Indian uttering a sound belonging to one of these two series, you are often at a loss to select a character to express it. His labial will often sound as much like *m* as like *b*, or as much like *w* as *m*. Among linguo-dental sounds, it is often impossible, even after several repetitions of a word by an Indian speaker, to decide between *d* and *r*, or between *d*, *l*, and *n*, as the best suited to represent the sound that smites your ear. In other words, there are labial, lingual, and dental sounds which *we* have not yet learned to distinguish, and which we have no characters to represent. I marvel not that old Charbonneau should have "candidly confessed" to Prince Maximilian, after a residence of thirty-seven years among the Minnetarees, that he could never learn to pronounce their language correctly.[*]

In the Grammar (¶¶ 19–23), where this subject is further discussed, it will be seen that I have selected a standard letter to represent each series,—*m* for the labial, and *d* for the lingual or linguo-dental. When I first commenced to form my vocabulary, I adopted a different course, and put down each word in all the forms in which I heard it; but, in time, I discovered that I might fill a large volume with these repeated words, and, in the end, only confuse the student, obscure the truth, and misrepresent the language.

When I first obtained some insight into the extent to which these permutations existed, I could scarcely trust my senses, and often feared that I labored under some subjective difficulties. At other times, when, in the mouth of the same speaker, and almost in the same breath, I would hear a well-known word suddenly change its form, I would puzzle myself by supposing that the change took place in accordance with some inscrutable grammatical rule. But when I came into the possession of vocabularies collected by others, I became better satisfied with the results of my own observations. In the compared vocabularies presented below, it will be seen how differently each author spells one and the same word, and that their differences arise chiefly from the transmutability of the sounds to which I have referred. In the first column (Say), the vowels have the English sound; and, in the second column (Hayden), they have the continental sound.

ENGLISH.	SAY.[1]	HAYDEN.[2]	VARIOUS AUTHORS.[3]	MATTHEWS.
axe,	weepsa,[4]	biipsa,		miiptsa [bi-].
bear,	lahpetze,		nohpittsee, Boller.[5] / lachpizi, Max.[6] / daßpitsi. / [naßpitsi].	
blood,	ehre,	ide,		idi.
cold,	cerea,	éidia,		tsidia.
crow,		peritska,	pehriska, Max.,[7]	pedetska.
earth,	amah,	awa,	awa. Max.,[8]	ama.
fire,	beras,	bida,		mida [bi-].
hair,	arra,	ada,		ada.
I,	mee,	bi,		mi [bi].
ice,	merohhe,	baruhe,		maduhi.
knife,	matze,	baéi,		maetsi [baetsi.]
man,	mattza,	bautse,		matse [watse, batse].
Minnetaree,		biuatsa,[9]	Elahsa, Max.,[10] / Idatza, De Smet,[11] / Hoeraeansch, Boller,[12]	hidatsa.
no,	najes,	desha,		desha [nesha].
skin,	laughpa,	daßpe,		dahpi [oahpi].
my son,	mourisha.	badisha,		madisi.
tongue,	neighje,	deze,		dezi [nezi].
two,	noöpah,		ruhpa, Max.,[13]	dopa [nopa].
water,	mene,	bidi,		midi [bidi].
white man,	boshe[14] and wasshe[15]	bashi,	moshee, Boller,[16]	mashi.
winter,	málá,	mana,		mada.
woman,	meya,	mia,	bea, Catlin,[17] / wea, Lewis and Clarke,[18]	mia [wia, bia].

From Dr. Say's Vocabulary in Long's Expedition, pp. lxx–lxxviii and p. lxxxiv.

[2] From Dr. Hayden's Minnetaree Vocabulary in Hayden's *Ethnography and Philology*, pp. 421–'46.

[3] Taken from various parts of the works of the authors to whom referred.

[4] "Tomahawk, weep-sa-lan-ga", p. lxxxv. (See miiptsa daka, in Dictionary.)

[5] "Noe-pitta-ee-toapish, or Four-Bears." Boller, p. 56.

[6] "Lachpizi-sihrish (the yellow bear)." Maximilian, p. 180. The letters have here their German sounds probably.

[7] "Pehriska-Ruhpa (the two ravens)." Max., p. 180.

[8] The first two syllables of "Awachawi", p. 178. (See amahami in the Dictionary.)

[9] "Indian, hinatsa."

[10] Max., p. 178. (See Ethnography, § 18. *Hidatsa*.)

[11] "The Idatzas, miscalled Grosventres." From letter in *Report of the Commissioner of Indian Affairs* for 1864, p. 276.

[12] "Men of the Hee-rae-an-seh", p. 97.

[13] "Pehriska-Ruhpa, (the two ravens)." See note 7 above.

[14] "French, bo-she", p. lxxxiv.

[15] "Spaniard, was-she-o-man-ti-qna", p. lxxxiv. (See mashi and umatikoa in Dictionary.)

[16] "Leaving the 'moshees' (whites) to reflect", etc., p. 187.

[17] In the feminine ending of the name "Seetsehea", p. 188. (See Grammar, ¶ 93.)

[18] In the feminine ending of the name "Sacajawea", p. 279.

Lest some should urge that these variations in orthography might be sufficiently accounted for by taking into consideration the changes which time may have produced in the language—for the quoted authors wrote at different dates—or by supposing the vocabularies to have been written from the dictation of men who spoke different dialects, I must call attention to the fact that there are many instances where one word, in different connections, is spelled with different interchangeable consonants by the same author. (In the following examples, the Hidatsa words in parentheses are forms given in the accompanying Dictionary.) Thus, Say presents us with two different forms of duetsa or luetsa, *one*, in "nowassa-pa" (duetsapi), *nine*, and "ape-lemoisso" (ahpiduetsa), *eleven;* with two forms of daka, *child, a diminutive ending*, in "sacanga-nonga" (tsakaka-daka), *egg*, and "weepsa-langa" (miiptsa-daka), *tomahawk;* with two forms of masi, *white man*, in "French, boshe", and "Spaniard, wasshe-omantiqua" (the latter is doubtlessly intended for masi umatikoa, *white men at the south*—see note 15, page 82); and with two forms of dohpaka, *people*, in "Snake Indians, mabuesho-rochpanga" (mapoksa, dohpaka), and "Les Noire Indians, ateshupesha-lohpanga" (ati, sipisa, dohpaka). In Hayden's vocabulary, we find two different spellings of matse, *man*, in "bautse-itse" (matse-etsi), *chief*, and "makariste-matse" (makadista-matse), *boy;* two spellings of adui, *sour, pungent, etc.*, in "adawi", *sour*, and bidi-arawi (midi-adui), *whisky;* and two spellings of midi, *sun*, in "midi-ewukpi" (midi-imahpi), *sunset*, and "bidi-waparepehe" (midi-mapedupahi or bidi-waperupahi), *midday, noon.* I regret that, in preparing these remarks, I have not had access to a copy of Maximilian's original work, which contains a vocabulary of the Minnetaree language; but I have no doubt that instances of this kind might be drawn from it.

Besides making the various labial interchanges mentioned above, they sometimes, but very rarly, use b for p; and occasionally, too, they combine the sounds of b and w, thus ama may be pronounced abwa. A third series of interchangeable consonants might be mentioned, namely, a sibilant series. To some extent they confuse the sounds of s, ṡ (English *sh* in *shun*), and ts (see Grammar, ¶¶ 17, 18), and illustrations of this confusion might be taken from the vocabularies I have quoted; but these sibilant interchanges do not occur to such a marked extent as do the labial and lingual changes, and, when heard, they are not so perplexing to the English student.

§ V. SONANT CHARACTER.—The Hidatsa language is sonorous and pleasing to the ear; but I consider it less musical than the Dakota. One of the chief reasons for the difference in tone between the Hidatsa and Dakota languages, I believe to be the almost total absence, in the former, of the nasal-vowel ending (ŋ) so common in the latter (see Grammar, ¶¶ 4, 14). The aspiration of the vowel in the Hidatsa takes the place of the nasal ending to a great extent. Another reason for difference of tone is that the Hidatsa shorten and obscure their vowels to a greater extent than the Dakotas. The Hidatsa is spoken with much inflection, and the vowels are often increased in quantity to express different shades of meaning.

If a party of Indians should be seated in an adjoining room, or at a short distance from the listener, conversing, where the voices can be heard, but not a syllable distinguished, the accustomed ear has little difficulty in discerning which one of the many languages of the plains the Indians are speaking. Each language has its own peculiar sonant character. It is more difficult to distinguish by this character the Hidatsa from the Crow than from the Dakota or Mandan, and more difficult to distinguish it from the latter than from the former of these two. The tones of these four languages belonging to the Dakota group are somewhat alike; so much alike that a person possessing but limited acquaintance with them might mistake one for another, hearing it at a distance as I have described. But the contrast in tone between these tongues and the neighboring, but alien, Arickaree is well marked, and any quickeared person might learn at once to distinguish it from them.

§ VI. CHANGES IN COURSE OF TIME.—I have said that the three languages spoken in the village at Fort Berthold show no perceptible inclination to coalesce (Ethnography, § 13). I have said this, well knowing that the statement was somewhat at variance with the opinions of earlier observers.* The few Mandan and Minnetaree words given by Lewis and Clarke in proper names show, as far as they go, that the languages have not materially changed since 1804. There are now, and doubtlessly there were in 1804, many points of correspondence between the Mandan and Hidatsa languages; but there are none which may not be more easily explained by supposing the two languages to have sprung from a common source than by supposing them to have been reciprocally changed by contact. I never could discover that the Hidatsa and Mandan spoken by the rising generation resembled one another more than did those languages as spoken by the old men. I do not claim that the long and intimate intercourse which has existed between these two tribes has produced no approximation or coalescence of their languages. It is but reasonable to suppose that the contrary is the case; but I could never get an Indian to point out to me, nor could I ever otherwise discover, a satisfactory instance of such coalescence.

Throughout the past hundred years, the Mandans have had as much intercourse with the Arickarees as with the Minnetarees; yet I never could trace any resemblance between the modern Mandan and Arickaree tongues. As far as I have observed them, there is not a single word alike in both. It is not likely that intercourse has produced a noteworthy approximation of languages in one case and none whatever in the other. There is no doubt that the Hidatsa language has changed in the course of time; but the change has resulted chiefly from causes other than the influence of the Mandan tongue. Some of the old men occasionally converse among themselves in terms which younger members of the tribe do not understand, and, when asked what they mean, they say they are trying to speak the old language.

* Lewis and Clarke, p. 97.—Maximilian, pp. 393, 405.

HIDATSA GRAMMAR.

HIDATSA GRAMMAR.

I. LETTERS.

1. Twenty letters, exclusive of the apostrophe, are used in this work to express in writing the Hidatsa language. Fifteen of the letters are essential, and five non-essential.

Essential Letters.

2. Of the essential letters, five are vowels, and ten, consonants.

3. The vowels are a, e, i, o, u.

   a has three sounds;—a (unmarked) has the sound of English *a* in *father;* ă (short) has the sound of English *a* in *what;* ą (obscure) has the sound of short *ŭ* in *tun.*

   e has three sounds;—e (unmarked) has the sound of English *ai* in *air;* ĕ (short) has the sound of English *e* in *ten;* ē (long) has the English sound of *e* in *they.*

   i has two sounds;—i (unmarked) has the sound of English *i* in *marine;* ĭ (short) has the sound of English *i* in *tin.*

   o has the sound of English *o* in *tone.*

   u has the sound of English *u* in *rude.*

4. The apostrophe (') is placed after vowels to denote a peculiar force or aspiration, not initial, in pronouncing them, which slightly modifies the sound.

5. The consonants are c, d, h, ħ, k, m, p, s, ṡ, t, z.

   c has the sound of German *ch* in *ich.*

   d has the common English sound before consonants; but before vowels it has a slight sound of English *th* in *this.* d is interchangeable with *n, l,* and *r.*

   h has the sound of English *h* in *hat.*

   ħ represents the guttural surd no longer in use in English; it is like the German *ch* in *machen,* but a somewhat deeper sound.

   k has the English sound, as in *took.*

   m has the ordinary English sound, as in *man;* it is interchangeable with *b* and *w.*

   p has the ordinary English sound, as in *pan.*

   s has the sound of English *s* in *sun.*

   ṡ has the sound of English *sh* in *shun.*

   t has, before consonants, the ordinary English sound, as in *tin;* but before vowels it has a slight sound of English *th* in *thin.*

   z has the sound of English *z* in *azure.*

Non-essential Letters.

6. The non-essential letters are five of the seven interchangeable consonants of the language; they are b, l, n, r, and w; they have all the
ordinary English sounds. The language might be written or spoken
without them. b and w are interchangeable with the essential letter m,
and l, n, and r with the essential letter d.

Remarks.

7. As no great advantage could be seen in retaining two sets of characters, capitals are, here, entirely dispensed with in writing the Indian
words; but, in the Ethnography, where a Hidatsa proper name is used,
temporarily, as an English word, the initial letter is a capital. Proper
names are easily recognized by the termination s̈.

8. The following letters of the English, it will be seen, are not included
in this alphabet: f, g, j, q, v, x, and y. The sounds of f, g,* and v are
not in the language. It is a difficult matter for these Indians, or any
one else, to pronounce i followed by a vowel (and many other vowel
combinations) without an intervening consonantal sound of y; elsewhere
in their tongue this sound is not heard, and a character to represent it
would be useless. ·k is the equivalent of q. English j might be represented by dz, and x by ks; but neither of these combinations has been
found in the Hidatsa.

9. Some of the tribe occasionally pronounce the first sound of a like
English a in hall, and make other slight variations of the vowel sounds,
which, however, seem to be only individual peculiarities of speech, or
modifications unavoidably produced by preceding or succeeding consonants. It is believed that all the standard variations are duly represented.

10. Often before a final ts, and more rarely before a final k or s̈, long
vowels may be shortened, e changed to ɪ, and a to ą. (¶¶ 30–33).

11. It was originally thought advisable to include a short ŭ in the
alphabet, or to introduce a new character to represent the sound of English u in tub; but it is now believed that wherever this sound constantly
occurs it is as a modification of a.

12. o is never shortened, as in the English word not; but a sound much
like short ŏ is heard in the modification of a, which is represented thus, ä.

13. The sounds of English u in pure and oi in oil, are not found in this
language; nor is the sound of ou in our ever used except occasionally
in the word ho or hao.

14. The nasal modification of vowels, so common in the Dakota, does
not properly belong to the Hidatsa, although a few of the tribe use it
with aspirated a in the words ä'tsi, idä'ti, ibä'taha, and liakä'ta.

---

* In the words lioki, iplioki, matslioki, and one or two others, I have
occasionally heard the k softened into a hard g.

15. The sound represented by c occurs only **after i, and in accented syllables** which are not terminal.

16. The English sound of *ch* in *chain* is represented **by tš.**

17. In words beginning **with ts, the t** is occasionally dropped by **women** and young people, who thus say sakits for tsakits, sitska for **tsitska,** etc.; but, according to the best usage of the language, the plain sibilant **is** never found **alone with** a **vowel and** never begins a syllable.

18. Sometimes tš is used where ts **is** to be regarded as the standard; **thus itsuašuka,** *a horse,* may be pronounced itšuašuka.

19. In acquiring the language, and making a correct analysis of its words, one of **the** greatest difficulties to be encountered is the interchangeability of certain consonants.

20. There **are two** important series of interchangeable consonants; a labial **series** consisting of m, b, and w, and a dental, or linguo-dental, series consisting of d, l, n, and r. The constituent sounds of each series are subject to interchanges so arbitrary and frequent **that no definite** rules can be given for them. The following remarks, however, will be **found** to apply: (¶¶ 21, 22).

21. m is regarded as the standard letter of the labial series; it is the one most commonly used by those who are considered the best speakers of the language. Before the vowel i, b is as commonly used as m **in** initial syllables, and w more commonly in median and terminal syllables.

22. d is the standard of the dental series. When r is substituted for d, it is more commonly done **by men** than by women, while the **latter** **appear to have** a greater **preference** for l and 'n than the former. A **desire for euphony seems sometimes to** determine speakers **in their choice.**

23. Whenever, **in** any **word, a** non-essential letter is heard as often, **or** nearly **as** often, as its corresponding essential, the fact is shown in **the** Dictionary in one of three ways: 1st, by putting the modified syllable in brackets and indicating its position in the word by dashes, thus "liamua [-bu-]" and "liami [-wi]" denote that these words are very often pronounced liabua and liawi; 2d, by placing the entire modified word in brackets; and, 3d, by giving the modified word in **its alphabetical** order, referring to the same word with the standard spelling. **Where** a non-essential letter is heard oftener than the standard letter, the fact is shown **by** prefixing *plus* [+] in the **brackets, thus,** "dopa [+ mopa].

II. SYLLABLES.

24. The words are **divided** into syllables in such a manner as to make the etymology as **clear as** possible. It is designed that each syllable shall represent one complete factor of a word, or, in case of contraction, more than one, but not the fragments of these factors joined together in an arbitrary way to simplify the task to the tongue and ear of the **English-speaking student.**

25. A very large proportion of the syllables end with vowels. The more common cases in which they end with consonants are given below. (¶¶ 26-33).

26. Initial and **median syllables** may end with c or k.   (¶¶ 27, 28).

27. Syllables ending in i occasionally take c after i when another syllable is suffixed (¶ 15); this most frequently happens when the added syllable begins with k, **p, or t;** thus we have micki from **mi, and** halipicti from halipi.

28. In the **prefixes** ak, dăk, and mąk, the k is seldom transferred to the following syllable.

29. Terminal syllables (and **consequently** words) may end in k, t, š, and ts.   (¶¶ 30-33).

30. A syllable may be closed **by k :** 1st, when verbs ending in ki form the imperative by dropping i, as amaki **is** changed to amak ; 2d, **when** ak, duk, and tok are used as suffixes; 3d, **when ak, dăk,** or mąk stand **alone;** and, 4th, in the words duk, tok, and **tsakąk.**

31. A syllable may be closed by t, when a verb **ending in ti** forms its imperative by dropping i, as kipšúti is changed to kipšút.

32. **Proper** names commonly end with š.

33. A word **which closes a sentence,** or stands alone forming a sentence by itself, commonly terminates in ts, if not with k, t, or š. ts answers the purpose of a vocal period in most cases.   (¶ 168).

34. Syllables are frequently contracted by the elision of their vowels.

35. A **contracted syllable,** when not terminal, belongs to the succeeding syllable.

36. A **syllable consisting of** a single vowel, when following immediately an accented vowel, or standing **immediately between two** other vowels, **may sometimes be omitted.**

III. WORDS.

37. Words will **be** considered under the usual eight heads (articles excluded) of nouns, pronouns, verbs, adjectives, **adverbs,** prepositions, conjunctions, and interjections.

Nouns.

38. For convenience of description, nouns may be divided into two classes, primitive and derivative.

Primitive Nouns.

39. Primitive nouns are such as, with our present knowledge of the language, we are unable to analyze either in whole or in part; as ma', snow ; i', mouth ; išta, eye, etc.

40. Nearly all the monosyllabic nouns are primitive, as are also the names of many things which are longest known to the people.

41. Many of the primitive nouns of the Hidatsa have, in kindred languages, their counterparts, which they closely resemble in sense and sound.

Derivative Nouns.

42. Derivative nouns are such as we are able to analyze in whole or in part.

43. Derivative nouns may be formed from words of any class, but chiefly from verbs, adjectives, and other nouns, either primitive or derived, by certain prefixes and suffixes, the commonest of which are i, adu, o, aku, ma, the possessive pronouns, and the diminutives dáka and káza.

44. i, prefixed to transitive verbs, forms nouns denoting the instrument or material with which the action is performed; thus, ita, *an arrow*, is from ta, *to kill*, and ikipakiši, *a towel*, from kipakiši, *to rub back and forth*. Nouns formed in this way are commonly prefixed by other nouns (denoting the recipient of the action), by the prefix ma, or by both; thus, maikipakiši, iteikipakiši, and maiteikipakiši are more commonly used than ikipakiši, although all these words denote the same thing. Nouns of the material are seldom heard without such prefixes; thus, maikikak, *ithread* (from kikaki, *to sew*), and maitëidušuki, *soap* (from ite, *the face*, and dušuki, *to wash*), are not heard in the simple forms of ikikaki and idušuki.

45. adu (an adverb of time and place when used alone) is employed as a prefix to form nouns under the following circumstances: (¶¶ 46–48).

46. adu, prefixed to verbs, forms nouns denoting the part on which the action is performed; as, adukikaki, *a seam*, from kikaki, *to sew*. Here ma, or the name of the thing to which the part belongs, precedes adu.

47. adu is also prefixed to verbs to form nouns, which signify the place where an action is performed; thus, from kidušá, *to put away carefully*, comes adukidušá, *a place of deposit*. In this case ma, or the noun denoting the object of the action, frequently precedes adu; *e. g.*, maadukidušá, *a place where anything is put away or stored*, matakiadukidušá, *a cupboard*.

48. adu is prefixed to intransitive verbs and adjectives to denote one or more of a kind or class which the verbs or adjectives describe; thus, from idákisa, *left-handed*, comes aduidakisa, *a left-handed person*, and from kiadetsi, *brave, skillful, etc.*, comes adukiadetsi, *one of the brave or skilled*. In this case, ma usually precedes adu.

49. o, prefixed to a verb, may form therewith the name of the action; as in odídi, *walking, gait*, from dídi, *to walk*.

50. o is used in the same way as adu, to denote the place where, or the part whereon, an action is performed; as in odútsi, *a mine*, from dútse, *to obtain*.

51. aku (a relative pronoun when used alone), prefixed to a transitive verb, forms a noun denoting the agent or performer of the act, and is nearly or quite synonymous with the English suffixes *er* and *or*. In this case, aku is commonly preceded by the name of the object; thus,

from mašipiša, *grapes*, and dúti, *to eat*, we have mašipišaakudúti, *grape-eater*, *i. e.*, the cedar-bird, or *Ampelis cedrorum*.

52. aku is sometimes used in the same sense as adu, in Par. 48. In this sense, it is common before the adjectives denoting color; as in akutohi, *beads*, from tohi, *blue*, and akušipiša, *black cloth*, from šipiša, *black*.

53. ma (to be distinguished from the pronoun ma) is a prefix of very extended use in the language. With some nouns, however, it is rarely used, while to a different class it is indispensable. It may be regarded as an indefinite particle, or as a universal noun or pronoun, qualified by the words to which it is prefixed. Some of the more common instances of its use are here given.

54. ma is prefixed to nouns of the instrument beginning with i, as in Paragraph 44, when the object on which the instrument is employed is not designated. When, for precision of definition, the object is named, its name takes the place of ma. When the name of the material of which the instrument is made is included, it commonly precedes ma; thus, from maidutsada, *a sled*, comes mida-maidutsada, *a wooden sled*.

55. ma is prefixed to adjectives to form the names of articles which possess in a marked degree attributes to which the adjectives refer; thus, from tsikoa, *sweet*, we have matsikoa, *sugar*.

56. ma is prefixed to verbs to form the names of objects on which the action denoted by the verb has been performed; thus, from kidutskiši, *to wash out*, comes makidutskiši, *a lot of washed clothes*.

57. Many words beginning with ma drop this prefix when incorporated with the possessive pronouns.

58. The possessive pronouns, (m), ma, mata, (d), di, dita, i, and ita, are placed before the name of the thing possessed; then, together, they are pronounced as one word, and the pronoun regarded as a prefix.

59. In many cases, where possessive pronouns are prefixed, the noun denoting the thing possessed loses its first syllable, has its accent removed, or is otherwise much changed; as in itápa, *his moccasins*, from hupa, *moccasins*; itaši, *his robe*, from maši, *a robe*.

60. Some words are rarely, others never,* heard without a prefixed possessive pronoun; as, itadsi, *leggings*, *his leggings*; isami, *a father's sister*; itsuka, *a man's younger brother*.

61. But few words, formed as shown only in Par. 58, are given in the Dictionary, while all known words in the 3d-person, formed as in Pars. 59 and 60, are laid down. In the cases of such words as are referred to in Par. 60, as never being heard without a pronoun, the noun, with the pronoun omitted, is given sometimes as a *hypothetical word*.

---

* This construction is only found with names of things, which necessarily belong to some one, and cannot otherwise exist (as blood relations), or are usually so conceived (as certain articles of personal property), and only to a limited number of such names.

Diminutives.

62. daka, which, when used alone, means the offspring or young of anything, is employed as a diminutive suffix of general application. Ex.—idaka, *his or its young* (the offspring of any individual or species mentioned); dalipitsidaka, *a bear's cub,* from dalipitsi, *a bear;* miiptsidaka, *a hatchet,* from miiptsi, *an ax.*

63. kaza is a diminutive suffix, whose use is limited to about twenty words of the language, including proper names. Ex.—masuakaza, *a puppy,* from masuka, *a dog;* miakaza, *a young woman,* from mia, *a woman;* amatikaza, *the Little Missouri River,* from amati, *the Missouri.*

64. The adjective kadista is also used as a diminutive.

Compound Nouns.

65. There are certain words which may be considered as compound nouns, because they closely resemble in structure compound nouns in English; although no definite distinction can be made in Hidatsa between compound and other derived nouns, since the so-called prefixes and suffixes are really words—the most of them capable of being used alone.

66. Compound nouns are formed in the various ways described in Pars. 44, 46, 47, 54, and 57, and also by simply placing two or more nouns together or by joining nouns to verbs, adjectives, and adverbs; e. g., istamidi, *tears,* from ista, the *eye,* and midi, *water;* masitadalipitsisui, *bacon,* from masi, *white man,* itadalipitsi, *his bear,* and sui, *fat;* istaoze, *eye wash, collyrium,* from ista, *eye,* and oze, *to pour into;* itahatski, the *Dakota Indians,* from ita, *arrows,* and hatski, *long;* amasitakoamasi, *the people of Prince Rupert's Land,* from amasitakoa, *at the north,* and masi, *white men.*

67. When a compound noun is formed by simply placing two nouns together, the first word commonly denotes the possessor, the second the thing possessed. (¶ 84).

68. Sometimes verbs, adjectives, and adverbs are used as nouns without undergoing any change of form; as oze, *to pour, a drink;* patsatikoa, *at the west, the west.*

Properties of Nouns.

GENDER.

69. Gender is distinguished by using, for the masculine and feminine, different words, which may either stand alone or be added to nouns of the common gender.

70. matse, *man,* sikaka, *young man,* itaka, *old man,* the terms used for male relations (as itsuka, idisi, etc.), for callings exclusively masculine, and the compounds of these words (as makadista-matse and itakalie), are nouns of the masculine gender, applied to the human species.

71. mia, *woman*, kadulie, *old woman*, terms used for female relations (as idu, itakiša, etc.), for those employed in labors exclusively feminine, and the compounds of these (such as miakazi, *a young woman*), are nouns of the feminine gender, applied to the human species.

72. kedapi, *bull*, when used alone, means a buffalo bull; but as a suffix, either with or without the interposition of adu, it designates the male of any of the lower animals.

73. mite, the generic name for *buffalo*, means also a buffalo cow.

74. mika, *a mare*, is used as a suffix to denote the females of the lower animals. It follows the specific name, with or without the intervention of adu.

75. When the species has been previously mentioned, or is otherwise understood, the specific name need not be prefixed to kedapi, adukedapi, mika, or adumika.

NUMBER.

76. Hidatsa nouns suffer no change of form to indicate the difference between singular and plural.

77. Some nouns we know to be singular or plural from their original meaning or from the sense in which they are used. In other cases, our only means of making a distinction is by the use of numeral adjectives, or such adjectives as ahu, *many*, etsa, *all*, kanšta, *few*, etc.

CASE.

78. In view of their syntactical relations, Hidatsa nouns may be parsed as having the same cases as nouns of other languages; but they are not inflected to indicate case except, doubtfully, in the possessive.

79. Possession is ordinarily shown by the use of the possessive pronouns, which stand before the noun denoting the thing possessed, and are usually considered as prefixed to it.

80. Two kinds or degrees of possession are indicated in the language. One of these may be called intimate, integral, or non-transferable possession; such as the possession we have in the parts of our body, in our blood-relations; the possession which anything has in its parts or attributes—the words idakoa, *his friend or comrade*, and iko'pa, *her friend or comrade*, are put with this class. The other kind, or degree, is that of acquired or transferable possession; it is the possession we have in anything which we can acquire, or transfer from one to another.*

81. Intimate or non-transferable possession is shown by the use of the simple possessive pronouns, i, *his, her, its*, di, *your*, ma, *my*, and the contractions, m and d. Ex.—šaki, *hand*, išaki, *his or her hand*, dišaki, *your*

---

* The terms here employed for the different classes of possession, as shown by the different kinds of pronouns, are the best which, at present, present themselves; but they do not accurately cover all cases.

hand, mašaki, *my hand;* iaka, *a man's elder brother*, diaka, *your elder brother*, miaka, *my elder brother.*

82. Transferable possession is shown by the compound possessive pronouns, ita, dita, and mata, which are formed by adding the syllable 'ta' to the simple pronouns. Ex.—midaki, *a shield*, itamidaki, *his shield*, ditamidaki, *your shield*, matamidáki, *my shield.*

83. The noun denoting the possessor is placed before the noun denoting the thing possessed, and, when the former appears in a sentence, only the possessive pronoun of the third person can, of course, be used.

84. Possession may be indicated by simply placing the name of the possessor before that of the thing possessed, without the use of an intervening pronoun; the two words may be written separately, or as a compound word (¶¶ 66, 67), if the signification requires it. Some cases of this mode of showing possession may be regarded as simply an omission of the pronoun i; others, as the use of one noun, in the capacity of an adjective, to qualify another noun.

85. When the name of the possessor ends with a vowel, the 'i' of ita may be dropped, in which case the names of possessor and possessed, with the interposed 'ta', may be written as a compound word with a vowel or syllable elided, as shown in Pars. 34 and 36. But if we regard the 'ta' as belonging to the noun denoting the possessor, we have as true a possessive case as is made by the English "apostrophe and s". The possessive particle ta is never used alone as a prefix.

86. The position of a word in a sentence and the conjugation of the verb which follows, usually show whether it is in the nominative or objective. Often, too, the case is rendered unmistakable by the meaning of the word and by the context.

Proper Nouns.

87. Proper names, whether of persons, domestic animals, or places, are usually terminated with the consonant š, if not already closed by another consonantal sound, as t or k.

88. š may be regarded as the regular sign of a proper noun. It is well to end any proper name with š, where another terminal consonant does not interfere, but it may be omitted when, in calling a person, we accent the last syllable of his name, when we annex the word azi to the name of a river, and occasionally under other circumstances.

89. š is not suffixed to the names of tribes or nations when the whole people are referred to. Perhaps such words are not regarded as proper nouns by this tribe; but if the name of the tribe is used to distinguish one member of it, and is thus employed as a proper name, it takes the terminal š.

90. Words temporarily employed as proper names (as terms of relationship, etc.), may take the terminal š, if there would be danger of ambiguity without it.

91. The name of a person may consist of a single word, usually a

7

noun; as, tsatsĕś, *Eagle* (the spotted eagle), motsaś, *Coyote*, amaziś, *Beans.*

92. Personal names are, however, more **commonly compound words** formed—(1) **of two nouns;** as, pedetskiliś (pedĕtska and ilii), *Crow-crop.* ista-uetsĕś, *Iron-eye;*—(2) of a noun and a verb; as, tsakaka-amakiś, *Sitting bird,* dalipitsi-iduhiś, *Rising bear;*—(3) of a noun and an adjective; as, tšeša-liadaliiś, *Lean-wolf,* tsakaka-tohiś, *Blue bird;*—(4) of a noun and adverb; as, midikoa-miiś, *Woman-at the water;*—(5) of a pronoun, noun, and adjective; as, itamidaki-iliotą! iś, *His white shield,*—and in various other ways.*

93. Names of females often begin with the word mia (wia, bia), or end with mia, miiś (wiiś), all of which mean *woman.* Ex.—miahopaś, *Medicine-woman;* miadalipitsiś, *Bear-woman;* tsakakawiiś, *Bird-woman;* matąliimiiś, *Turtle-woman.*

94. Localities are named from **physical peculiarities** or historical associations. The **names of various localities** known to the tribe are appended to the Dictionary.

Syntax of Nouns.

95. A noun **precedes a** verb, adjective, noun **in apposition, or any** part of **speech used as** its predicate. Since there is **no verb** *to be,* used as in English, any word except a conjunction or interjection may be employed as the predicate of a noun.

96. The name of 'the person spoken to' commonly follows a verb in the imperative; but in almost all other cases a noun, whether subject or object, stands before the verb.

97. When the **names of both** subject and object **appear, the** former usually precedes the latter.

98. The name of the possessor precedes that of **the thing possessed.**

PRONOUNS.

99. Hidatsa pronouns may **be divided into four** classes, namely, *personal, relative, interrogative,* and **demonstrative.**

Personal Pronouns.

100. Personal pronouns are of two kinds, simple and compound.

101. **Simple,** or primary, personal pronouns consist, in the singular, of but one syllable; they may stand **alone, as** separate **words, but are** usually found incorporated with other words.

102. Compound **personal pronouns consist of** more than one syllable, are derived from **simple pronouns, and,** except those in the possessive case, are used as separate words.

103. Personal pronouns exhibit, by their different forms, their *person, number,* and *case.*

---

* See Ethnography, § 25.

104. They have the first, second, and third *persons*, the singular and plural *numbers*, and the nominative, possessive, and objective *cases*.

SIMPLE PERSONAL PRONOUNS.

105. The simple personal pronouns are five in number; they are ma and mi (sometimes contracted to m) for the first person, da and di (sometimes contracted to d) for the second person, and i for the third person.

106. They stand alone when used for repetition and emphasis, but otherwise are incorporated with other words.

107. ma, *I*, and da, *thou*, are the proper nominative forms; they are used as the nominatives of transitive verbs, but may also be employed as the nominatives of certain intransitive verbs which have an active sense; as, amáki, *he sits*, amamaki, *I sit*, adamaki, *you sit*. They may be prefixed or suffixed to, or inserted into, verbs; thus we have kikidi, *he hunts*, makikidi, *I hunt*, dakikidi, *you hunt;* kạtsihe, *he extinguishes*, kạtsima, *I extinguish*, kạtsida, *you extinguish;* akakạṣi, *he writes*, amakakạṣi, *I write*, adakakạṣi, *you write*.

108. ma, *my*, is used in the possessive case, prefixed to the noun denoting the thing possessed, in intimate or non-transferable possession; as in masạki, *my hand*, from sáki, *hand;* matsi, *my foot*, from itsi, *his foot*. (¶ 81).

109. mi, *me*, di, *thee*, and i, *him, her, it*, are prefixed to transitive verbs to denote the object; as, from kideši, *he loves*, we have mikideš`, *he loves me*, dikideši, *he loves thee*, ikideši, *he loves him, her*, or *it*, midakideši (*me thou lovest*), *you love me*, and dimakideši (*thee I love*), *I love you*.

110. mi and di are, however, used as the nominatives of such intransitive verbs as imply only quality or state of being, and of qualifying words used as verbs.

111. di, *thy, your*, and i, *his, her, its, theirs*, are also used in the possessive case, prefixed to the name of the thing possessed, to denote non-transferable possession. (¶ 81). Examples.—dišaki, *your hand*, išaki, *his hand*, from šaki, *hand;* ditsi, *your foot*, itsi, *his foot* (the hypothetical word, tsi, is not used without the possessive pronouns).

112. ma and mi, da and di, are commonly contracted, when placed before vowels, according to orthographic rules already given (¶¶ 34, 35); as in makulii, *my ear*, dakulii, *your ear*, from akulii, *ear;* mišta, *my eye*, dišta, *your eye*, from išta, *eye*.

113. The possessive pronoun, i, is often omitted before words beginning with a vowel, where possession is intimated; thus, akulii, *ear*, is also *his* or *her ear;* išta, *eye*, also *his* or *her eye*.

114. When the pronoun of the third person, singular, stands alone, it is often pronounced hi.

115. The plural forms of simple pronouns are not incorporated; they are mido, plural of ma and mi; dido, plural of da and di; and hido, plural of i.

Compound Personal Pronouns.

116. The compound personal pronouns are formed from the simple pronouns by means of suffixes. The words most readily recognizable, as of this class, are micki, dicki, and icki (with their plurals), and the possessives, mata, dita, and ita.

117. micki (1st person), dicki (2d person), and icki (3d person) are used in an emphatic and limiting sense, and are nearly synonymous with the English words *myself*, *thyself*, and *himself* or *herself*. They may be used alone, as nominatives or objectives to verbs, but are commonly repetitions, being followed by the simple incorporated pronouns with which they agree.

118. Their plurals, used in the same way as the singular forms, are midoki (*ourselves*), didoki (*yourselves*), and hidoki (*themselves*).

119. máta, *my*, *our*, dita, *thy*, *your*, and ita, *his*, *her*, *its*, *their*, are compound possessive pronouns, which are ordinarily used to indicate an acquired or transferable possession (¶¶ 80–82), and are prefixed to nouns, denoting the thing possessed. (¶ 83).

120. In compound words, formed of the names of possessor and possessed with the pronoun ita, the i of ita may sometimes be dropped. (¶¶ 36, 85).

121. mata, dita, and ita have not separate forms for singular and plural.

122. The words matamae (1st pers.), ditamae (2d pers.), and itamae (3d pers.), are used respectively as the equivalents of the English words *mine* or *my own*, *thine* or *thy own*, and *his*, *hers*, *its*, *theirs*, or *his own*, etc., and also as the equivalents of the Dakota words mitawa, nitawa, and tawa. The Hidatsa words, however, I regard not as pronouns, but as nouns formed by prefixing the compound possessive pronouns to the noun 'mae'. According to the usual custom with interchangeable consonants, these words are often pronounced matawae, nitawae, and itawae.

Synopsis of Personal Pronouns.

Simple.

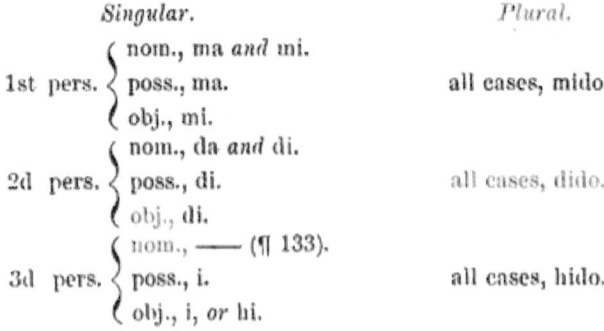

	Singular.	Plural.
1st pers.	nom., ma *and* mi. poss., ma. obj., mi.	all cases, mido.
2d pers.	nom., da *and* di. poss., di. obj., di.	all cases, dido.
3d pers.	nom., —— (¶ 133). poss., i. obj., i, *or* hi.	all cases, hido.

Compound.

With 'ki' for emphasis and limitation.

Singular.	Plural.
1st pers., micki.	midoki.
2d pers., dicki.	didoki.
3d pers., icki.	hidoki.

With 'ta' to denote transferable possession.

Singular and Plural.

1st pers., mata.
2d pers., dita.
3d pers., ita.

Relative Pronouns.

123. The interrogatives tapa, *what?* tapé, *who?* aku (¶¶ 51, 52), and some other words are used as relative pronouns.

Interrogative Pronouns.

124. Interrogative pronouns, and all other interrogative words of the language, begin with t, which, being always followed by a vowel in these words, has a slight sound of English *th* in *thing*. (¶ 5).

125. tapé, *who?* tapa, *what?* taka, *what?* to, *which* or *where?* tua, *which? how?* are the principal interrogative pronouns.

126. Their compounds, tapeitamae, *whose?* tapata, takata, tota, *whither?* todu, *where?* tuami, *how many?* etc., etc., are sometimes used as pronouns, although usually filling the offices of nouns, adjectives or adverbs.

Demonstrative Pronouns.

127. The demonstrative pronouns are hidi, *this*, hido, *that*, with ku and sa or šia, *that, him*, distinctive or emphatic forms.

128. Their compounds are bidimi, *this many*, bidika, *this much*, biduka, *this way*, kutapa, *what is that?* kuadu, *that place*, kutsąki, šetsąki, *that alone*, šedu, *just there*, etc., etc. These, like the compounds of interrogative pronouns, are used as pronouns, but more commonly as other parts of speech.

Syntax of Pronouns.

129. All simple pronouns in the objective case, or used separately for emphasis, and usually all compound pronouns in any case, precede the verb.

130. Personal pronouns in the objective commonly precede those in the nominative.

131. When mi or di is used as the nominative of an intransitive verb (¶ 110), or of any word used as such, it stands before the verb.

132. When ma or da is used as an incorporated pronoun in the nominative (¶ 107), its position in the verb is usually determined as follows: (1st) In a verb formed directly from a verbal root and beginning with any consonant (except m followed by a), the pronoun is prefixed in the indicative; as in kikiški, *he measures*, makikiški, *I measure*, dakikiški, *you measure*; patšaki, *he cuts*, mapatšaki, *I cut*, dapatsaki, *you cut*. (2d) In a verb formed directly from a verbal root and beginning with a vowel, or the syllable ma, the pronoun is inserted in the indicative; while the verb, if beginning in the third person with i or o, is made to begin with a in the first and second persons. Ex.—ašadi, *he steals*, amašadadi, *I steal*, adašadadi, *you steal*; maihe, *he tries*, mamahe, *I try*, madahe, *you try*; iku'pa, *he hates*, amaku'pa, *I hate*, adaku'pa, *you hate*; odapi, *he discovers*, amodapi, *I discover*, adodapi, *you discover*. (3d) In a transitive verb formed from an intransitive verb by the addition of be, ha, or ke, the pronoun is suffixed.

133. There is no incorporated pronoun in the third person nominative.[*]

134. The use of incorporated pronouns being necessary to the conjugation of verbs, they cannot be omitted when several verbs refer to the same subject or object.

135. Incorporated possessive pronouns must be prefixed to the name of each thing possessed, even when but one possessor is indicated.

136. A demonstrative, relative, or interrogative pronoun usually stands at the beginning of the clause to which it belongs.

137. When a relative and demonstrative pronoun appear in the same sentence, the clause containing the former usually stands first.

138. Some modifications of the above rules will be discussed under the head of verbs.

VERBS.

139. Almost any word in the language may be used and conjugated as an intransitive verb, and may again, by certain suffixes, be changed to a transitive verb, and be conjugated as such.

140. Adjectives, nouns, adverbs, and prepositions are often thus treated; pronouns, conjunctions, and interjections rarely.

141. But there is a large number of words in the language which are used only as verbs and are not derived from other parts of speech; these may be called verbs proper.

142. Many verbs proper we cannot analyze, and therefore consider them as primitive verbs. Such are ki, *to bear* or *carry*; hu, *to come*; de, *to depart*; eke, *to know*, etc.

---

[*] Possibly in maihu and maihe we have exceptions to this rule. (¶ 199).

143. Other verbs proper, which we **call derivative, are formed, by the use of** certain prefixes and **suffixes, from verbal roots, from primitive verbs,** and from other derivative **verbs.**

Verbal Roots.

144. Verbal roots **are not** used **as** independent words. A **great** number have been found **in the** language; but satisfactory meanings have been discovered **for a very** few only, some of which are here **given for** illustration: kiăpi, *bark, peel ;* lieše, *tear through ;* liolii, *break across ;* lin, *spill,* **overset;** kahe, *spread, stretch ;* kape, *tear into, lacerate ;* kaɔtsi, *notch ;* kide, **push;** kiti, *clear off ;* ktade, *pound* **in, peg;** midi, *twist ;* mitsi. **mince;** mu, *make noise ;* mudsi, *roll up ;* **papi, roughen,** *chap ;* pi, **penetrate ;** plin, or pliuti, *squeeze or press out ;* pkiti, *smooth* **out** (? fr. kiti); pšu, **dislocate ;** ptsu or ptsuti, *thrust forth ;* šipi, *loosen ;* **ški, open out ; šku, extract;** šaki, *erase ;* ta, *destroy ;* taki, *place in contact,* **shut;** tapi, **squeeze ;** tsa, *separate ;* tsada, *slide ;* tsa'ti, *stick, polish ;* tsiti, *raze ;* **tski, squeeze** *on a small surface from different directions, shear, strangle,* etc. ; **tski**pi, *pare ;* tskiše, *wash ;* tskupi, *bend.* Some of these may be modified roots, containing something more than the simplest **radical idea,** but could not be well further analyzed.

Prefixes and Suffixes.

145. Some of **the** prefixes **and** suffixes referred **to** are independent words, but many of **them are** used only when connected with verbs. Some are to **be regarded as** adverbs, others perhaps as auxiliary verbs.

PREFIXES.

146. **The more important** prefixes, **whose** meanings have been **determined,** are ada, ak, da, dak, du, ki, mak, and pa.

147. ada immediately precedes the root, and denotes that the **action is** performed by the foot, or by means of heat or fire ; as in adaliolii, *to break across with the foot,* from liolii, *break across,* and adakite, *to clear off by fire,* as in burning a prairie, from the root kite, *clear off.*

148. ak denotes that the action is performed with or on something ; as, akšnĕ, *to* **spit** *on,* from šuĕ, *to spit.*

149. da denotes that the action is done, or may properly be done, with the mouth ; it stands immediately before **the** root, and is often **pronounced** ra **or** la. Ex.—datsa, *to bite off,* from tsa, *separate ;* dalieše, *to tear with the teeth,* from the root lieše, *tear.*

150. dăk (or dăka) stands immediately before a root or verb to denote that the action is performed **with a** sudden forcible impulse, or with great force applied during a short **time,** and usually repeated at short intervals; **as in** dăktsaki, *to chop,* from tsaki, *cut ;* dakaliolii, *to break across with a blow,* from the root liolii, *break across.* n is often used as the initial sound of this **prefix.**

151. du is prefixed to roots, to convert them into verbs, without materially adding to their significance; it may be said to denote general or indefinite causation; is sometimes pronounced ru or lu. Ex.—duliolii, *to break across in any way or by any means*, from liolii, *break across;* dumidi, *to twist in any way*, from the root midi, *twist.*

152. ki is sometimes added directly to verbal roots, but more commonly to verbs. It may be added to any verb, no matter how formed, and is the most extensively used verbal prefix in the language. It intensifies the meaning; denotes that the action is done forcibly, repeatedly, completely, with difficulty, or over the entire object. Sometimes it merely strengthens, without altering the meaning of the verb; in other cases, it totally changes its application. Some verbs are never used without it. Ex.—dalipa, *to put the arms around*, kidalipa, *to hug;* pạti, *to fall down*, kipạti, *to fall from a great height.* The words kime, *to tell*, and kideši, *to love*, have not simpler forms.

153. mak (or maki) is prefixed to verbs to denote opposition or reciprocity; that the action is performed by two contending parties, that the motion is from opposite directions, that two actors mutually and reciprocally perform the action; thus, from patạki, *to close*, comes makipatạki, *to close anything which has both sides moved in the act*, as a book or a pocket-comb, and from iku'pa, *to hate*, makiiku'pa, *to hate mutually, to hate one another.*

154. pa is a causative prefix, denoting that the action is done by the hand, or by an instrument held in the hand, or that it may be properly so performed. It stands immediately before roots and primitive verbs. Ex.—paliu, *to pour with the hand*, from liu, *spill;* pamidi, *to twist with the hand*, from midi, *twist.*

SUFFIXES.

155. The principal suffixes to verbs are adsi, adui, de, he, ha, ke, kša, and ti, with duk and tok for the subjunctive, di, diha, mi, and miha for the future indicative, and ts for the closing of sentences.

156. adsi denotes a resemblance or approach to the standard described by the simpler form of the verb; it is most commonly, however, used with adjectives, rarely with verbs proper. (¶ 226). Ex.—mitapa,*to lie, to deceive*, mitapadsi, *to equivocate.*

157. adui denotes progression and incompleteness in action on condition; it answers sometimes the purpose of the English termination *ing* in present participles. Verbs ending in adui are intransitive and usually preceded by ki. Ex.—titsi, *thick*, titsadui, or kititsadui, *gradually increasing in thickness;* išia, *bad*, išiadui, *deteriorating, to become progressively worse.*

158. Verbs lose their final vowels when adsi and adui are suffixed.

159. de may be translated, *almost, nearly, about to*, and denotes an incomplete action or condition. It is added to, and forms, intransitive

verbs. Ex.—tsipiti, *to fall upon* **the water, to be in a condition to sink,** tsipitide, *to be about to fail,* or *nearly* **falling,** *on the water.*

160. he, signifying generally to make or cause, **changes some intran**sitive verbs, and words used as such, to transitive. Verbs take it in the third person indicative, but rarely retain it in the first **person;** while in the second **person** indicative, and in the imperative, it is dropped or changed **to** ha. The incorporated pronouns are suffixed to verbs formed by **the** addition of he, which suffix they sometimes follow, but **more** commonly replace. Ex.—komi, *complete, finished,* komihe, *he finishes,* komima, *I finish,* komida, *you finish,* komihada, *finish thou!*

161. **ha** is the form of 'he' used in the second person.

162. ke, signifying to cause, to change, to use for, is added to intransitive verbs, to form transitive verbs. It is more extensive in its application than he, and may be added to any of the numerous words of the language which are capable of being used as intransitive verbs. It is retained in all persons, tenses, and modes, and followed by **the incor**porated pronouns. When ke is suffixed, the verb is most commonly put in the intensive form. The more familiar instances, only, of its use are given in the Dictionary. Ex.—hiši, *red,* hišike, *to dye or color red, dyed red;* išia, *bad,* išiake, *to make bad, change from good to bad, damaged, debased,* kiišiake (intensive), *he damages,* kiišiakema, *I damage,* kiišiakeda, *you damage;* **ati,** *a house,* kiatike, *to use for a dwelling,* **or** *convert into a dwelling;* midi, **water,** kimidike, *to liquefy.*

163. kša denotes that an action is performed habitually or excessively, or that a quality exists **to a** constant or excessive degree ; it is used with verbs proper and adjectives. Ex.—mitapa, *to lie* or *deceive,* mitapakša, *to lie habitually* or *excessively;* ide, *to speak,* idekša, *to speak garrulously* or **unguardedly, to say too** *much.* (¶ 231).

164. ti, denoting a favorable condition or readiness **to** perform an act, **is** added to intransitive verbs, forming new intransitive verbs. Ex.— hua, *to cough,* huati, *to be about to cough, to feel a desire to cough;* halipi, *to sneeze,* halipicti, *to desire to sneeze;* tsipi, *to sink,* tsipiti, *to fall upon the water, to be placed in a condition favorable for sinking.*

165. duk, used alone as an adverb of future time, is suffixed **to sub**joined **verbs, to** denote doubt or condition **in regard to future time, and** is therefore equivalent to a sign of the subjunctive **mode in the** future tense. Ex.—miadéheduk ditamamits, *if I am angered, I will kill you.*

166. tok, an adverb used to denote doubt and interrogation, is usually used independently, but may be suffixed to verbs **to** indicate **the** past and present tense of the subjunctive mode; as in madetok diamakatats, *had I gone, I would not* **have seen you.**

167. di (2d person singular), diha (2d person plural), mi (1st person singular), and miha (1st person plural) denote the future tense, indicative mode, and may follow any **verb which** takes **ma** and **da** for its incorporated nominative pronouns. **They have the appearance of** being

only repeated pronouns, but are probably different forms of a regularly conjugated auxiliary verb.

168. A verb, or any word used as such, in the indicative mode, when closing a sentence, and therefore when standing alone and forming a sentence by itself, is terminated in ts; if in other situations it ends in a vowel. (¶ 33). By comparison of this with previous rules, it will be seen that a large majority of the words of the language are capable of receiving this termination. In the conjugations following, some of the verbs are shown with the terminal ts. (¶¶ 196, 198).

169. ta' (not) and ta (only) are often pronounced as if suffixed; they are regarded, however, as independent adverbs.

170. There are verbs which are heard to end sometimes in i and sometimes in e, and apparently when a passive sense is meant by the former and an active by the latter. Owing, however, to the indistinct manner in which final vowels are so often pronounced, and to certain individual liberties taken with vowel sounds, the value of this peculiarity, as a grammatical rule, cannot now be estimated. A few words, where this change of terminal vowels was often heard, are given in both forms in the Dictionary.

171. Many verbs ending in i or e change these letters to a in the second person indicative, and also in the imperative, when the final i or e is not dropped.

Properties of Verbs.

PERSON.

172. The first and second persons are shown by the incorporated pronouns, ma and mi for the former, da and di for the latter. The third person is shown by the simple form of the verb.

NUMBER.

173. In the conjugation of the verb, number is indicated only in the future indicative, where mi and di are used in the singular, for the first and second persons respectively, and miha and diha in the plural. (¶ 167).

MODE.

174. Three modes only, the *infinitive*, *indicative*, and *imperative*, are shown in the conjugations of verbs. The subjunctive and potential are indicated by adverbs or additional verbs.

Infinitive.

175. The infinitive mode is the same as the third person indicative, the simple form of the verb. It is, however, rarely used, finite verbs being employed instead; thus, "I try to cough" is more frequently rendered mahua mamahets, *I cough I try*, than hua mamahets, *to cough I try.*

176. In the third person, **no distinction is made between the infinitive and** indicative; thus, hua **maibets may be rendered either** *to cough he tries* **or** *he coughs he tries.*

Indicative.

177. The simple **form of** the verb is used as the third person indicative. For the **first** and second persons this is modified by the incorporated **pronouns; and for the future tense, as show**n in Pars. 167 and 173.

Imperative.

178. **The imperative** mode has five forms.

179. **The first** consists in using the same **form** as **the second person** indicative; **this is done** mostly in **verbs which have the incorporated** pronouns suffixed.

180. The second is made **by** changing final i **or e of the infinitive to** a, **or** using an infinitive ending **in a or** u.

181. The third is formed by dropping **the final i of verbs ending in** ki, and sometimes of those ending in ti; **thus, we have amak, imperative of** amaki.

182. In the fourth form, the auxiliary da is added to the second form of the imperative; **it** is usually, but not invariably, placed after the verb. da seems **to** be a form of the verb de, *to* ***depart*, meaning** *go thou!*

183. The **fifth form** of the imperative mode **is made by adding** diha instead of **da.**

184. **The fourth and fifth** forms are used **when immediate compliance** with **the** order is desired.

TENSE.

185. **But** two distinctions, in regard to time, are made in conjugating **verbs; one of these** is for *indefinite,* the other for *future* time.

186. Other varieties of time are expressed by adverbs, suffixed **or** independent, or by other words used independently.

187. The *indefinite tense,* used for both present and past time, is shown **by** the simple **form** of the verb, with **or** without the **incorporated** pronouns.

188. For the *future tense,* indicative **mode, mi and miha** are added to the indefinite for **the** first person, and **di and diha for** the second person; in the third **person, the form is** the same as in the indefinite.

189. Sometimes, to a **verb in the third** person, future tense, at the close **of** a sentence, they **are heard to add** hits, pronouncing it as a separate word. This may **be a part** of the conjugation, but is, more probably, **a** personal pronoun **of the** third person, hi, with the ending ts, added for emphasis.

CONJUGATION.

190. All transitive and some intransitive verbs are properly conjugated, having different forms for the different modes and tenses.

191. The greater part of the intransitive verbs, and words used as such, are not properly conjugated, since they suffer no change of form in the different modes and tenses.

192. The verbs which are conjugated may be known by taking ma (*I*) and da (*thou*) for their incorporated pronouns in the nominative; while those which are not conjugated have the pronouns mi and di incorporated in the nominative case.

Conjugated Verbs.

193. The conjugation has three principal forms. In the first form, the pronouns are prefixed; in the second, inserted; and, in the third, suffixed.

194. In adding the pronouns, however, some additional changes are made in the verb, producing in all ten varieties of the conjugation.

195. In the first variety, the incorporated pronouns are simply prefixed to the third person, or simple form of the verb; while the latter remains unchanged. Ex.—kidĕśi, *to love*, or *he lores*.

INFINITIVE MODE.
kidĕśi, *to love*.

INDICATIVE MODE.

Indefinite Tense.
Singular and Plural.

3d person. kidĕśi, *he, she,* or *it lores* or *lored, they lore* or *lored.*
2d person. dakidĕśi, *thou lovest, you love* or *lored.*
1st person. makıdĕśi, *I* or *we love* or *lored.*

Future Tense.
Singular.

3d person. kidĕśi, *he, she,* or *it will love.*
2d person. dakedĕśidi, *thou will love.*
1st person. makidĕśimi, *I will love.*

Plural.

3d person. kidĕśi, *they will love.*
2d person. dakídĕśidiha, *you will love.*
1st person. makidĕśimiha, *we will love.*

IMPERATIVE MODE.
kidĕśa, kidĕśada, kidĕśadiha, *love thou, love ye.*

196. In the second variety, the first letter of the simple form is dropped when the pronouns are prefixed, and the pronouns are contracted to m

and d. The words belonging to **this variety are not numerous; they all begin with** d, and consequently **in the indicative mode, indefinite tense, the forms** of the second and **third persons are the same. Ex.—**dúti, *to eat, to chew.*

INFINITIVE MODE.

duti, *to chew* or *eat.*

INDICATIVE MODE.

Indefinite Tense.

Singular and Plural.

	(without terminal ts.)	(with terminal ts.)
3d *person.*	duti, *he eats,* etc.	**dutIts.**
2d *person.*	duti, *you eat,* etc.	dutIts.
1st *person.*	muti, *I eat,* etc.	mutIts.

Future Tense.

Singular.

3d *person.*	duti, *he will eat,* etc.	dutIts.
2d *person.*	dutidi, *thou will eat.*	dutidIts.
1st *person.*	mutimi, *I will eat.*	mutimIts.

Plural.

3d *person.*	duti, *they will eat.*	**dutIts.**
2d *person.*	dutidiha, *you will eat.*	dutidihats.
1st *person.*	mutimiha, *we will eat.*	mutimihats.

IMPERATIVE.

dut. da' dut, etc. *eat, eat thou.*

197. The third variety **of** the conjugation **has** the pronouns prefixed **to the** unaltered simple form; but the letter a is in turn prefixed to **the** pronouns, causing them to appear inserted in the verb; further, the pronouns are contracted by the omission of their vowels. **Most verbs** beginning with o belong to this variety. Ex.—ókipapi, *to find, to recover* **something lost,** but not to make an original discovery.

INFINITIVE MODE.

okipapi, *to find.*

INDICATIVE MODE.

Indefinite Tense.

Singular and Plural.

3d *pers.*	okipapi, *he, she,* or *it finds,* or *found,* or *they,* etc.
2d *pers.*	adokipapi, *you find* or *found.*
1st *pers.*	amokipapi, *I* or *we find* or *found.*

Future Tense.

Singular.

3d pers. okipapi, *he, she, or it will find.*
2d pers. adokipapidi, *thou wilt find.*
1st pers. amokipapimi, *I will find.*

Plural.

3d pers. okipapi, *they will find.*
2d pers. adokipapidiha, **you** *will find.*
1st pers. amokipapimiha, *we will find.*

IMPERATIVE MODE.

okipapa, okipapa da', okipapa diha.

198. In the fourth variety, the incorporated pronouns are inserted in the verb by being placed immediately after the first syllable of the simple form, while **no** change is made in the latter, **except the** separation of the syllables. Verbs conjugated thus have a **or e for their** first syllables. Ex.—éke, *to know, to recognize.*

INFINITIVE MODE.

eke, *to know.*

Indefinite Tense.

Singular and Plural.
  (without terminal ts.)   (with terminal **ts.**)
3d pers. eke, *he,* etc., *knows,* or *knew.*   ekĕts.
2d pers. edake, **you** *know* or *knew.*   edakĕts.
1st pers. emake, *I know* **or** *knew.*   emakĕts.

Future Tense.

Singular.
3d pers. eke, *he,* etc., *will know.*   ekĕts.
2d pers. edakedi, *thou will know.*   edakedits.
1st pers. emakemi, *I will know.*   emakemits.

Plural.

3d pers. **eke,** *they will know.*   ekĕts.
2d pers. edakediha, *you will know.*   edakedihats.
1st pers. emakemiha, *we will know.*   emakemihats.

IMPERATIVE MODE.

ekn, eka da', eka diha.

199. To the fifth variety, belong verbs beginning with **ma**. In it, the incorporated pronouns come after the first syllable, and **are substituted** for the second syllable of the simple form, which is, **therefore,** changed by the loss of a syllable. Ex.—maihu, *to trade, to buy.*

INFINITIVE MODE.

maihu, *to trade.*

INDICATIVE MODE.

Indefinite Tense.

Singular and Plural.

3d pers. maihu, *he or she trades or traded, they,* etc.
2d **pers.** madahu, *you trade or traded.*
1st pers. mamahu, *I or we trade or traded.*

Future Tense.

Singular.

3d pers. maihu, *he or she will trade.*
2d pers. madahudi, *thou wilt trade.*
1st pers. mamahumi, *I will trade.*

Plural.

3d **pers.** maihu, *they will trade.*
2d **pers.** madahudiha, *you will trade.*
1st pers. mamahumiha, *we will trade.*

IMPERATIVE MODE.

madahu **da', maihu da'.**

200. In the sixth variety, the incorporated pronouns are inserted in the same way as in the fourth; but the syllable da is inserted, in the first and second persons, immediately before the last syllable of the verb. This extra interpolated syllable does not seem to answer the purpose of either pronoun, adverb, or auxiliary; its utility has not been discovered. ašádi, *to steal,* atádi, *to go out of a house,* and perhaps a few other verbs, are conjugated in this way.

INFINITIVE MODE.

ašadi, *to steal.*

INDICATIVE MODE.

Indefinite Tense.

Singular and Plural.

3d pers. ašadi, *he or she steals or stole, they steal or stole.*
2d pers. adašadadi, *you steal or stole.*
1st pers. amašadadi, *I or we steal or stole.*

Future Tense.

Singular.

3d pers.   ašadi, *he or she will* **steal.**
2d pers.   adašadadidi, *thou wilt steal.*
1st pers. amašadadimi, *I will steal.*

Plural.

3d pers.   ašadi, *they will steal.*
2d pers.   adašadadidiha, *you will steal.*
1st pers. amašadadimiha, *we will steal.*

IMPERATIVE MODE.

ašada da', ašada diha.

201. To the seventh variety belong **verbs beginning in i** (*not* the incorporated pronoun of the third person **objective**). Here the incorporated pronouns are inserted, but i is changed **to a.** Ex.—íka, *to see.*

INFINITIVE MODE.

ika, *to see.*

INDICATIVE MODE.

Indefinite Tense.

Singular and Plural.

3d pers.   ika, *he or she sees or saw, they see or saw.*
2d pers.   adaka, *you see or saw.*
1st pers. amaka, *I or we see or saw.*

Future Tense.

Singular.

3d pers.   ika, *he or she will see.*
2d pers.   adakadi, *thou wilt see.*
1st pers. amakami, *I will see.*

Plural.

3d pers.   ika, *they will see.*
2d pers.   adakadiha, *you will see.*
1st pers. amakamiha, *we will see.*

IMPERATIVE MODE.

ika, ika da', ika diha.

Besides these, ika has a reduplicated form in the imperative, used in an exclamatory manner, ikaka! *See there! Behold!*

202. The eighth variety is distinguished by the incorporated pronouns of the nominative being substituted for the last syllable of the infinitive form. Nearly all transitive verbs formed from intransitive verbs by the suffix he belong to the eighth variety. Ex.—ḣapihé, *to lose*.

INFINITIVE MODE.

ḣapihe, *to lose.*

INDICATIVE MODE.

Indefinite Tense.

Singular and Plural.

3*d pers.* ḣapihe, *he* or *she loses* or *lost,* or *they lose* or *lost.*
2*d pers.* ḣapida, *you lose* or *lost.*
1*st pers.* ḣapima, *I lose* or *lost,* or *we lose* or *lost.*

Future Tense.

Singular.

3*d pers.* ḣapihe, *he will lose.*
2*d pers.* ḣapidadi, *thou wilt lose.*
1*st pers.* ḣapimami, *I will lose.*

Plural.

3*d pers.* ḣapihe, *they will lose.*
2*d pers.* ḣapidadiha, *you will lose.*
1*st pers.* ḣapimamiha, *we will lose.*

IMPERATIVE MODE.

ḣapida, da' ḣapida, ḣapihada.

203. The ninth variety is the same as the eighth, with the addition of the simple possessive pronouns, in full or contracted, prefixed to the verb. In this variety are found but few verbs; they are formed from nouns by the addition of the suffix he; they undergo a double inflection, one to denote possession of the noun, and the other to show person, tense, etc., in the verb. Ex.—ṅahe, *to make* or *cause to be a wife,* to wed, from na, *a wife.* ṅahe, in its active sense, or used personally, is said of the male.

INFINITIVE MODE.

ṅahe, *to make a wife,* to wed.

INDICATIVE MODE.

Indefinite Tense.

Singular and Plural.

3*d pers.* ṅahe, *he makes his wife, he* or *they wed* or *wedded,* etc.
2*d pers.* duada, *you make your wife* or *wives, you wed* or *wedded,* etc.
1*st pers.* mnama, *I make my wife, I* or *we wed,* etc.

8

Future Tense.

Singular.

3d pers.   uahe, *he will make his wife,* **or** *wed.*
2d pers.   duadadi, *thou wilt make thy wife,* **or** *wed.*
1st pers.   muamami, *I will make my wife,* **or** *wed.*

Plural.

3d pers.   uahe, *they will make their wives,* or *wed.*
2d pers.   duadadiha, *you will make your wives,* etc.
1st pers.   muamamiha, *we will make our wives,* or *wed.*

IMPERATIVE MODE.

duada, duaha da', duaha diha.

204. In the tenth variety, the pronouns are suffixed to the simple form, which in itself remains unchanged. Transitive verbs formed from the intransitive by the addition of ke are conjugated in this way. Ex.— kitsakíke, to *render completely good, to make* whole **or** sound, *to change from bad to good,* etc., from tsaki, *good.*

INFINITIVE MODE.

kitsakike, *to make good.*

INDICATIVE MODE.

Indefinite Tense.

Singular and Plural.

3d pers.   kitsakike, *he, she, it,* or *they make* or *made good.*
2d pers.   kitsakikeda, *you make* or *made good.*
1st pers.   kitsakikema, *I* **or** *we make* **or** *made good.*

Future Tense.

Singular.

3d pers.   kitsakike, *he, she,* **or** *it will make good.*
2d pers.   kitsakikedadi, *thou wilt* **make good.**
1st pers.   **kitsakikemami,** *I will make good.*

Plural.

3d pers.   kitsakike, *they will make good*
2d pers.   kitsakikedadiha, *you will make* **good.**
1st pers.   kitsakikemamiha, *we will* **make good.**

IMPERATIVE MODE.

kitsakikeda, kitsakike diha.

Unconjugated Verbs.

205. All adjectives, adverbs, nouns, etc., used as predicates of nouns, are regarded as intransitive verbs, there being no copula in the language. These intransitive verbs, and such others as denote only quality or condition, suffer no change of form to denote different modes and tenses. They may, however, take the incorporated pronouns mi and di for their nominatives.

206. These pronouns are prefixed. To verbs beginning with consonants they are usually prefixed in full. Ex.—liié, *old, to be old.*

> liié, *he*, *she*, or *it is* or *was old, they are* or *were old.*
> diliié, *thou art* or *wert old, you are* or *were old.*
> miliié, *I am* or *was old, we are* or *were old.*

207. Before verbs beginning with vowels, the pronouns are often contracted. Ex.—adáliiše, *to be ignorant.*

> adaliiše, *he is* or *was ignorant, they are* or *were ignorant.*
> dadaliiše, *thou art* or *wert ignorant,* etc.
> madaliiše, *I am* or *was ignorant,* or *we were ignorant,* etc.

208. Transitive verbs in the third person, or used in a passive sense or impersonally, with pronouns in the objective case prefixed, have the same appearance as the unconjugated intransitive verbs, except that for the third person the objective pronoun i is used; thus, from alióa, *to conceal,* we have

> ialioa, *he conceals it,* or *it is concealed.*
> dialioa, *he conceals you,* or *you are concealed.*
> mialioa, *he conceals me,* or *I am concealed.*

Irregular and Defective Verbs.

209. There are a few irregular and defective verbs in the language, of which the following are examples:

210. hi, *to draw into the mouth, to drink* or *inhale,* may, with terminal ts, be conjugated thus:

> 1. hits, *he drinks* or *drank* or *will drink, they drink,* etc.
> 2. dats, *you drink* or *drank.*
> 3. mats, *I drink* or *drank.*
> 4. dadits, *you will drink.*
> 5. mamits, *I will drink.*

Here, in the fourth and fifth forms, there are (with the terminal) but the pronouns and signs of the future tense, and in the second and third forms, only the pronouns.

211. matú, *there is* or *there are,* has no other form.

212. muk (sometimes pronounced as the English word *hook*) signifies *give me.* It may be an irregular imperative of the verb ku, *to give,* but is more probably a defective verb.

Compound Verbs (so called).

213. Sometimes two verbs are used together to express an idea for which there is no single word in the language. When both verbs are in the third person indicative, or when one is in the infinitive, they often appear to us as a single word, particularly if their English equivalent is a single word; but when conjugated, it is found that each assumes its own proper form, the same as if used independently. Ex.—Ákhu, *to bring*, consists of ak, *to be with*, and hu, *to come*. This, when inflected, appears as two separate words, one conjugated, the other unconjugated; thus, ak-hu, *he brings*; dak-dahu, *you bring*; mak-mahu, *I bring*; dak-dahudi, *you will bring*; mak-mahumi, *I will bring*, etc.

214. Again, a noun and a verb may be used together to express an idea for which there is no single word in the language; thus, from hi, *to draw into the mouth*, we have ope-hi, *to draw tobacco into the mouth, i. e., to smoke*, and midi-hi, *to draw water into the mouth*, or *drink*.

215. Some expressions, such as these, are, for convenience of definition, put in the Dictionary as compound verbs.

Syntax of Verbs.

216. Almost all sentences are closed by verbs or words used as such; the principal exception being where interrogative adverbs are used to qualify an entire sentence.

217. When a verb denoting quality or condition, and another denoting action, are used in the same sentence with a common subject, the former precedes the latter; or, in other words, conjugated verbs commonly follow unconjugated verbs.

218. Verbs in the infinitive usually precede those in the indicative.

219. Any word used alone, with the terminal ts, in answer to a question, may form a sentence by itself; for it is used as a verb in the simple form, where a personal pronoun of the third person is understood to be in the nominative.

220. In this language, as in other languages, "active transitive verbs govern the objective case". It might be said that all transitive verbs govern the objective case, for the existence of a passive form is questionable. (¶ 170). When an objective pronoun is followed by the simple form of a transitive verb, the latter may be parsed as in the third person indicative; although, in translating the expression into English, a verb in the passive voice may be used.

221. Other points connected with the syntax of the verb have been referred to in the discussion of the etymology.

ADJECTIVES.

222. There are certain intransitive verbs in the Hidatsa, which are used in the same sense as the adjectives of European languages, and may be translated by them. For the convenience of the English student, these verbs will be called adjectives, and described as such.

223. There are a large number of the adjectives, which we cannot analyze with our present knowledge of the language, and which may be called primitive.

224. Derivative adjectives are formed from primitive adjectives, from other derivatives, from nouns, adverbs, etc., by forming **compound words, or by the use of suffixes having** the force of adverbs.

225. The force of the adjective is modified by the adverbial suffixes and also by adverbs **used** independently, as shown in the following paragraphs.

226. **adsi is suffixed to** denote an approach to the standard quality or positive **degree,** as indicated by the simple form of the adjective; **thus, from hiši,** *red, scarlet,* comes hišadsi, *of a dull red color, crimson* or *purple.* (¶ 156).

227. **iša,** or iše, is of much the same signification as adsi, but some-**times applied** differently; it signifies *like* or *resembling.* Ex.—From **tohi,** *blue, sky-blue,* comes tohiša, *of an impure or uncertain blue, bluish;* from šipi, *black,* comes šipiša, *resembling black, i. e.,* of a deep color hardly to be distinguished from black. adsi may follow iše to denote a **wider** variation from the standard quality.

228. **de** is a suffix, which may be translated *almost* or *nearly.* Ex.— kakilii, *round,* kakiliade, *almost round;* **tsamutsi,** *straight,* tsamutside, *almost straight.*

229. **di** increases the signification **of** the adjective **to** which it is **suffixed;** its use is not very extended; it seems to be suffixed only to words of three syllables, ending with i and accented on the penult. Ex.— padopi, **short, low-sized,** padopidi, **very** *short;* tamulii, *minute,* tamuliidi, *very minute.*

230. tsąki, **good, takes, as** an increased or intensified form, tsąkicti, which may be a compound of tsąki and ictia, *great.* tsakicti commonly takes the suffix **di;** thus, tsąkictidi denotes a very high degree of excellence.

231. **kša** denotes that the quality **exists** excessively, habitually, **or** continuously. Ex.—išia, *bad,* išiąkša, *persistently bad.* (¶ 163.)

232. **ka'ti,** *much, true, truly,* is a word **used** independently **as an adjec-**tive and adverb. As an adverb, it is used **to** limit **the significance of adjectives to the** true or standard qualities; **as in hiši-ka'ti,** *true red,* **bright red,** išia-ka'ti, *truly bad, unqualifiedly bad.*

233. **When two nouns** are compared together in regard to quality, and **either** one used **as the standard of comparison for** the **other,** the ex-pressions itadotadu and itaokadu are used. The former **means** *at the near side of it,* and indicates the less degree; the latter signifies *on the far side of it,* or *beyond it,* and indicates the greater degree. These ex-pressions give us more nearly the **equivalents** of the comparative degree **of** English than anything else in the Hidatsa.

234. An adjective may be formed of a **noun and an adjective.** Ex.—

From mika', *grass*, and tohiśa, *bluish*, comes mika'tohiśa, *green (grass-bluish)*.

235. Some adjectives are compounds of two other adjectives; as, tsidiśipi, *bay*, from tsidi, *yellow*, and śipi, *black*.

Numerals.

236. The Hidatsa system of numeration is strictly decimal; consequently, there need not be more than ten primitive numeral adjectives.

237. There are, however, not more than eight; these eight are—

dnétsa (or luetsa), *one*,   kíliu, *fire*,
dópa (or nopa), *two*,   akáma (or akawa), *six*,
dámi (or nawi), *three*,   śápua, *seven*, and
tópa, *four*,   pítika, *ten*.

238. dópapi, *eight*, is a compound of dopa, *two*, and pi (which seems to be the root of pitika); it probably signifies *ten less two*.*

239. duétsapi, *nine*, is a compound of duetsa, *one*, and pi, and seems to mean *ten less one*.

240. Multiples of ten less than one hundred are named on the same principle as in English; thus we have—

dopápitika (two tens), *twenty*,   akámaapitika, *sixty*,
dámiapitika, *thirty*,   śapúapitika, *seventy*,
topápitika, *forty*,   dópapiapitika, *eighty*, and
kiliúapitika, *fifty*,   duétsapiapitika, *ninety*.

It will be seen that the first word of each of these compounds, if not ordinarily ending in a, is made to do so in this connection, and that the accent is sometimes removed.

241. The word for one hundred, pitikictía, signifies *great ten*. The term for one thousand is, *pitikictia-ákakodi*,—the meaning of akakodi, I know not.

242. Numbers over ten, but not multiples of ten, are named by the addition of the word alipi (*portioned; a part or division*), thus:

alipiduétsa, *eleven*,   dopápitika-alipiduétsa, *twenty-one*,
alipidópa, *twelve*,   dopápitika-alipidópa, *twenty-two*,
alipidámi, *thirteen*,   dámiapitika-alipidámi, *thirty-three*,
alipitópa, *fourteen*,   topápitika-alipitópa, *forty-four*, etc.

243. With the exception of the word for *first*, itsika, the ordinals are formed by prefixing i to the cardinal numbers; thus, we have idópa, *second*, idámi, *third*, itópa, *fourth*, etc.

Syntax of Adjectives.

244. Adjectives usually immediately follow the nouns or pronouns which they qualify.

---

* Some judicious remarks on this paragraph, and on Par. 239, may be found in a paper *On Numerals in American Indian Languages*, etc. By J. Hammond Trumbull, LL. D. Hartford, 1875. pp. 28, 29.

245. Qualifying words are often seen used as nouns or pronouns; this is particularly the case with numeral adjectives, and such words as ahu, *many*, etsa, *all*, iha, *other*, kauśta, *few*, etc.

ADVERBS.

246. There are adverbs which are apparently primitive; as, tä, *not*, duk, *when*, tia, *a long time*, etc. Many primitive adverbs are used as suffixes, as already shown when describing verbs and adjectives.

247. A large number of adjectives are used as adverbs, without undergoing any change of form. When primitive adjectives are thus used, they appear as primitive adverbs. Ex.—śua, *slow*, *slowly*, hita, *fleet*, *fleetly*, ätsa, *near*, tiśa, *far*.

248. Derivative adverbs are formed from nouns, from demonstrative and interrogative pronouns, from adjectives, and from other adverbs.

249. A large number of adverbs of place are formed from nouns by suffixing the prepositions (postpositions), du, lia, ka, koa, and ta; thus, from dumata, *the middle*, we have dumatadu, *in* or *through the middle*, dumatalia, *toward the middle*, dumátaka, *on the middle*, dumatakoa, *at the middle*, and dumatata, *facing the middle*, or *in the direction of the middle*.

250. Words formed thus (¶ 249), might be regarded as merely nouns in the objective, with their governing prepositions; but they are pronounced and used as if belonging to the same class of words as the English adverbs *windward* and *forward*. Since every noun in the language is capable of taking one or more of these postpositions, the number of adverbs of this character is very great.

251. From nouns, adverbs of time are formed by suffixing du, duk, and śedu; the first of these means *in* or *during any time*, the second *in* or *during future time*, the third *in* or *during past time*; thus, from maku, *night*, we have makudu, *during the night*, *nightly*, makuduk, *during the coming night*, "*to-night*", makuśedu, *during the past night*, or "*last night*"; from oktsia, meaning also *night*, we have oktsiśedu, oktsiadu, and oktsiaduk; from ata, *daylight* or *dawn*, we have ataduk, *to-morrow*, etc.

252. From pronouns, adverbs are formed in much the same way as from nouns; thus, from the demonstrative śe, we have śedu, *in that time* or *place*, śekoa, *at that place, just there*, śeta, *in that direction*, and from the interrogative to, we have tóta, *whither*, tódu and tóka, *where*, *wherein*, *whereat*.

253. When adjectives are used as adverbs, the same suffixes, to modify their force and meaning, are used in the one case as in the other. Adjectives which can denote the manner of performing the action are those chiefly used as adverbs.

254. Adverbs are formed from numeral adjectives by suffixing to the names of the cardinal numbers du, and the compound preposition tsakoa; thus we have dópadu, *at two times*, or *on two occasions, twice*,

dámidu, *thrice*, tópadu, *four times*, and also dópatsakoa, *at* or *in two places*, dámitsakoa, *at* or *in three places*, tópatsakoa, *in four places*, etc.

255. From ordinals, adverbs are formed by the addition of du; thus, ítsikadu, *in the first place* or *order*, *firstly*, idópadu, *in the second place* or *order*, *secondly*, idámidu, *thirdly*, itópadu, *fourthly*, etc.

256. In adverbs of time, formed by adding to nouns du, duk, and sedu as indicated in Par. 251, the numeral adjectives are inserted between the noun and the adverbial suffix in the manner and for the purpose here indicated; thus from óktsi or óktsia, *night :*

    oktsíadu, *during the night.*

    oktsidópadu, *during two nights.*

    oktsitópadu, *during four nights.*

    oktsíaduk, *during the coming night* or *to-night.*

    oktsidópaduk, *two nights hence*, or *during the night after next.*

    oktsidámiduk, *three nights hence.*

    oktsitópaduk, *four nights hence.*

    oktsísedu, *last night, during last night.*

    oktsidópašedu, *night before last, two nights ago.*

    oktsitópašedu, *four nights ago.*

257. Adverbs formed from nouns are often used as nouns; thus, átaduk, *during to-morrow* or *to-morrow*, oktsísedu, *during last night*, or *last night*, adésedu, *during last summer*, or *last summer*.

258. Adverbs are used as predicates to nouns, and in this position, there being no copula, fill the office of intransitive verbs.

259. "Adverbs qualify verbs, adjectives, and other adverbs", as in other languages.

260. Adverbs usually precede the words which they qualify; but ka'ti, *much*, or *truly*, tă, *not*, ta, *only*, and the interrogative tok, more commonly follow the words they qualify.

PREPOSITIONS.

261. ak (¶ 148), which is prefixed to verbs, and du, *in* or *during*, hia, *toward*, ka, *in*, koa, *at*, ta, *in the direction of, facing*, which are suffixed to nouns (¶ 249) to form adverbs, fill more fully the office of prepositions than anything else in the language. They are not, however, used as independent words; and, from the position which they occupy in regard to nouns, would be more properly called *postpositions*.

262. aka, *on,* and api, *with*, are perhaps to be regarded as independent or separate prepositions.

263. There are many adverbs which answer the purpose of prepositions, and may be translated by the English prepositions. Adverbs formed from nouns which are the names of place, belong particularly to this class; thus, from míkta, *the bottom*, comes miktákoa, *below*, and miktáta, *down;* from ámaho, *the interior*, amahóka, *within* or *in;* from atáši, *all out of doors*, atášikoa, *out.*

264. Prepositions, separate and incorporated, and all adverbs used as prepositions, follow the nouns which they govern.

265. When incorporated, they may be found suffixed to the nouns which they govern, or prefixed to the verbs which follow; but in either case they come, of course, after the noun.

CONJUNCTIONS.

266. There are two words which are possibly simple conjunctions; they are Iśa, *and, also,* and duma, *but.*

267. Other words used in joining words and sentences perform also the duties of adverbs and prepositions, and are properly to be classed as such.

268. Conjunctions commonly stand between the words, clauses, or sentences which they connect.

INTERJECTIONS.

269. There are not many words which are purely exclamatory or interjectional; a large number of the words which are used as interjections being verbs.

270. The following words, however, cannot be well analyzed, and may be regarded as true interjections:

n! *oh!* expressing pain or astonishment, and commonly preceding a sentence.

iḣó! *there now! does that satisfy you?* etc.

ki! is used in doubt and astonishment.

hidi! used by children when teased; perhaps from the demonstrative pronoun hidi.

hukahé! used by men to express surprise and delight; as when much game is killed at a volley, etc.

tsakak'! an expression of disgust and impatience, may be a derived word.

HIDATSA DICTIONARY.

a.

a

a, *n.:* a tree, a plant; the entire plant as distinguished from its parts;—used after 'ma' or as a suffix to nouns; as, kohati, *corn,* kohatia, *a stalk of corn.*

a, *n.;* a muscle.

a á te, *r. t.;* to strike by throwing; to hit or bruise with a stone or other missile.

a á ti, *v.;* hurt or bruised by a missile.

á da [ara], *n.;* the arms; the forelegs of quadrupeds.

ă da, *n.;* the hair of the head; the locks.

ă dă, a causative prefix to verbs, denoting that the action is done by the foot, or by heat or fire. (¶ 147).

a da a du ic ti a, *n., fr.* ada *and* aduictia; the *brachium,* the upper part of the arm.

a dă du i, *v. i., fr.* ade *and* adui; becoming painful.

ă da lia, *v. i.;* to be burning; burnt, parched, charred.

ă dă lia he, *r. t.,* 3d pers.; to parch or burn.

ă dă lia ke, *v. t., fr.* ădălia; to cause to burn; to be burned or parched.

ă dă liă pe, *r. t., fr.* ădă *and* liăpi; to kick; to bark or denude by kicking.

ă dă lié lie, *v. t.;* to seize, take hold of, cling to;—also ădălielii.

ă dă lié se, *r. t., fr.* ădă *and* liese; to tear with the foot; to tear with the paws, as a beast.

ădă

a dă li se, *r. t.;* to be ignorant of.—madăliisets, I don't know, I am ignorant.

a dă li se ke, *r. t.;* to make ignorant; to leave in ignorance.

ă dă lió li, *r. t., fr.* ădă *and* liolii; to break with the foot.

a dă lipa ko a, *n.;* the Mandan Indians.

a dă lipi, *n., fr.* adu *and* alipi; a part of anything;—also adălipi.

a dă lipi ke, *r. t.;* to make or be made a portion; to make one thing a part of another.

ă dă liu, *r. t., fr.* ădă *and* liu; to spill with the foot; to upset by kicking;—also adaliue.

ă da í du ti [-ruti], *n., fr.* ăda *and* iduti; ribbon or braid used in tying up the hair.

ă da ka, *r. t.,* 2d pers. of ika, to see.

ă da kấ da ho [ara-], *n.;* the Arickaree Indians; perhaps from ădă, *the hair* or *locks.* This name, it is said, was originally applied to the Arickarees from their manner of wearing their hair. The meaning of the last three syllables is now unknown.

ă da kấ pĕ, *r. t., fr.* ădă *and* kape; to scratch with toe-nails, or with paws, as a dog;—also, adakapi.

ă dă kǐ de, *r. t., fr.* kide; to push with the foot.

ă dă ki tĕ, *r. t., fr.* ădă *and* kite; to burn off; to clear by fire.

ădă

ă ,dă kí ti, *v.*; cleared off by fire, as a burned prairie.

ă da ku″pa, *v. t., 2d pers. of* iku′pa, *to hate.*

ă dă mí di [-widi], *v. t., fr.* ădă *and* midi; to twist with the foot.

ă dă pa pă du i, *v. i., fr.* ădă-papi; becoming scorched or sunburnt.

ă dă pa pi [ăla- or ĕla-], *r. i.*; scorched; sunburnt.

ă dă pá pi de, *r. i., adj.*; almost scorched.

ă dă pa′ pi he, *r. t., 3d pers.*; to scorch or chap.

ă dă pá pi ke, *v. t.*; to cause to become scorched or sunburnt; to expose to sun or fire.

ă dă pe, *v. t.*; to kick.

ă dă sú ki, *v. t., fr.* ădă *and* suki; to erase with the foot.

ă dă tá lipi, *v. i.*; to snap or crackle in the fire.

ă dă tá lipi he, *v. t.*; he makes snap by fire.

ă dă tá lipi ke, *v. t.*; to cause to snap by fire.

ă dă tá pi, *v. t., fr.* ădă *and* tapi; to squeeze with the foot; to trample on.

ă dă te, *v. i., fr.* ădă *and* te; to be bruised under foot; to be trampled to death.

ă dă té he, *v. t., 3d pers.*; to trample to death.

a dă ti, *n., fr.* adu *and* ati; a camping-ground; a place marked with the remains of old camps.

ă dă to″ ti, *v. t., fr.* to′ti; to agitate or shake to and fro with the foot.

ă da tsa, *n., adv.*; a place behind something else; behind.

ă dă tsá ki, *v. i., fr.* tsáki; to be severed by fire.

adé

ă dă tsá ki he, *v. t.*; to sever by fire.

ă da tsa ko a, *adv., fr.* adatsa *and* koa; behind.

ă dă tská pi, *v. t., fr.* ădă *and* tskapi; to press with the toes; to walk on tiptoes.

ă dă tská ti, *v. t., fr.* ădă *and* tskati; to enter or pass through on tiptoes.

a da tsku ă du i, *v. i.*; becoming progressively moist.

a dá tsku i [aratskui], *adj.*; moist, wet.

a dá tsku i de, *v. i., fr.* ada-tskui; almost wet.

a dá tsku i ke, *v. t.*; to wet or moisten; wetted.

a dé, *v. i., adj.*; to be warm; unpleasantly warm; painful.

a dé, *n.*; warm weather; summer.

a dé a du i, *v. i.*; *same as* ada-dui.

a dé dĕ, *adj.*; almost painful.

a dé du [-ru], *adv., fr.* adé; during the summer.

a dé duk [-ruk], *n.* and *adv., fr.* ade; next summer; during next summer. — ade-dopa-duk, two summers hence. ade-dami-duk [ade-nawi-ruk], three summers hence. ade-topa-duk, four summers hence.

a dé he, *v. i., fr.* ade; to be angered; he is angry.

a dé he ke, *v. i., fr.* adehe; to make angry.

a dé ke, *v. t., fr.* ade; to make warm or painful; changed from a comfortable to a painful condition.

a dé kša, *adj., fr.* ade *and* kša; sultry.

a dé še du [-ru], *n.* and *adv., fr.* ade *and* šedu; last summer; during last summer.—ade-dopa-šedu

[ade-nopa-šeru], t w o summers
ago. ade topa-šedu, four summers ago.

a dí [arí], *n.*; a road, a trail.

ă di a šá dsi, *adj.*; poor, destitute.

ă di a šá dsi ke, *v. t.*; to impoverish.

ă di i tă du i, *v. i., fr.* ădiiti *and*
adui; becoming hungry.

ă di í ti, *v. i., adj.*; hungry.—mă-
diiti, or bădiitits, I am hungry.

ă di í ti ke, *v. t.*; to cause to be
hungry; to be made hungry.

ă di ša, *n.*; the little raven of the
northern plains, probably the
Corvus columbianus of Wilson.

ă di ša i ta pa″ hiš, *n.* (See
Local Names.)

ă dsi, a suffix to verbs and adjectives denoting an approach to
the standard. (¶ 156).

ă du [aru], *prob. fr.* du; a suffix
denoting time and place; an adverb of time and place.

ă du, a prefix to verbs forming
nouns; a part, a place, one of a
kind. (¶¶ 45–47).

ă du ă dă pa pi, *n., fr.* ădăpapi;
a sunburnt surface.

a du ă du i, *v i., fr.* adui; becoming bitter.

a du ă ka, *n., fr.* adu *and* aka;
outside part; skin or rind.

a du ak šá ki, *n., fr.* adu *and*
akšaki; a contusion; a contused
wound.

a du á ptse, *n., fr.* aptse; the
edge of a knife.

a du é di, *n., fr.* adu *and* edi;
ordure.

a du ĕ ta, *n.*; a sore place, a scar
or ulcer.

a du hi dă, *n., fr.* hida; new
goods or articles.

a du hi dú, *n., fr.* hidu; the skel-
eton; the bony part of any member.

a du hó pi, *n., fr.* adu *and* hopi;
a perforated or excavated place;
a hole.

a du hú pa, *n.* See hupa.

a du ña kú pi, *n., fr.* adu *and*
ñakupi; a groove or crease; a
longitudinal depression.

a du ñá pi, *n., fr.* ñapi; any place
to lie down; a bed, either tem-.
porary or permanent.

a du ñẽ pi, *n., fr.* adu *and* ñepi;
a shallow place in a lake or river;
a shoal.

ă du i, a suffix to verbs signifying
continuation or progress. (¶ 157.)

ă du i, *v., adj.*; bitter; sour; pungent.

ă du í, *n., fr.* adu *and* i; hair;
feathers; the entire plumage of
a bird or pelage of an animal.

a du ic tí a, *n., fr.* adu *and* ictia;
the main part, the larger part of
anything as distinguished from
its smaller parts.

a du i dă ñpi, *n., fr.* idañpi; an
incised wound, a knife-cut.

a du i dă ki ša, *n., fr.* adu *and*
idakiša; a left-handed person;
the left side.

a du i dé, *n., fr.* adu *and* ide;
speech, language; a word.

ă du i de, *v. i., adj., fr.* ădui; almost bitter or sour, as changing
milk.

a du i dĭ tsi, *n., fr.* adu *and* iditsi;
scent, smell, odor.

a du i dĭ tsi-i ši″ a, *n.* (išia,
bad); a stench.

a du i dĭ tsi-tsa″ ki, *n.* (tsaki,
good); an agreeable odor.

ă du i ke, *v. t., fr.* adui; to change
from sweet to bitter.

ădu

ă du Ї kša, *adj.*; excessively bitter.

a du Ї ptsi, *n., fr.* adu *and* iptsi; an upright, a perpendicular support, as a chair-leg.

a du i ša mi ke, *n., fr.* adu *and* išamike; young twigs sprouting from a stump.

a du Ї ši, *n., fr.* adu *and* iši; rind; covering; exterior;—nearly synonymous with aduaka.

a du i ši a, *n., fr.* išia; an inferior or rotten portion; — used sometimes as a term of contempt for persons.

a du í ti pe, *n., fr.* itipe; a hole dug, or a place in any way arranged for a trap.

a du kạ ti, *n.*; cultivated ground; a field or garden.

a du kạ tí lia, *adv.*; toward the field.

a du kạ tí ka, *adv.*; in the field; among the fields.

a du kạ tí ko a, *adv.*; at the field.

a du ké da pi, *n.*; the male of any species.

a du kí a dĕ tsi, *n., fr.* kiadetsi; a brave, skillful, or enduring person; a good hunter or warrior; one intelligent or ingenious.

a du ki a kạ ma ke, *n., fr.* akamake; one-sixth.

a du ki dá-de ša [-neša], *n., fr.* kida *and* deša; a maiden.

a du ki dá-ma tu, *n.*; a woman who is or has been married.

a du ki dá mi he ke, *n., fr.* kidamiheke; one-third.

a du ki dá mi ke [+-kina-wike], *same as* adukidamiheke.

a du ki dó pa he ke, *n., fr.* kidopaheke; one-half.

adu

a du ki dó pa ke [+-nopa], *same as last word.*

a du ki du ĕ tsa pi ke, *n.*; one-ninth.

a du ki du ša, *n., fr.* adu *and* kiduša; a place where anything is laid away or put in order.

a du ki du ša ko a, *adv., fr.* adukiduša.

a du ki kạ ki, *n., fr.* kikaki; a seam.

a du ki kї liu a ke, *n., fr.* kikiliuake; a fifth part.

a du ki ša pu a he ke, *n., same as the next word.*

a du ki ša pu a ke, *n., fr.* kišapuake; a seventh part, one-seventh.

a du ki tó pa ke, *n., fr.* kitopake; a fourth part.

a du má di he, *n., fr.* adu *and* madihe; prepared food; preparation of food; cooking.

a du má di he a ti, *n., fr.* adumadihe *and* ati; a kitchen.

a du mí ta pa, *n., fr.* mitapa; falsehood, deceit.

a du ó ki pa di, *n., fr.* adu *and* okipadi; young trees, saplings.

a du ó ktsi, *n., fr.* adu *and* oktsi; a shadow.—aduoktsi mahewits, I will make a shadow, *i. e.*, erect a screen to keep off the sunlight.

a du pạ lia du i, *n., fr.* paliadui; a blister; a chafed or blistered part.

a du pạ lii, *n.*; a corner or angle.

a du pạ lii-dá mi [+-nawi], *n.*; a triangle.

a du pạ lii-tó pa, *n.* (topa, *four*); a quadrangle.—adupạlii kiliu, a pentagon.—adupạlii-ahu, a polygon.

a du pá tska, *n.*, *fr.* adu and pa-tska; a side; an even surface; a facet. The compounds of this word and of adupaḣi are often used synonymously; b u t the former commonly refer to flat surfaces and short solids, the latter to long prismoidal bodies.

a du pa tska dá mi [-nawi], *n.*, *fr.* adupatska and dami; a three-sided needle, a glover's needle.

a du pá tska ko a, *adv.*, *fr.* adupatska; at or on the side.

a du pa tska tó pa, *n.* (topa, *four*); any long, four-sided, object, as a hewn log.

a du pi, *n.*, *fr.* adu and pi, *to tattoo or paint*; a tattooed mark on the body; tattooing.

a du pí di e, *n.*, *fr.* pidie; a ruffled edging.

a du pó a da mi [-wi], *n.*, *fr.* adu and poadami; a bullet; bullets.

a du pó a da mi-ka di″ ṡta, *n.* (kadiṡta, *small*); shot.

a du pú a, *n.*, *fr.* adu and pua; a swelling.

a du ṡä ṡa, *n.*, *fr.* adu and ṡaṡa; a fork or branch, a bifurcation.

a du ṡí pe, *n.*, *fr.* adu and ṡipe; a piece of broken ground, a succession of steep hills and deep ravines.

a du ṡó ki, *n.*, *fr.* adu and ṡoki; the back of a knife; dull part of any cutting instrument.

a du ṡú ka, *n.*, *fr.* adu and ṡuka; a joint; a condyle.

a du tä ka, *n.*, *prob. fr. same root as* itaka; a grandfather; a granduncle in the male line.

a du tsí di a ma tu″, *n.*, *lit. it has yellow spots*; a rattlesnake.

9

a du tsó hi, *n.*, *fr.* tsohi; a point; a tapering end or part.

a du tsú a, *n.*; a seed.

a du ú, *n.*, *fr.* adu and u; a wound, more particularly a bullet or arrow wound.

a du ú ĕ, *n.*, *fr.* adu and ue; a fire-place.

a du ú ĕ ḣa, *adv.*, *fr.* aduue; toward the fire, i. e., in the direction of the centre of the lodge, opposite to atutiḣa.

a du ú ĕ ko a, *adv.*; at the fire-place.

a du ú ĕ-u″ ĕ tsa, *n.* (uetsa, *metal*); a stove.

a du wí ta pa. See adumitapa.

a hi″, *n.*; the "*pomme-blanche*", or *Psoralea esculenta*, a plant bearing an edible root, growing wild in Dakota. Recently, the name has been applied to turnips introduced by the whites, and now cultivated by these Indians.

a hi″ mi ka, *n.*, *fr.* ahi and mika; the "*female pomme-blanche*", or *Psoralea argophylla*.

a hú, *adj.*, *adv.*; much, many.—ahuts.

a hú ke, *v. t.*, *fr.* ahu; to increase, to multiply; increased.

a ḣó ä, *v. t.*; to conceal, to hide; also aḣoe.

á ḣo ka, *n.*; the kidneys.

á ḣpi, *adj.*, *n.*; portional; not entire; a part.

a ḣpi a ká ma [+-wa], *num. adj.*, *fr.* aḣpi and akama; sixteen.

a ḣpi dá mi [+-nawi], *adj.*, *fr.* aḣpi and dami; thirteen.

a ḣpi dó pa [+-nopa], *adj.*, *fr.* aḣpi and dopa; twelve.

a ḣpi dó pa pi, *adj.*, *fr.* aḣpi and dopapi; eighteen.

alip

a lipi du ĕ tsa [+-lu-], *num. adj., fr.* alipi *and* duetsa; nine.

a lipi du ĕ tsa pi, *n. adj., fr.* alipi *and* duetsapi; nineteen.

a lipi ki liu, *adj., fr.* alipi *and* kiliu; fifteen.

a lipi šă pu a, *adj., fr.* alipi *and* šapua; seventeen.

a lipi tó pa, *adj., fr.* alipi *and* topa; fourteen.

a liŭ a, *v. t., same as* alioa.

ak, *v. i., prep.*; with; upon; to be or have with.

ak, a prefix to verbs signifying on or with. (¶ 148).

ă ka, *prep., adv.*; above; exterior to; surrounding.

ă ka, *n., prob. fr. last word*; rind, peel; *same as* aduáka.

a kă lipi, *v. t.*; to cross over; to step over.

ắ ka kạ ši, *v. t.*; to write in characters, or in Indian symbols; to make a pictorial record, but not to paint for mere ornament.—ámakakạši, I write. ádakakạši, you write.

ă ka ko di. (¶ 241).

a kă ma, *num. adj.*; six.

a kă ma a pi ti ka, *num. adj.*; sixty.

a kă ma he, *v. t.*, 3d pers., *fr.* akama; to make or divide into six.

a kă ma ke, *v. t.*; to divide into six parts; divided into six.

ắ ka pe, *v. t.*; to court, to seek one of the opposite sex.—mia akapets, said of the man.

a kă ški, *v. t.*; to pull out; to hold between the fingers.

ắ ka ta, *adv., fr.* aka; up; upwards.

a kă ta, *n.*; the palate.

a ka″ ta a du hi dú, *n., fr.*

ăku

akáta *and* aduhidu; the palate-bonĕs.

a kă wa, *num. adj., same as* akáma.

a kă wa a pi ti ka, *same as* akamaapitika.

ă ka za, *n., dimin. of* a; a tendon.

ak′ de, *v. t., comp. of* ak *and* de; to take away with one, to carry something off.—makmadets, I carry away.

ak′ hu, *v. t., comp. of* ak *and* hu; to bring, to come and take with.—makmahuts, I bring.

ă ki, *v. i.* and prefix to verbs; on or with; nearly synonymous with ak, from which it may be derived, or the latter may be a contraction of aki.

ă ki lii, *v. t., fr.* aki *and* elii; to urinate on; to stain or soil in this way.

a ki kă hi, *v. i.*; to be with; to be taken back with.

a ki kă he, *v. t.*; to take back with; to capture and bring home; to take from and bring away.

ă ki tsa, *v. t.*; to overshoot; to miss in throwing.

ă ko ka, *adv., fr.* ak *and* oka; upon, on top of.

ắ kši ĕ, *v. t.*; to support; to hold in the hand, as a light.

ắ kšu ĕ, or **ak-šu-e,** *v. t., fr.* šuĕ; to spit upon.

ak′ tsi šĕ, *v. t.*; to look through an aperture at something, to look in or out through a window or door, to glance through at.

ă ku, *n.*; color; kind, description. akuto? what kind?

ă ku, a relative pronoun, prefixed to verbs, forming nouns; it denotes the subject; with transi-

ăku

tive verbs the agent, with intransitive verbs the object of the action; with adjective verbs, it denotes something of the color, or kind referred to; it is prefixed also to nouns used as verbs.

ă ku á ka pe, *n., fr.* aku *and* akape; a beau, a suitor.

ă ku a ma o" ze, *n., fr.* amaoze; a farmer.

ă ku há tski, *n., fr.* aku *and* hatski; giants.

ă ku hí de, *n., fr.* aku *and* hide; a maker, a manufacturer of anything.

ă ku hí ši, *n., fr.* aku *and* hiši; red cloth; scarlet shrouding.

a kú lia, *adv., apparently from* oka *and* lia; yonder, off, in the direction of the more distant side.

a kú li, *n.*; **the human ear;** the pinna.—makulii, my ear.

a ku" li a du hó pi, *n.* (aduhopi, *a hole*); the *meatus auditorius externus.*

a ku" li a du lia kú pi, *n.* (aduliakupi, *a groove*); *fossa* of helix of auricle.

ă ku lió ta i šé, *n., fr.* aku *and* liotaišč; something of a grayish color; an iron-gray horse.

ă ku i dí tsi tsą ki, *n., fr.* iditsitsąki; scent, material for scenting.

ă ku i ší a, *n., fr.* aku *and* išia; a worthless or impecunious person; a person not respected.

ă ku kí kše, *n., fr.* aku *and* kikše; one who fixes, mends or arranges.

ă ku kí ta he, *n., fr.* aku *and* kitahe; a butcher.

ă ku má di he, *n., fr.* aku *and* madihe; a cook.

ă ku má di he a ti, *n.* (ati, *a*

ăma

house); a temporary screen or shed erected for cooking purposes; a kitchen.

ă ku ma i kú tski, *n., fr.* aku *and* maikutski; one who copies, patterns after, follows an example, or carries out instructions.

ă ku ma i šké, *n., fr.* aku *and* maiške; one who commands, directs, or sets an example.

ă ku ma ki kú a, *n., fr.* kikua; a soldier; the Soldier Band of the Hidatsa; a member of the Soldier Band. This band consists of a number of the bravest and most influential men of the tribe; it enforces laws, administers punishments, has great power, and may discipline even the chief of the tribe. This term is applied also to white soldiers, who, for special distinction, are sometimes called maši-akumakikua.

ă ku ma tse é tsi, *n., fr.* aku *and* matseetsi; men belonging to the class or order of chiefs, men of consequence in the tribe.

ă ku pú zi, *n., fr.* aku *and* puzi; anything striped or spotted, particularly printed fabrics; calico. See mašiiliipuzi.

ă ku ší pi ša, *n., fr.* aku *and* šipiša; dark blue cloth; black strouding.

ă ku tó hi, *n., fr.* aku *and* tohi; glass beads used in garnishing. Possibly the beads first introduced by the traders were blue, and hence the name.

ă ma [áma, ábwa, áwa], *n.*; the earth; earth, clay; country, land.

ă ma ă da lia, *n., fr.* ama *and* adalia; lignite.

áma

á ma á da tsa, *n., fr.* ama *and* adatsa; **the** high upland, the open uninhabited prairie.

á ma á da tsa ko a, *adv., fr.* amaadatsa; **o n** t h e uplands, away from the river-valleys.

ä ma a du lia ku″ pi, *n., fr.* ama *and* aduliakupi; a ravine, an old water-course.

ä ma a du śi″ pe, *n., fr.* ama *and* aduśipe; "bad-lands".

a ma a lio ka, *n., fr.* ama *and* alioka; straw**berries.**

ä ma däk tsą́ ki, *n., fr.* ama *and* däktsąki; a deep gully.

ä ma dé ta, *n., fr.* ama *and* deta; a bluff; a steep river-bank; high steep hills bordering a valley.

ä ma dé ta ko a, *adv., fr.* amadeta; on or at the bluff.

a ma de ta ku hä́ li, *n.* (lialii, *striped*); a bluff of many-colored, stratified rocks.

ä ma de ta ku mä́ ku, *n., fr.* amadeta, aku, *and* maku; a high **bluff;** a bluff forming the edge **of** a lofty plateau, a s distinguished from t h e **banks of** a river where it passes **through its** flood-plain.

ä ma de ta ku śí diś, *n.* See Local Names.

ä ma de ta ma pä́ hiś, *n.* See Local Names.

a ma dí a, *n., fr.* ama; an ordinary low hill, a prairie knoll.

ä ma dí a di da″ zi, *n., ? fr.* amadia; a ringworm.

ä ma ĕ, *n.;* a hoe.

ä ma ĕ a ku tsu″ ka, *n.* (tsuka, *flat*); a spade.

ä ma hä́ tski, *n., fr.* ama *and* hatski; a long ridge; a "divide".

ä ma ho, *n.;* the inside, the interior.

ama

ä ma hó a de, *v. i., fr.* amaho *and* ade; to feel internal pain, to be griped.

ä ma hó ka, *adv., v. i.;* within, inside; to be within.—ati amahoka amamakits, I am sitting in the house.

ä ma hó ka ke, *v. t., fr.* amahoka; to put into, to place within.

ä ma lia kú pi, *n., fr.* ama *and* liakupi; farrowed land, a tract of land containing one or more ravines; often used synonymously with amaaduliakupi.

ä ma liä́ mi [-wi], *n., fr.* ama *and* liami; a mountain-chain; mountainous country.

ä ma liä́ mi [-wi], *n.;* a tribe of Indians who formerly **dwelt** in a village of the same name on Knife River. See Ethnography, § 11.

ä ma liä́ mi ko a, *adv., fr.* amaliami; at the mountains; said when referring to the Rocky Mountain region.

ä ma liä́ ti, *v.* and *n., fr.* ama *and* liati; to shine; light; light proceeding from an original source, not reflected.

ä ma liä́ wi; alone and in its derivatives 'amaliami' is often thus pronounced.

ä ma lió ta, *n., fr.* ama *and* liota; salt.

ä ma ic′ pu, *n., fr.* ama *and* icpu; a pointed or conical butte or hill; the point of such a butte; a collection of such **buttes.**

ä ma ic pu śä́ śaś [or -śaśe]. See List of Local Names.

ä ma i dą́ li śe, *n., fr.* ama *and* idaliśe; a shovel.

a mak′, *v., imperative of* amaki; sit down, be seated.

ǎ ma ka, *n., prob. fr.* ama *and* ka; a badger. The name may allude to the proximity of his body to the earth as he walks, or to his dwelling.

a má ka, *adv., fr.* ama *and* aka; overground; upon the land.

a má ka do lipa ka, *n., fr.* amaka *and* dolipaka; Indians; a name of special distinction, used when dolipaka would be ambiguous.

a má ka noli pa ka, *n., same as* amakadolipaka.

a má ki, *v. i., prob. fr.* ama *and* aki; to sit.

a má ki ke, *v. t;* to put sitting; to cause or oblige to sit.

ǎ ma mạ ki má ka da. See Local Names.

ǎ ma má ku, *n., fr.* ama *and* maku; high ground; a general name for a hill or ridge of any kind.

ǎ ma ó ze, *v. t., fr.* ama *and* oze; to plant.

ǎ ma sǐ", *n.;* an eagle-trap, a trap in the ground. See Ethnography, § 27, *Eagle—Hunting.*

ǎ ma sǐ' a, *n., fr.* ama *and* iśia; "bad-lands".

ǎ ma sǐ pe, *n., same as* amadusape.

ǎ ma sǐ pi śa, *n.* (sipiśa, *black*); a dark mineral pigment, obtained by these Indians from various places in the neighborhood of their village, and used in symbolic writing, decorating robes, etc. Of late years, the name has been also applied to black ink obtained from the whites.

ǎ ma sǐ ta, *n.* (śita, is said to mean *cold*, but I have never heard it so used but in this

word); the north, the land north of the Hidatsá country.

ǎ ma sǐ tá ko a, *adv., fr.* amaśita; northward; at the north; northern; used also as an adjective and noun.

ǎ ma sǐ ta" ko a-a ma liá ti, *n., literally, northern lights; aurora borealis.* See apaliadalia, which is the more common name.

ǎ ma sǐ tá ko a-ma si, *n., lit., white men of the north;* the white inhabitants of Hudson's Bay Territory.

ǎ ma só di śa, *n.;* the mud-swallow.

ǎ ma ta, *adv., fr.* ama; turned in the direction of the ground, facing the earth.

a má te, *1st pers. indicative of* ite, *to admire.*

a má ti, *n.;* the Missouri River. See Local Names.

a má ti", *n., fr.* ama *and* ati; an earth-covered lodge; a number of such lodges; hence, a permanent village of earth-covered lodges.

a má ti a du śa śaś. See Local Names.

ǎ ma ti dá tạ li [-natạli], one of the old villages near or on Knife River.

ǎ ma ti lia, *n.;* another of the Knife River villages.

ǎ ma ti liá mi, *same as* amaliami; name of former tribe and village.

a má ti ka za, *n.;* the Little Missouri River. See List of Local Names.

ǎ má tsa ka" du i, *v. i., fr.* amatsaki; becoming stained with earth.

ămă

ă mă tsa ki, *adj.,fr.* ama *and* tsaki; stained with earth.

ă mă tsa ki he, *v. t.*; he stains with earth.

ă mă tsa ki ke, *v. t.*; to stain with earth; to cause to be soiled with earth; soiled with earth.

ă ma tsí di, *n.,fr.* ăma *and* tsidi; a yellow mineral pigment obtained by the Indians; ochre.

ă ma tsí di o du tsi, *n.* See Local Names.

ă ma tsú ka, *n., fr.* ama *and* tsuka; a flat meadow; a bottom.

ă ma ú ti, *n.,fr.* ama *and* uti; the skirt or base of a hill; a foot-hill.

ă ma ú ti ko a, *adv.* of place, *fr.* amauti.

a mă zi, *n.*; beans; any leguminous plant.

a ma zi-sí pi sa, *n.,fr.* amazi *and* sipisa; black beans. The name is also sometimes applied to roasted coffee.

ă mpa, *n.*; the neck.

ă ntsi. See a'tsi.

ă pa, *n.*; ears, particularly the ears of the lower animals.

ă pă, *n.*; the nose of man and the lower animals; the beak of a bird.

ă″ pă a du hó pi, *n.,fr.* ăpă *and* aduhopi; nostrils.

ă″ pă a du sú ka, *n.,fr.* ăpă *and* adusuka; the bridge of the nose.

ă pă dă ka, *n., dimin. of* ăpă; alæ of nose.

a pă di, *v. i.*; to sprout and grow, to increase by growth.

a pă di, *n.*; the Canadian porcupine (*Erethizon dorsatum*). The animal is common on the Upper Missouri, and its quills are used

ăpi

for embroidering. This word is also used to designate the quills.

a pă di hi', *n.,fr.* apadi *and* hi'; porcupine quills.—apadi is the more usual term.

a pă di kě, *v. t.,fr.* apadi; to cause to grow; grown.

ă pă hé da pi, *n.,fr.*'apa *and* hedapi; the juncture of the nose with the forehead.

a pă hi, *n.*; the sky; clouds.

a pa hi ă dă lia, *n.,fr.* apalii *and* ădălia; the *aurora borealis*.

a pă hi a du i ho″ ta ki, *n.* (iliotaki, *white*); white clouds; cirrhus clouds.

a pă hi a du si″ pi sa, *n.* (sipisa, *black*); dark, heavy clouds.

a pa hi tă tsi, *n.* (tatsi, *thick*); a sky completely overcast with clouds.

a pa hi tó hi, *n.* (tohi, *blue*); the blue sky.

ă pă ic' pu, *n.,fr.* ăpă *and* icpu; the point of the nose.

a pá ka, *n.*; mosquito.

ă pă sĭ ki, *n.,fr.* ăpă *and* saki, *the hand;* a pelican (*Pelecanus trachyrhynchus*). The name alludes either to the shape of the bird's bill or to the use which he makes of it.

ă pă sa kŭ pi, *n.,fr.* ăpă *and* sakupi; a hooked or Roman nose.

ă pă tsi tú ki, *n.,fr.* ăpă *and* tsitnki; a pug-nose.

ă pi, *prep., etc.*; with; to be with.

a pic tí a, *n., fr.* apa *and* ictia; a mule.

ă pi ka, *adv.,fr.* api; together, together with.

ă pi ke, *v. t.,fr.* api; to place together.

ă pi sa, *n.*; the liver.

a pĭ tsa, *n.*; sand-bill crane (*Grus canadensis*).

a pi tsa tó hi, *n.*; blue heron (*Ardea Rerodias*).

ą pi tska, *n.*; bristles on lips of *Felidæ*, etc.

a pó ka, *n.*; a head-dress of any kind, a hat or bonnet.

a pó kŝa, *n.*; a pendant jewel; an ear-jewel.

â pú ti, *n.,fr.* äpä *and* uti; the upper lip, the entire upper lip. (See ideta). These Indians seem to regard the upper lip as the "root of the nose".

á pú ti a du lia ku'' pi, *n.,fr.* äputi *and* aduliakupi; the *sulcus* of the upper lip.

a rí, *n.*; a trail; *same as* adi.

â ru; alone and in its compounds adu is often thus pronounced.

a ŝá di, r. t.; to steal, to take anything illegally or occultly.— adi aŝadi, "to steal the road", to run away secretly, to abscond.

ă ŝu, *n.*; a string or cord; also a fishing-line; a snare.

á ŝu ka, *n.*; testes.

a'' ŝu ka-ma tú, *n.*; a stallion.— aŝuka-deŝa, a gelding.

ă ta, *n.*; day; daylight.—ata-ka-diŝta, sometimes said of early in the day.—atąts, it is day.

á ta dĕ, *n.*; almost day, near daylight.

a tá di, r. i.; to go out of doors; also to menstruate.

á tá di ke, r. t.; to put out of doors, or out of the house.

á ta duk [-ruk], n.,fr. ata *and* duk; to-morrow.

ă ta duk, adr.; when to-morrow comes.

a tá i ŝe, adj.,fr. ata *and* iŝĕ; bright as day.

ą tą́ ka, *n.*; the end or extremity;—perhaps, also, *in* the end.

ą tą́ ka du, *n.,* and *adr.,fr.* ata-ka; in or through the end; the terminal portion.

a tą́ ka du i, r. i.,fr. atą́ki *and* adui; bleaching, gradually whitening.

ą tą́ ka lia, adr.,fr. ątąka; endwards, towards the end.

ą tą́ ka ko a, adc.; at the end.

a tą́ ki, adj.; white; *same as* iliotąki.

a tą́ ki ke, r. t.,fr. atąki; to cause to whiten; whitened, bleached.

á ta ruk, *n.*; to-morrow; *same as* atadnk.

á taŝ, n.,fr. ati; one's own house; a home.

a tá zi, *n.*; out of doors; outside.

a tá zi lia, adr.,fr. atazi; toward the outside.

a tá zi ko a, adc.; at the outside; out of the houses.

á tĕ, *n.*; a father; a father's brothers and male cousins.

a tĕ́, r. i.; to appear, to come in sight.

a tĕ́ de, r. i.; to be almost in sight, nearly appearing.

a tĕ́ he, r. t.,fr. ate; to make appear, to show.

a tĕ́ he ka, r. t., imper. *of* atcheke; show it, let us see it.

a tĕ́ he ke, r. t.; to cause to appear, to hold up to view, to exhibit.

á tĕ ka'ti, n.,fr. atĕ *and* ka'ti; a true or real father, not a father's brother.

á ti, n.; a house of any kind.

a ti du tĭ du, n.; the roof of an earth-covered lodge.

á ti he, r. t.,fr. ati; to make a camp.

ati

a ti í pki ti, *n., fr.* ati *and* ipkiti; the **mixture** of **white** earth and water which they use in coating **log cabins.** Lately this term has been applied to whitewash made of lime.

á ti ke, *v. t., fr.* ati; to change into a house; to use for a house.

a tí ši, *n.*; the hole in the top of **the** lodge to let out the smoke; (recently) a stove-pipe.

a ti ší a, *n., prob. fr.* ati *and* iši; heavy, dressed elk or buffalo skin, such as is used in making skin lodges.

a ti tsó hi, *n.*; *same as* atitsuahe, but less used.

a ti tsú a he, *n., fr.* ati *and* tsuahe; a skin lodge. The name alludes to its shape.

a ti tsú ka, *n., fr.* ati *and* tsuka; the side of the fire, a seat in the **lodge** neither opposite nor **next** the door.

ă tsa, *prep., adv.*; **near by, close** to;—also átsĕ.

a″ tsi, *n.*, the *mammæ*; the udder of an animal.

a″ tsi bi di, *n., same as* a'tsimidi.

a″ tsi hi, *v., comp. of* a'tsi *and* hi; to suck.

a″ tsi hi ke, *v. t.*; to give to suck, to nurse, to suckle.

a″ tsi ic pu, *n., fr.* a'tsi *and* icpu; the nipple.

a″ tsi mi di, *n., fr.* a'tsi *and* midi; milk.

ă tska, *adj.*; cross, fierce,—as a dog.

ă tskă de, *adj.*; surly, almost fierce.

ă tskă du i, *v. i.*; becoming fierce.

ă tska ke, *v. t., fr.* ătska; to enrage.

azi

ă tskă kša, *v. i., adj., fr.* ătska *and* kša; habitually **cross.**

ă tskă kša ke, *v. t.*; to render habitually cross, to sour one's temper.

á tu, *n.*; the head.

a tú a de, *v. i., comp. of* atu *and* ade; to have headache.

a tú i tsa ti, *n., fr.* atu *and* itsati; hair-grease.

a tú ka, *n.*; the seat opposite the door of a lodge; "at the head".

a tú ti, *n., fr.* ati *and* uti; "the bottom of the lodge". In a skin lodge, **this** signifies the space between the poles and the ground, near where they meet; in **an** earth-covered lodge, the space between the short uprights, the outer wall, and the ground.

a tú ti lia, *adv., fr.* atuti; **in the** direction of the bottom of **the** lodge, away from **the fire.**

a tú ti ko a, *adv.*; at or in the bottom of the lodge.

a tú ti ko a-i″ ptsa, *n., fr.* atutikoa *and* iptsa; the shorter uprights of an earth-covered lodge, the outer row of supporting-posts.

a tú ti ko a-i″ ptsi, *same as* last word.

a tú ti ko a-mi da″, *n.* Synon. atutikoaiptsa.

á zi, *n.*; a river.

á zi, *n.*; a horn.

á zi, *n.*; a spoon or ladle. The Hidatsa make their spoons of horn; hence, perhaps, the name.

a zi a du ší ša, *n., fr.* azi *and* adnšaša; a branch or fork of a river.

a zic tí a, *n., fr.* azi *and* ictia; the big-horn or Rocky Mountain sheep, *Ovis montana.*

azi

a zi dé ḣi, *n.*, *fr.* azi *and* deḣi ; a spoon or ladle made from the horn of the *Ovis montana*.

a zi liá mi, *n.*, *fr.* azi *and* liami ; antlers; animals bearing antlers; males of the *Cervidæ*.

a zi liá wi, *same as* aziliami.

a zi ic′ pu, *n.*, *fr.* azi *and* iepu ; the source **or** head waters of a river.

a zi ic′ pu ko a, *adv.*, *fr.* aziiepu.

a zi ic′ pu ša ša, *n.*, *fr.* aziiepu *and* šaša ; the affluents which join a river near its source.

ú zi ka za, *n.*, *dimin. of* azi ; a creek or rivulet.

úzi ka zi, *n.*, *same as* azikaza.

a zi ší pi ša, *n.*, *fr.* azi *and* šipiša ; a black spoon, one made of buffalo-horn.

a zi ú e tsa, *n.*; metal spoons, such as are obtained from the whites.

a zi ú ti, *n.*, *fr.* azi *and* uti ; the mouth of a river.

b.

b. Words heard as beginning with the sound of b may be found under **m**.

c.

c is not an initial sound.

d.

d, a common abbreviation of the pronouns da and di.

da [na, la, ra], *pers. pron.*, *simple*, 2d *pers.*; thou, you, ye.

dáḣi

da, *adv.*, prefix to verbs; denotes departure or motion from; **as in** damakoa, *I go away*, from makoa, *I go.*

da′ [+ na], *probably a form of the last word, or of* de, *to go*; suffixed to verbs it makes an imperative form ;—go thou ! do thou do it !

dá da [nana], *v. i.*; to shiver, to tremble.

dá di [na-], *n.*; a party of Indians travelling with their effects, a moving camp.

dá dsa, *n.*; the calf of **the leg.**

da hé, *v. t.*; to work, to labor at anything; to make or form.

da he ka″ ti [lahekanti], *v. i.*, *? from* dahé *and* ka′ti ; to be tired.—madaheka′ti, I am **tired.**

da he ka″ ti he, *v. t.*, 3d *pers.*; to tire; to fatigue.

da he ka″ ti ke, *v. t.*; to cause to tire; fatigued.

da he ku ti di ki, *v. t.*, *fr.* diki, *to strike*—I know not the meaning of the rest of the word ; to strike an enemy first, to " count first *coup* ".

dá hu [nahu, lahu], *v. i.*, *fr.* da *and* hu ; to come away from.—damahuts, I come away from. dadahuts [nalahuts], you come away from.

da liá dé [la-], *v. t.*, *fr.* liadé ; to shell with the teeth, as corn.

da liá ḣi [na-], *n.*; the elongated, vertebral, spinous processes between an animal's shoulders ; a " hump-rib ", a buffalo-hump.

da lia ḣi má ku, *n.*, *fr.* daliaḣi *and* maku ; a high hump, a buffalo-hump.

dá lia mi [-wi], *adj.*, *prob. fr.* liami ; fringed, having long ornamental ends.

dali

da liạ pe śi, *adj.*; steep; perpendicular.

da liạ pi [la-] *v. t., fr.* hạpi; to peel off; to bark a tree.

da liạ pi he śi, *same as* daliạpeśi.

da lié śe, *v. t., fr.* lieśe; to tear with the teeth.

da lié śi, *v., adj.*; torn with teeth.

da lié śi ke, *v. t.*; to cause to tear with teeth; torn by teeth.

dá lii [na-], *n.*; a dim shadow or shade; hence also a soul or ghost; seldom used alone. See idalii and dokidalii.

da liY lii, *n., prob. fr.* dalii; the reflection of an object as seen on a polished surface; perhaps a hypothetical word. See idaliilii.

da lií pi, *v. t.*; to flay.

dạ lii śe, *v. t.*; to dash or throw away; to dig or shovel.

dạ liki śi [na-], *n.*; a pillow.

dạ liki śí śi, *n., fr.* dalikiśi *and* iśi; a pillow-case.

dá lio, *n.*; the lungs.

dá lio ke [na-], *? fr.* dalio; a saddle of any kind.—dalioke-hidu, a bone saddle or horn saddle. daboke-mida, a wooden saddle. See matạtsidalioke.

da lió ki, *v. t., fr.* lioki; 2d and 3d pers.; to row a boat.—malioki, I row.

dạ lipa, *v. t.*; to place the arms around, to enfold in the arms.

dạ lipi [nálipi], *n.*; a pelt of any kind; a buffalo-robe.

dạ lipi ke [nálipike], *n.*; the annual religious ceremony of the Hidatsa. See Ethnography, § 22.

dạ lipY tsi [nálipitsi], *n., fr.* dálipi *and* tsi; a bear.

dạ lipi tsi-a du a ma" kiś, *n.* See Local Names.

dak

dạ lipY tsi-i tsíc pu [na-], *n., fr.* dalipitsi and itsicpu; a bear's claw.

dạ lipY tsi-i tsY ti [na-], *n., fr.* dálipitsi *and* itsiti; a bear's track.

dạ lipY tsi-o dạ lipi [na-], *n., fr.* dalipitsi *and* odalipi; a bear-skin.

dạ lipi tsó ki [na-], *n.* (tsoki, *hard*); raw-hide, "*parflèche*".

dạ litsí a, *adj.*; *same as* daktsia, which is the more common pronunciation.

dá liu, *v. t., fr.* liu; to spill, overset, or topple.

da liú e, *v. t.*; *same as* dáliu.

da liú pi, *v. t., prob. fr.* liupi; to drink dry, to drain with the mouth; also, to absorb as a sponge. 3d pers.

dạk [nạk], a prefix to verbs and verb-roots, usually indicating that the action is performed by a sudden, forcible impulse. In the 1st and 2d persons, the 'd' is sometimes dropped.

dạk' a [nạka], *same as* dạk, from which it may be derived, or the former may be a contraction of dạka.

dá ka, a diminutive suffix.

dá ka, *n.*; the offspring or young of anything. See idaka.

dá ka, *v. i.*; to remain, to continue in one condition unchanged; to be; to live.

dá ka a du mi di, *n., fr.* daka, *offspring*, adu *and* midi; *liquor amnii.*

da ka dú tska [-lu-], *n.*; a twin, twins. They are very rare among these Indians.

dạ kạ he, *v. t.*; to pull toward; to pluck, but not pluck out; to stretch or spread out.

dak

da kǎ hi še, *v. t.*; to hold in the arms.

da kǎ hi ši, held in the arms.

dǎk a hó hi, *v. t., fr.* dǎka *and* hohi; to break across with a blow.

dǎk a kí ti [nǎk-], *v. t., fr.* dǎka *and* kiti; to shave or remove hair.; to clear off by blows, as these Indians do in removing hair, with a flint or iron scraper, from a skin, preparatory to dressing it.

dǎk a mí di [nǎkawidi], *v. i.* and *t., fr.* dǎka *and* midi; to twist by sudden force; said if a saddle turns while a horse is running, etc.

dǎk a mí di ke, *v.*; to cause to turn; turned by sudden force.

dǎk a mí tsi [-witsi], *v. t., fr.* dǎka *and* mitsi; to cut fine by blows, to mince, to chop into small fragments.

dǎk a pǎki, *v. i.*; to blossom.

dǎk a pǎ ki ke, *v. t.*; to cause to blossom.

da kǎ pe, *v. t., fr.* kape; to lacerate with the teeth.

da kǎ pi, *v. t.* See kidakapi, which is the more common form.

dǎk a pǐ hi, *v. t.*; to float in air or on water; to flap.

dǎk a pǐ hi he, *v. t.*; to float; to allow to float. 3d pers.

dǎk a pǐ hi ke, *v. t.*; to cause to float, to make float; floated.

dǎk a pú ši, *v. i.*; to be puffed out, inflated.

dǎk a pú ši ke, *v. t.*; to cause to increase in diameter; to puff out.

da kǎ ptsi, *v. i., fr.* kaptsi; to be nicked, to have numerous small notches.

dak

da kǎ ptsi he, *v. t.*, 3d pers.; to nick, to cut fine notches, to keep a record or tally by cutting notches.

dǎk' a ta, *v. t., fr.* daka *and* ta; to smash to pieces by throwing violently or by hitting.

dǎk a tǎ hi, *v. i.*; to make a noise by stamping, pounding, etc.

dǎk a tí, *v. i.*; to be stretched out or shaken out forcibly, as in shaking blankets.

dǎk a tí i, *same as* dǎkati.

dǎk a tí he, *v. t.*, 3d pers.; to unfold; unroll; shake out.

dǎk a tí ke, *v.*; to cause to unroll; unrolled; unfolded; shaken out.

dǎk a to" ti, *v. t., fr.* dǎka *and* to"ti; to ruffle or shake with force suddenly and briefly applied.

dá ka tsa, *adj., v., fr. v. i.* daka, remaining unchanged; alive.

dak a wí di, *same as* dakamidi.

dá ke, *a form of* daka; to continue, etc.

da" ki [na'ki], *n.*; a prisoner of war.

dá ki, *v. i.*; to squeal as a child.

dá ki [naki], a band or clan in a tribe. In the Hidatsa daki, we have apparently a modification of the totem system.

da ki dá mi [nakináwi], *fr.* daki *and* dami *or* idami, *i. e.*, **three** *bands (consolidated) or the* **third** *band;* one of the Hidatsa clans.

da' ki ši, *n.*; *same as* dalikisi.

da kí ti, *v. i., ? fr.* kiti; to close up like a pocket-knife.

da ki tó pa [na-], *lit., four bands or the fourth band;* the

dák

,name of one of the Hidatsa clans, or bands.

dá ko a [na-], *v., fr.* da *and* koa; to go away from, to abscond.—damakoa, I go away.

da kó ĕ [la-], *n.*, a man's friend or comrade; a hypothetical word. See idakoe and madakoe.

dăk sá ke, *v. t.*; to produce a wound by throwing.

dăk sá ki, *v. i.*; wounded by a missile.

dăk' si, *v. t.*; to bundle, to wrap in skins or cloth.

dak sí pi [nak-], *adv., v.*; after in point of time, later, subsequent to.

dăk tá dĕ, *v. t., fr.* ktade; to nail with heavy blows, to drive a spike.

dăk tsá da ke, *v. t.* and *i.*; to slide or cause to slide with sudden, forcible impulses, as in skating.

dăk tsá ki, *v. t., fr.* dăk *and* tsaki; to chop, to cut with heavy blows as in chopping wood.

dăk tsa'' ti, *v. t., fr.* dak *and* tsa-ti; to thrust into with force suddenly applied, as in sticking with a spear.

dăk tsi a, *v. i,* *adj.*; heavy, weighty.

dăk tsi á du i, *v. i.*; gradually increasing in weight.

dăk tsí a ke, *v. t.*; to make heavy.

dá ktsi di, *n., fr.* daka *and* tsidi; a name applied to light-colored buffalo-calves.

dăk tsí ke, *v., adj.*; to place in a row; to be in single file; aligned, as the posts of a palisade or the teeth of a comb.

dăk tsú a [nak-], *n.*; a mink; the *Putorius vison.*

dám

dăk tsú ti, *v. t.*; to hit hard; to beat with a stick.

dăk tsú ti, *v. t.*; to braid.

dăk ú di, *r.*; to produce a current of air by a sudden motion, as in fanning.

dăk ú dsi, *v. i.* and *t.*; to oscillate, to swing; pronounced so much like dakudsi, 2d pers. of kudsi, that it is difficult to distinguish.

dăk ú liti [nák-], *adj.*; light, not heavy.

dăk ú liti hé, *v. t.*, 3d pers; to make light.

dăk ú liti ke, *v. t.*; to make light; reduced in weight.

da'' ku pe [na-], *n.*; a bed-curtain.

dá mi [nawi], *num. adj.*; three. It is more commonly pronounced nawi, both alone and in its derivatives.

dá mi a pi ti ka [+ na-], *num. adj.*; thirty.

dá mi de [+ na-], *adj., v.*; almost three, two and a large part of a third.

da mi hé ke [+ na-], *v. t.*; to make into three, to divide into three; *pass.* divided into three parts.

dá mi ke, *v. t.*; *same as* damiheke.

dá mi tsa ko a, *adv.*; in three places or directions.

da mí tsi, *v. t., fr.* mitsi; to chew fine.

da mó ki [-wo-], *v. i.*; to sink down, to ebb.—kidamoki is the more common form.

dá mu [nawu], *adj., etc.*; deep; said of water.

dá mu ke [nawu-], *v. t.*; to deepen; become deep.

dǎ nä, *same as* dǎdä—midanats, I shiver.

dá pē, *r. t., fr.* da *and* **pe**; to eat by tearing, as a dog eats.

da psú ti, *r. t., fr.* psn; to shove out of place; to jog the arm.

dǎ śa, *r. t.*; to lacerate with the teeth.

dǎ śi [naśi], *n.*; a name, a proper name; pronounced also dázi.

dǎ śi e [la-], *r. t.*; to take off with the teeth, as in eating corn from a cob.

da śĭ pi [la-], *r. t., fr.* śipi; to untie with the teeth.

dǎ śku, *r. t., fr.* śku; to extract with the teeth.

dǎ śtĕ, *r. t.*; to munch, to chew fine; also to pound fine.

dǎ' ta [+ na-], *n.*; the heart. This word is also used figuratively, as in English; and various emotions and feelings are attributed to conditions of the heart, as shown in words which follow.

da' ta dé śa [na'tanéśa], *r. i., adj., fr.* da'ta *and* deśa, " heartless"; giddy, foolish, inconsiderate.

da' ta dé śa ke, *r. t., fr.* da'tadeśa; to cause to be foolish or inconsiderate.

da' ta dé śe, *same as* da'tadeśa.

da' ta lie pá du i, *r. i., fr.* da'taliepi; becoming indolent.

da' ta lié pi, *r. i., fr.* da'ta *and* liepi; to be lazy; indolent.

da' ta lié pi ke, *r. t.*; to cause to be lazy.

da' ta i śi a, *r. i., fr.* da'ta *and* iśia, *bad;* to be angry, morose, disagreeable; unhappy or **sorry**.

da' ta i śi á du i, *r. i.*; becoming angry, etc.

da' ta i śi a ke, *r. t.*; to cause to be morose, **angry**, etc.; angered.

da tá ki, *r. i.*; to be hurt, to be in pain.—midataki, I am hurt.

da tá pi, *r. t., fr.* tapi; to hold or press between the teeth.

da tá ti, *r. t.*; to squeeze with the teeth.

da' ta tsá ki, *r. i., fr.* da'ta *and* tsaki, *good;* to be happy, pleasant, agreeable.

da' ta tsa kí ke, *r. t.*; to make or cause to be happy.

da' ta tsó ki, *r. t., fr.* da'ta *and* tsoki, *hard;* firm, resolute, self-denying.

da' ta tsó ki ke, *r. t.*; to make resolute, etc.

dá' ti, brother-in-law; a hypothetical **word**. See ida'ti.

da tĭ pi, *n.*; a ravine.

da tó ti, *r. t., fr.* to'ti; to shake to and fro in the mouth, as a cat worries a mouse.

dǎ tsa [la-], *r. t., fr.* tsa; to bite.

da tsá' ti [la-], *r. t., fr.* tsati; to stick the teeth into; to hold in the teeth for the purpose of cutting, as these Indians do with meat.

dǎ tsi [la-], *r. i., prob. fr.* datsa; dented.

da tsĭ pi, *r. t.*; to loosen with the mouth; to lick off with the tongue.

da tská pi [la-], *r. t., fr.* tskapi; to pinch with the teeth; to nibble or bite, but not to bite off.

da tská ti [la-], *r. t, fr.* tskati; to pass or press through a small opening; to squirt or leak.

da tskĭ pi, *r. t.*; to pare off, to peel.

dat

da tski ti [la-], *v. t., fr.* tskiti; to clip, to dock.

da tsó pe, *v. t.*; to draw in with the lips, to smack. See kidatsope.

da tsú ki, *v. i.*; to draw in or suck with the lips, but not to nurse.

dá wi, *num. adj., same as* dami; more commonly pronounced nawi.

da wí tsi, *v. t., same as* damitsi, and more common.

da wó ki. See damoki.

dá wu, *v. i., same as* damu; but more commonly pronounced nawu.

dá zi [nazi], *n.*; a proper name; *same as* daši.—dazi taká, or nazi taká? what is his name?—manazi, my name.—dadazi, or nanazi, your name.

de, *v. i.*; to go, to depart; gone.—dets, he is gone, departed.

dě, a suffix to verbs and adjectives, signifying incompleteness, a degree less than the positive; almost, nearly.

dé li, *v., adj.*; clear, transparent; white, when referring to the tail of a horse, and some other things.

dé pa, *n.*; certain deformities artificially produced.

dé ša [+ neša], *v. i., adv.*; no; there is not; there is none, etc.

dé ša ke, *v. t.*; to cause to be not, to cause to cease or disappear; *pass.* disappeared, extinct, cured (as a disease).—kidešake is the more common form.

dé še, *same as* děša.

dé ta, *n.*; a boundary, edge, or border.

dé ta ko a, *ad., fr.* deta; at the edge or border.

dik

dé zi [nezi], *n.*; the tongue.

dé zi a ziš, *n.* See Local Names.

di, *v. t.*; to shoot; to shoot *at*, whether you kill or not; also to hunt. See kidi.

di, a suffix to adjectives, increasing their force; as in padopidi and kaustadi.

di [ni], *pron.*; thou; thee; thy.

dic' ki [nic-], *pron. comp.*; thyself.

di da kó e [nílakoe], your friend. See dakoe and idakoe.

di dá' ti, *n.*; your brother-in-law. See ida'ti.

di de, ⎰ *v. i.*; to travel, to march,
di di, ⎱ to walk; also said of the motion of a snake, of swimming, etc.

di di, *n.*; a travelling party, a party moving or marching; a step, a walk. See matsedidi and paduididi.

di dí ki, your leg. See diki and idiki.

di dí ši [ni-], your son. See diši and idiši.

dí do [ni-], *p. pron.*, 2d pers., plur.; ye.

dí do ki [ni-], *pron., fr.* dido; yourselves.

dí ha [ni-], *v. t.* and *auxil.*, 2d pers., imper.; do thou do it; about the same as da', but more emphatic; added to verbs, it gives one form of the imperative.

di ha, *? aux. verb*, suffixed to form the second person, future, indicative of conjugated verbs.

dí lio, your body. See lio and ilio.

dik, *v. t., imperative of* diki; strike.

dí ki, *v. t.*; to strike, to whip; to "count *coup*".

di ki, a hypothetical word; leg; lower extremity.

dĭ pi, *v.*; to bathe; to be bathing; to bathe one's self.

dĭ pi ke, *v. t.*; to cause to bathe; to clean by bathing; to bathe another person.

di śa mi [**niśawi**], your aunt; *fr. hypothetical word* śami.

di śi, *n.*; a son; probably a hypothetical word. See idiśi, didiśi, and madiśi.

dĭ śi, *v. i.*; to hasten, to hurry, to be fast.

dĭ śi di śi, an imperative form of śidiśi; be thou in haste, **hurry** up! hurry thyself.

dĭ śi ke, *v. t.*; to cause to hurry; hurried.

di ta [**ni-**], *pers. pron.*, 2d pers. possessive; denotes transferable possession.

di tá du [**nitaru**], your mother's brother. See itadu.

di ta má e [**nitawae**], *n., fr.* dita *and* mae; your own, your property.

di ta mé tsa [**nitawetsa**], your brother. See itametsa.

di tsą ki, *v., pron.*; you alone; you unaided, or by yourself.

dĭ tsi [**nitsi**], *v. t.*; to massacre.

di tú hi [**+ ni-**], *n.*; your dress or shirt. See itulii.

dó do pa [**loropa**], *n.*; the cheek.

doli [**noli**], a prefix limiting a noun to the human species; also pronounced nok and dok.

doli pä ká [**noli-**], *n.*; living human beings; formerly applied only to Indians, but now often used to include all races. See amakadolipaka.

dok, *same as* doli.

dok i dá hia ti [**nók-**], *n., fr.* dokidalii *and* ati; the village of the dead, the hereafter of the Hidatsa.

dok i dá lii, *n., fr.* dok *and* idalii; a human shade, a ghost.

dok i da″ hi ta i ko zi, *n., lit.* ghost's *whistle*; the *Equisetum hyemale.*

dok i da″ hi ta má tsu, *n., fr.* dokidalii, ita, *and* matsu, *i. e.,* ghost's **cherry**; the Virginia creeper; the fruit of the Virginia creeper or *Ampelopsis.*

dok i da″ hi ta ma tsu ä, *n.*; the Virginia creeper, the entire plant.

dok i dá lii ta pa hiś, *n.* See Local Names.

dok pá ka, *n., same as* dolipaka.

dok té, *n., fr.* dok *and* te; a corpse.

dok té o du śa [**nokteoruśa**], *n., fr.* dokte *and* oduśa; a place of deposit for the dead, a scaffold, grave, or graveyard.

dó pa [**+ nopa**], *num. adj.*; two. In compounds, this is sometimes pronounced nupa and dupa.

dó pa he, *v. t., fr.* dopa; to make double, to form in two parts.

dó pa he ke, *v. t.*; to form into two parts, to divide in two; divided in two.

dó pa ke, *same as* dopaheke.

dó pa pi [**+ no-**], *num. adj., fr.* dopa *and* pi; **eight.**

do pá pi ti ka [**+ no-**], *num. adj., fr.* dopa *and* pitika; twenty.

dó pa tsa ko a, *adv.*; in two places or directions.

dó ta [**iota**], *n., adv.*; near to; the near side; neighborhood or proximity.

dót

dó ta du [-ru], *adv., n., fr.* dota; the near side; at or in the near side. See itadotada.

dó ta lia [lo-], *adv., fr.* dota; in this direction; denoting motion toward the speaker.

dó ta ko a, *adv., fr.* dota; in the neighborhood of the speaker; at a place nearer to the speaker than some object named; also, inferior to.

dó ti [lo-], *n.*; the throat.

do tic tí a, *n., fr.* doti *and* ictia; bronchocele,—a disorder not uncommon in the village at Fort Berthold.

du, a hypothetical word. See idu.

du [ru], a prefix to verb-roots, denoting general causation, that the action is done in some way not specified. *Same as* Dakota ' yu '.

du [ru], *prep.*; in, during, at that time or place. Suffixed to nouns, it forms adverbs of time and place. Suffixed to pronouns, it forms words which may be considered as pronouns or adverbs.

du é tsa [+ lu-], *num. adj.*; one.

du é tsa ke, *v. t.*; to cause to be one; united.

du é tsa pi [+ lu-], *num. adj., fr.* duetsa *and* pi; nine.

du é tsa pi ke, *v. t., fr.* duetsapi; to divide into nine parts.

du é tsa ta, *adj.*; only one.

du é tsa ti, *v. i., adj.*; one here and there; to be a scattered few.

dú ha, *v., imper. and 2d pers. indic. of* duhe; lift.—diduha, lift thyself, *i. e.*, arise (from sitting).

dú he, *v. t.*; to lift, to raise up.

dú hi, *v.*; lifted, raised; aroused.

dú hi ke, *v. t.*; to cause to arise; to assist in rising or raising.

dum

dú lia, *v. t.*; to spread, as bedding.—kidulia is the more common form.

du liä dĕ, *v. t.*; to collect by dragging; to rake.

du liä de, *v. t.*; to shell, as corn.

du lié mi, *v. i.*; said of the settling down of a river, the abating of a flood.

du lié śe, *v. t., fr.* heśe; to tear in any way, to tear such articles as cloth or paper.

du lié wi, *same as* duliemi.

du lió lii, *v. t., fr.* liolii; to break across by any means; to break by bending, as in breaking a stick.

du lió lii ke, *v. t.*; to cause to be broken; broken.

du lió ki, *v. t., fr.* lioki; to separate by dragging, as in combing.

dú lipi, *v. t.*; to take down something that is hanging on a nail or peg.

duk [ruk], an adverb of future time; when—will. It is also used to denote uncertainty or condition with regard to future events. It is suffixed.

du ká pi, *v. t., fr.* kapi; to lacerate by any means; to wound by tearing.

dú ki di, *v. t., fr.* kidi; to pull a skin back and forth across a rope, as is done in dressing hides.

du kí ti, *v. t., fr.* kiti; to clear off by plucking, to pluck clean.

du kú ti, *v. t.*; to pluck.

du mä lii ta, *v. i., adv.*; back and forth, going from side to side, changing direction rapidly.

du mä li'ta ti di e, *v.*; to run back and forth.

dum

du má ta [ru-, nu-], *n.*; middle, the middle of anything.

du má ta du [-ru], *adv., n.*; in or through the middle; the middle part of anything.

,du má ta lia, *adv.*; toward the middle.

du má ta ko a, *adv.*; at the middle.

du má ta ta, *adv.*; facing the middle, directed toward the middle.

du má ti tski, *v., fr.* dumata *and* itski; tied in the middle; cut or strangled in the middle.

du mí di, *v. t., fr.* midi; to twist or twill in any way.

dú mi lia [-wi-], *v., adv.*; to turn or point out of a straight line, in an oblique direction; said of a white man's track—toes outward, of the track of a man lost in a storm, etc.

du mú dsi [duwudsi], *v. t., fr.* mudsi; to roll up; nearly the same as pamudsi.

dú pi, *v. t.*; to break off a portion.

du pú pi, *adj.*; capable of stretching and recoiling, elastic.

dú sě [ru-, lu-], *v. t.*; to lay down, to release, to deposit.— dusa and dusa-diha are imperative forms.

du sĭ pi, *v. t.*; to untie; to open like a sack by pulling the edges apart.

dú ske [ru-], *v. t.*; to open, as a door or the lid of a box.—duska, imperative.—duski, opened.

dú sku, *v. t.*; to place an evil charm on, to bewitch.

du sú ki [ru-], *v. t., fr.* suki; to erase, to clean by rubbing; to wash as the face, but *not* as clothing.

dut

du tá, *v. i., fr.* ta; to crack; to go to pieces in any way.

dú ta [nuta, luta], *n.*; a rib; ribs.

du tá he, *v. t., fr.* duta; to cause to burst, or fly to pieces.

du tá pi [ru], *v. t., fr.* tapi; to squeeze; to hold and press, as in shaking hands; to squeeze in any way.

du tá ti, *fr.* tati; to poke or punch; to press with the finger-tip.

dú ti [nuti], *v. t.*; to chew; to eat, to partake of solid food.— duti is the form of the 2d and 3d persons;—muti, of the 1st person. See ¶ 196.

dú ti, *v. t.*; to bind, to confine. In this word, the initial d (or r) is retained throughout its conjugation (1st var. ¶ 195), which distinguishes it from duti, *to eat;* but in the 3d person and in the infinitive, these two verbs are homonymous.

du tĭ ksa, *v. t.*; to eat constantly, habitually.

du tó' ti, *v. t., fr.* to'ti; to shake as in casting pepper; to dredge or sprinkle.

dú tsa, *simple imperative of* dutsi, take it, get it.

du tsá da, *v. t., fr.* tsada; to slide or slip in any way.

du tsá ki, *v. t., fr.* tsaki; to dissever without cutting or burning; to pull apart.

du tsá ki de, *v., adj.*; almost dissevered, torn so as to be held only by a thread.

du tsá' ti, *v. t., fr.* tsa'ti; to stick, thrust through, impale; hold in readiness for cutting by sticking.

dút

dú tsĕ, v. t.; to take hold of; to obtain; to lift.

dú tsĭ [ru-], v; taken; procured.

du tsĭ pi, v. t.; to untie.

du tsĭ si, v. i.; to spring back, as something bent and released.—kidutsisi is the more common form.

du tsĭ ti, v. t.; to tear asunder; to tear down, to raze a building.

dú tska, v. or adj.; twin. See dakadutska.

du tská pi, v. i., fr. tskapi; to pinch with an instrument.

du tská ti, v. t., fr. tskati; to squeeze, force, or pass through, by any means.

du tskí pi, v. t.; to milk a cow. This word seems to be from same root as datskipi, but the connection is not obvious.

du tskĭ si, v. t.; to wash; said of washing clothing.

du tskí ti, v. t., fr. tskiti; to encircle the body, neck, limbs, or any object, with something which presses closely; to tie a string tightly around, to strangle, to kill by hanging, to tie a sack in the middle, etc.

du tská pi, v. t., fr. tskupi; to bend, to double by pressure or otherwise; to bend a stick for setting a spring-trap.

du tsú ki, v. t.; to knead the abdomen (kneading the abdomen is a common remedy for numerous complaints with this people); to engirdle.

du tú' ti, v. t.; same as duto'ti.

du wá li ta, v. i.; same as dumalita.

du wí di, v. t.; same as dumidi.

hah

e.

ĕ, adv.; yes.

e, v. t.; to keep, to retain.

é de de, v.; to bear, to lay.

é di, n.; the abdomen.

ĕ di, v. t.; to defecate.

ĕ dic' ti, v. t., fr. edi, with the suffix ti; denoting desire or readiness.

e dic tí a, v. i., fr. edi and ietia; to be pregnant.

ĕ di de, comp. v., fr. edi and de.

ĕ du i, adj.; same as adui; pungent, bitter.

é lii, v.; to urinate.

e liic' ti, v. i., fr. elii and ti; denoting desire or readiness.

é ke, v. t.; to know; to understand; to recognize.

é ke ta', v. t., negative of eke; to know not.—emaketäts is the true equivalent of I don't know, but madáliisets, I am ignorant, is more commonly used.

ĕ lu i, same as edui and adui; this pronunciation is quite common.

ĕ pĕ, v. t.; to grind or triturate; same as pĕ.

é ri, n.; same as edi.

é tsa, n., adj.; all, the aggregate of a number of individuals; not ordinarily applied to the whole of one thing. See liakahéta.

é tsa de, adj.; almost all.

h.

ha, v. and suffix to verbs, 2d pers. of he; you do; you make.

ha hé tĕ, v. t.; to divorce.—haheta, 2d pers.

hah

ha hé ti ; divorced.

hä lipi, *v. i.* ; to sneeze.

hä lipíc ti, *v. i., fr.* halipi ; to have a desire to sneeze, to be ready or about to sneeze.

hä lipi ke, *v. t.* ; to cause to sneeze, to produce sneezing.

ha kä' ta [hakänta], *2d pers. and imper. of* haka'ti ; wait, halt!

ha kä' ti, *v. i.* ; to stop, cease, leave off, halt.

ha kä' ti he, *v. t.* ; to stop or arrest.

ha kä' ti ke, *v. t.* ; to cause to stop ; stopped.—haka'ti and its derivatives are often used with li as the first letter. See liaka'ti.

hä kạ tsi, *v. t.* ; to butcher, to cut up meat.

hä ke, *v. t.* ; to gather and hold up with the hands, as the edge of a robe or skirt is held in wading.

hä ko ka, *adv.* ; above, overhead, but not in contact with ; nearly the same as akoka.

hä mi [hawi], *v. i.* ; to sleep.

ha mic' ti, *v. i., fr.* hami *and* ti ; to be sleepy.

hä mi de, *v. i.* ; almost asleep, dozing.

ha mï ksa, *v. i.* ; to sleep habitually and excessively.

hä o, *interj., adv.* ; a word used to denote approbation, gratification, agreement, assent, or greeting. It is common to many Indian languages. It is usually written "how" by travellers, and is often pronounced by Indians the same as the English word *how*. It is difficult to determine the best mode of spelling. Mr. Riggs in his Dakota Dictionary writes it hao and ho, both of

he

which forms are used here also, although the Hidatsa rarely say ho.

ha pä, *adj.* ; cold, chilly; refers to the sensation as experienced by living animals.

ha pä ke, *v.* ; to make cold; changed from warm to cold, chilled.

ha' pé sa, *v. i., adj.* ; dark, devoid of light.

ha' pé sa de, *adj., n.* ; almost dark; twilight.

ha' pé sa du i, *v. i.* ; darkening.

ha' pé sa ke, *v. t.* ; to darken; darkened.

ha sí si, *v. i.* ; to feel a stinging or smarting sensation.

ha sí si he, *v. t.* ; to sting, to smart.

ha sí si ke, *v. t.* ; to cause to smart; rendered sharply painful.

hä tsa, *v. t., fr.* tsa; to clean or separate by scraping.

hä tsa ke ki, *v. i.* ; to hiccough.

hä tsa ke kic ti, *v. i., fr.* hatsakeki; to have a desire to hiccough, to be about to hiccough, to be hiccoughing and likely to continue.

ha tsí te, *v. t.* ; to cook by roasting or baking.

ha tskä du i, *v. i., fr.* hatska; lengthening gradually.

hä tski, *adj.* ; long.

hä tski de, *adj.* ; almost long, nearly long enough.

hä tski ke, *v. t.* ; to make long; lengthened.

hä tski ksa, *v., adj.* ; continuously or excessively long.

hä wi, *v. i.* ; *same as* hami.

he, *v. t.* ; to make; to prepare.

hé

he, an auxiliary verb or suffix to verbs, forming transitive from intransitive ver bs; 3d pers.; signifies to make or cause. (¶ 160).

hé da pi, *n.*; the waist.

hé duts, *same as* heide, and apparently a contraction.

hé i de, *v. i.,* or sentence, *fr.* ide; "so he says"; "that is what he says"; said when quoting or repeating, and ordinarily used with the terminal ts; thus, heidets.

hi, *v. t.*; to draw into the mouth, as in smoking or drinking; an irregular verb. (¶ 210).

hi, *v.*; to touch, to come in contact with.

hi [or **i**], *n.*; a sharp point; the point of an instrument; commonly suffixed.

hi', *n.*; a common name for dermal appendages—hair, feathers, bristles, etc.; commonly used as a suffix, or terminal part of a compound noun.

hi, *pers. pron.,* 3d pers., singular.

hi dá, *v., adj., ? from* hídi ; new, recently made.

hi dá ka tsa, *v. i., fr.* daka; it lives; it continues.

hí da mi [-wi], *v. i.,* imperf. 3d pers., *same as* hami; he sleeps.

hí da mi de, *v. i., fr.* hidami; he dozes.

hi dá tsa, *n.*; *said to mean "willows"*; the name of one of the old villages of this tribe on the Knife River, and the present name of the entire tribe.

hí di, *v. t.*; to make; to form.

hi di', *interj.*; let me alone! there now! Used mostly by children when being teased.

híd

hí di, *dem. pron.*; this; is used for person, place, and time.—hidimape, this day, to-day.

hí di ka, *adj., fr.* hidi *and* ka; in this compass, this amount, so much.—hídika or hídikats is said when exhibiting a quantity, or giving an idea of quantity by signs.

hí di ko a, *adv., fr.* hidi *and* koa; at this place, here.

hí di mi, *adj., fr.* hidi; this many, so many. It is used in much the same way as hidika, but refers to number instead of quantity. It answers the question 'túami?' *how many?*

hí di še, *adv., fr.* hidi *and* iše; thus, in this manner.

hí di ta, *adv., fr.* hidi; in this way or direction; this part.

hí di wi or **hídiwits,** common modes of pronouncing hidimi. hidiwits is the terminal form.

hí do, *pers. pron.,* 3d pers., plural.

hi dó, *dem. pron.*; that, that person or place.

hi dó, *adv.*; in that place, there.

hi dó ka, *adv. fr.* hidó; in that place; by that way; therein.

hí do ki, *comp. pers. pron.,* 3d person, plur., *fr.* hido; themselves.

hi du, *n.*; a mother.

hi dú, *n.*; bone.

hi du" a du pu pú lii, *n.*; cartilage.

hi dú i mak i a, *n., fr.* hidu *and* imakia; bones used in gaming. The name has been recently applied to dominoes.

hi dú ka, *adv., same as* hidoka; also pronounced híduka.

hí du ši di, *n.*; the Assinneboine Indians.

hík

hí ke, *v. t., fr.* hi, *to drink;* to cause to drink, as in watering a horse.

hí sắ dsi, *v. i., adj., fr.* hisi; of a dull or doubtful red color, red but not scarlet, reddish.

hí sắ dsi ke, *v. t.*; to make of a reddish color; to dye reddish.

hí sắ du i, *v. i.*; reddening, becoming red.

hí si, *adj.*; red; bright red, scarlet.—hísi-délii-hisi, a light transparent red.—hísi-ámahu-liota, pink.

hí si de, *v. i., adj., fr.* hisi; almost red; said of an iron or stone that is being heated.

hí si he, *v. t.*; to redden.

hí si ke, *v. t.*; to dye red; to make red.

hí si ke, *v.*; reddened; dyed red.

hí si sắ du i, *v. i., fr.* hisise; assuming a reddish tinge.

hí si se, *adj., v. i., fr.* hisi and ise; having a reddish tinge; said of northern lights, the morning sky, etc.;—also hísisi.

hí si si ke, *v. t.*; to cause to assume a reddish tinge.

hí sú a, *n.*; mint, *Mentha canadensis.*

hí ta, *adj.*; fast, fleet; said of a good runner; used also adverbially.

hí tá du i, *v. i.*; becoming fleet, increasing in speed.

hí ta ha, *adv.*; fleetly, rapidly; a more proper adverbial form than hita.

hí ta ke, *v. t.*; to make fleet, to accelerate motion.

ho; the word hao (which see) is sometimes thus pronounced.

hó i ke or **hówike,** *v.*; to hum

huá

a child to sleep; to drone a lullaby.

hó pa, *adv.*; slowly; tediously, wearily.

ho pá, *v. i., adj.*; to be mysterious; sacred; to have curative powers; to possess a charm; incomprehensible; spiritual. Same as Dakota, *wakan,* but signifies also the power of curing diseases.

ho pá di, *n., fr.* hopá; mystery; medicine; incomprehensible power or influence, etc.

hó' pa du i, *v. i., fr.* ho'pi *and* adui; becoming more and more perforated in different places, as a target at which marksmen are shooting.

hó pa ke, *v. t., fr.* hópa; to make slow, to cause to be slow.

ho pá se, *v. t.*; to scare greatly, to terrify.—hopasíts, terrified.

ho pá ti, *n., prob. fr.* hupa; corn in the ear; roasting ears.

ho pá ti si, *n., fr.* hopati *and* isi; corn-husks.

hó' pi or **hópi,** *v. i., adj.*; bored, perforated; excavated.

hó' pi de, *adj.*; almost perforated, bored nearly through.

hó' pi ke, *v. t.*; to perforate; bored through; supplied with an excavation or opening.

hu, *v. i.*; to come.—hu', imperative.

hu, *n.*; a mother. This word is said to be of amaliami origin.

hú a, *v. i.*; to cough.

hú a ke, *v. t.*; to cause to cough.

hu á ksa, *v. i.*; to cough habitually or continuously, as with a bad cold.

hu á ti, *v. i.*; to have a desire to cough; to be about to cough.

húd

hú di śe du [huriścru], *n.*, *adv.*; yesterday. See śedu.

hú duk, *adv.*, *fr.* hu *and* duk; when it comes to pass, at a future time specified.

hu ka hé! *interj.*; hallo! etc.

hú pa, *n.*; soup.

hú pa, *n.*; moccasins. See itápa.

hú pa, *n.*; a stem or handle; a corn-cob; a pipe-stem, etc.

hu pa a ku i kú tski, *n.*, *fr.* aku *and* ikutski; a "measuring worm".

hu té, *n.*; a screech-owl.

hú tsi, *n.*; wind.

ḥ.

ḥa, *prep.*; toward, in the direction of; suffixed to nouns, it forms adverbs, which qualify verbs denoting motion.

ḥa, *adj.*; coarse, rough, scaly, etc; used only as a factor of compound words.

ḥa bú a, *same as* ḥamua.

ḥá da ḥá du i, *v. i.*; growing lean.

ḥá da ḥi, *adj.*; lean.

ḥá da ḥi ke, *v. t.*; to cause to be lean; to starve; starved, reduced to a condition of leanness.

ḥá da ḥi kśa, *adj.*, *v.*; habitually lean; emaciated.

ḥá da ḥí kśa ke, *v. t.*; to cause to be emaciated.

ḥá de, verbal-root; shell, as corn.

ḥa dé, *n.*; rain.

ḥa dé, *v.*; to rain.—ḥadets, it rains.

ḥa dí e, *v.*; to rain; *same as* ḥade.

ḥá ḥa, *v. i.*, *fr.* ḥa; very rough, prickly, echinate.

ḥak

ḥa ḥá du i, *v. i.*; becoming very rough.

ḥá ḥa dsi, *v. i.*; roughish, having the appearance of being rough.

ḥa ḥá tu a, *n.* (*Dakota*, ḥaḥatonway); the Chippeway Indians.

ḥa ḥá tu a-ma śi, *n.* (maśi, *whites*); the Red River half-breeds.

ḥá ḥi, *v.*, *adj.*; striped, marked with parallel bands or lines.

ḥá ḥi he, *v. t.*, 3d pers.; to stripe, to mark with parallel bands.

ḥá ḥi ke, *v. t.*; to stripe, to cause to be striped.

ḥa ḥú a, *v. i.*, *adj.*; to be set closely together; thickly studded.

ḥa ḥú a ke, *v. t.*; to cause to set closely together, to compel a large number of persons or things to occupy a small surface, to plant closely, to pitch camp with the lodges close together.

ḥa ḥú a kśa, *adj.*; continuously or constantly close, or thickly set.

ḥá ka, *v. i.*; to be rocking, oscillating, shaken, or agitated.

ḥá ka, *v. i.*; to itch; to be afflicted with itching sores, as in small-pox.

ḥá ka du i, *v. i.*; becoming itchy or more itchy.

ḥá ka he, *v. t.*, *fr.* ḥáka; to rock, shake, or agitate.

ḥá ka hé ta, *v.*, *n.*, *adj.*; whole, entire; the entire of one thing.

ḥá ka hé ta de, *adj.*; almost entire.

ḥá ka hé ta ke, *v. t.*; to make whole or entire; completed.

ḥá ka ke, *v. t.*, *fr.* ḥaka; to make

liak

itchy, to produce an itchy sensation or an itching sore.

lia ká' ta, *same as* haka'ta. In the derivatives of this word also, li is often substituted for the initial h.

lia kú pi, *v. i., adj.*; hollowed longitudinally, having a crease or furrow.

lia kú pi he, *v. t.*; to make a crease or furrow.

lia kú pi ke, *v. t.*; to furrow, to mark with creases or grooves; grooved.

liá ma dsi [-wa-], *v. i., adj., fr.* liami; having a diverging appearance.

liá ma du i [-wa-], *v. i., fr.* liami; becoming progressively more branched, forked, or diverging.

liá mi [-wi], *v. i., adj.*; to be forked; scattering or diverging.

liá mi ke, *v. t., fr.* liami; to cause to diverge or scatter, as in tossing the hair.

lia mú a [-bu-], *v. i., fr.* mua; to make a rough noise, to rattle.

liá pa du i, *v. i., fr.* liapi *and* adui; becoming thinner; wearing thin.

lia pa tá du i, *v. i., fr.* liapati; becoming satiated.

lia pá ti, *v. i.*; to have a feeling of satiety, to have hunger or thirst fully satisfied, to be satisfied or satiated in any respect.

lia pá ti de, almost satisfied.

lia pá ti he, *v. t.*; to satisfy.

lia pá ti ke, *v. t.*; to satisfy; to cause to be satisfied, to supply with food sufficient for satisfaction; satisfied.

lia pá ti ksa, *v. i., adj.*; habitually satiated; gorged, satisfied to disgust.

hém

liá pe, | verbal **root**; denude, re-
liá pi, | move surface, peel.

liá pi, *v. i., adj.*; thin, as paper or finely dressed skin.

liá pi, *v. i.*; to lie down.—liap, imperative.

liá pi, *v. i.*; to be lost.

lia pi hé, *v. t.*; to lose; he loses or lost; they lose. (¶ 202).

lia pi hé ke, *v. t.*; to cause to lose.

liá pi hé ksa, *v.*; to lose frequently or excessively; to be careless of things; to be in the habit of losing.

liá pi ke, *v. t., fr.* liapi; to make thin, to wear thin, to cause to be thin.

liá pi ke, made thin, worn thin.

liá pi ke, *v. t., fr.* liapi; to cause to be lost, to lose.

liá pi ksa, *v. i.*; excessively thin; constantly thin.

liá ta ta ka, | *adv.*; rapidly,
liá ta ta ka ha, | in frequent and rapid succession.

liá ta ta ká du i, *v. i., fr.* liáta-taki; becoming gradually accelerated in motion.

liá ta ta ki, *v. i., adj.*; to be rapid, to move rapidly.

liá ta ta ki ke, *v. t.*; to make rapid, to accelerate motion.

liá ti, verbal root; to brighten or lighten; hence, amaliati **and** oliati.

liá wi, *same as* liami.

lie, *adj., probably a contraction of* liie; old.

lié mi [-wi], *v. i., adj.*; lonesome.

lié mi ke [-wi-], *v. t.*; to make lonesome.

lié mi ksa, *v. i.*; continually lonesome; melancholy.

liép

lié pa du i, *v. i., fr.* liepi; becoming more shallow.

lié pi, *v. i., adj.*; shallow; applied to water, etc.

lié pi de, *v. i.*; almost shallow.

lié pi ke, *v. t.*; to make shallow, to bail out or drain out.

lié pi ke, made shallow, drained or evaporated to shallowness.

lié pi kša, *v. i.*; very shallow; continually shallow.

lié pi kša ke, *v. t., fr.* liepikša.

lié še, verbal root; tear through, separate.

lié wi, a common pronunciation of liemi, either when used alone or in its derivatives.

lii di a, *v. i.*; to experience an itching sensation; to feel other abnormal or peculiar sensations.

lii di a ke, *v. t.*; to make itchy or sensitive.

lii di á kša, *v. i.*; persistently or habitually itchy or sensitive.

lii é, *adj.*; old, advanced in age; decrepit as if old; said of organized beings.

lii é ke, *v. t.*; to cause to be old or decrepit.

lii é kša, *adj., v.*; superannuated.

lii pa du i, *v. i., fr.* liipi; becoming wrinkled, as a person advancing in age.

lii pe, verbal root; skin, flay.

lio, hypothetical word; the body; the trunk; the entire body. See ilio, dilio, and malio.

lió li, verbal root; break across, break by bending.

lió lio i, *v. i.*; to experience the peculiar weak or painful feeling in the eyes resulting from deferred sleep.—mišta liolioits, my eyes are sleepy.

i

lió ka, *n.*; a skunk, *Mephitis mephitica.*

lió ka di ti, *v. t.*; to close up by tying.

lió ki, verbal root, denotes the pulling of a hard instrument through something that yields, as in pulling a comb through the hair, an oar through water.

lio pá še, *v. t., same as* liopaše.—liopaše is the more common pronunciation.

lio pá ši, *v.*; scared, startled, terrified.

lio pá ši ke, *v. t.*; to cause to be scared.

lió ta, *adj.*; gray; whitish-gray.

lió ti ša, } *adj., fr.* liota *and* iše;
lió ti še, } grayish, iron-gray; said in describing horses.

liu, verbal root; upset, spill, throw down.

liú a lia, *n.,* ? hypothetical; the knees. See iliualia.

liú e, *v. t. and i.*; to upset; to topple over, as a stick set upright.

liú e de, *v. i., fr.* liue *and* de; to be almost falling; to stumble.

liú liu i, *same as* liolioi.

liu pi, verbal root; drain dry; drink, absorb. See daliupi.

liu ti, verbal root, or ? modified *fr.* liu; to be in a condition to fall, placed insecurely.

liú' ti, *n.*; gloves; mittens.

i.

i, *n.*; point, edge; tooth; *same as* hi.

i', *n.*; hair of animals; *prob. fr.* hi'.

i or i', *n.*; the mouth.

i

i, *pers. pron.,* incorporated, 3d pers., masc., fem., and neut., sing. and plur., objective and possessive. In the objective, it may denote the combined agent and object of a reflexive verb. In the possessive, it usually denotes non-transferable possession.

i, a prefix forming, with verbs, nouns of the material or instrument. Prefixed to cardinal numbers, it forms ordinals.

í a lia lia, *v. t.;* to encircle or surround; surrounding it.—alialia is perhaps the simple word.

í a lio a, *v., reflex of* alioa; also, ialioe.

í a ka, *n.;* a man's elder brother.—miaka, my elder brother. diaka, your elder brother.

í a pa ti, *n.;* a stopple of any kind; a cork.

ic kǎ, *n.;* a star.

ic kǎ dǎ mi [-nawi], *n., fr.* icka *and* dami; the Belt of Orion.

ic kǎ dé lii, *n., fr.* icka *and* delii; Sirius.

ic kǎ lia liú a, *n., fr.* icka *and* lialiua; the Pleiades.

ic kǎ ic tí a, *n., fr.* icka *and* ictia; Venus and Jupiter.

ic kǎ sǎ pu a, *n., fr.* icka *and* sapua; Ursa Major.

íc ke, *n.;* bands, societies, or secret orders among the Hidatsa; each having its own songs, dances, and ceremonies, which are to a certain extent esoteric.

íc ki, *comp. pers. pron.;* himself; herself; itself; themselves.

íc pa, *n.;* the wing of a bird.

íc pa tǎ ki, *n., fr.* icpa *and* tǎki; a species of hawk.

íc pe, *n.;* a magpie, the *Pica hudsonica.*

ida

ic pe, *n.;* the tail of a bird.

ic pu, *n.;* point, top, extremity, small end; *same as Dakota* inkpa *or* iutpa. For examples, see amaicpu, aziicpu, midaicpu, and sakiicpu.

ic ta tǎ ki, *n.;* the kill-deer, *Ægialitis vocifera.*

ic tí a, *adj.;* great, large.

ic tí á du i, *v. i., fr.* ictia; increasing.

ic tí a he, *v. t. and i.;* to increase.

ic tí a ke, *v. t.;* to cause to enlarge or increase; to change from small to large.

ic tí a ke, enlarged.

i da, *v. i.;* to yawn.

i dǎ lii, *n., fr.* dalii; a shade; its or his shade, shadow, or ghost.

i da lii lii, *n., fr.* daliilii; a reflection; his, her, or its reflection.—madaliilii, my reflection. didaliilii, your reflection.

i dǎ lii se, *n., fr.* i *and* daliise; a shovel; *same as* amaidaliise.

i dǎ lipi, *v. t.;* to make an incised wound.

i dǎ ka, *n., fr.* daka; his or her offspring; their offspring.

i dǎ ka kí ti, *n. fr.* dakakiti; a robe-scraper. The term has been recently applied to razors.

i dǎ ki sa, *n., adj.;* left; left hand; left side.

i dǎ ki sa ko a, *adv.;* at the left; to the left.

í da ko a ka de, *n.;* the parting in the centre of hair of head.

i da kó c [-la-], *fr.* dakoe; his friend, his comrade.

i da kú dsi, *n., fr.* dakudsi; a swing. See maidakudsi and makadistaidakudsi.

idá

i dá mi [+ -nawi], *ord. num.,*
fr. dami ; third.

i dá mi de [-nawi-], *v., adj.* ;
almost third.

i dá mi du [ináwiru], *adv.* ;
thirdly, in the third order or
place.

i dá mi ke, *v. t.* ; to make third,
to place in the order of third ;
made third.

í da pa, *n., adj.* ; right ; right
side ; right hand.

i da pá lia, *adv.* ; toward the
right.

i da pá ko a, *adv.* ; at the right.

í da pu di, *adj.* ; wild or unman-
ageable, as a wild horse.

i dá špa, *n.* ; shoulder ; shoulders.

i dá špa ki pĕ, *comp. v.* ; to carry
on the shoulders.

i dá! ti, *n.* ; a wife's brother, or a
man's sister's husband.—dida'ti,
your brother-in-law. mada'ti,
my brother-in-law.

í da tska ti, *n., fr.* i and datskati ; a syringe.—maidatskati is
the more common form.

i dá wi. See idámi and its derivatives.

i dé, *v. t.* ; to say ; to speak.

i dé kša, *v. t.* ; to talk excessively, to say too much ; to be garrulous or too communicative.

i dé ta, *n., fr.* i, mouth, *and* deta ;
the lips, more properly the mu-
cous surface of the lips.—ideta-
aku-akoka, upper lip. ideta-aku-
miktakoa, lower lip. See aputi.

i di, *n.* ; blood.

ï di, *n.* ; penis.

i di a lii, *v. i.* ; to sigh.

i di é or **idiéts,** *v. t.,* 3d pers. ;
he thinks, believes, or supposes.—
dadiets, or nadiets, you think.
madiets, or badiets, I think.

idí

í di hu, *v. comp., fr.* idi *and* hu ;
to bleed.

í di í pšą ki, *n., fr.* ipšaki ; a
breech cloth.

i di ká lia, *n., ? fr.* idiki ; popliteal space.

i dí ké di kša, *n., fr.* idiki ; a
garter, or string for securing the
legging.

i dí ki, *n.* ; the leg ; the entire
lower extremity. — madiki, my
leg.

i dí ki ú ti, *n., fr.* idiki *and* uti ;
head of femur.

i dí ki ú ti o ki, *n., fr.* idikiuti
and oki ; acetabulum.

I di ko a—ma tu″, said of a
woman's jealousy.

i di pá du i, *v. i., fr.* idipi *and*
adui ; fattening.

í di pi, *v. adj.* ; fat, fleshy.

í di pi ke, *v. t.* ; to make fat ;
fattened.

í di pi ksa, *adj.* ; obese.

i dí ši, *n., fr.* diši ; his or her son ;
their son.

i dí tsi, *adj., v. i.* ; to have a scent
or smell, agreeable or disagreea-
ble.

i dí tsi i ší a, *v. i., fr.* iditsi *and*
išia ; to smell disagreeably, to
stink.

i dí tsi i ší a ke, *v. t.* ; to cause
to smell badly ; changed from an
agreeable to a disagreeable odor.
The intensive form is more commonly used.

i dí tsi ke, *v. t.* ; to supply with
an odor, to cause to smell.

i dí tsi tsą ki, *v. i., fr.* iditsi *and*
tsąki ; smelling sweetly, sweet-
scented.

i dí tsi tsą kí ke, *v. t.* ; to cause
to smell sweetly, to put scent
upon, to remove a disagreeable

idó

odor; sweetly scented. See kiiditsitsąkike, which is the more
common form.

i dó pa [+ ·nopa], *ord. num.,fr.*
dopa ; second.

i dó pa du [inóparu], *adv.;*
secondly, in the second place.

i dó pa du ke, *v. t.;* to put in
the second place or order.

i dó pa ke, *v. t.,fr.* idopa ; to
place second, to make second.

i dú, *n.;* a woman's elder sister ;
her or their elder sister. See
madu and didu.

i dú hi, *v. reflex.,fr.* duhi ; to lift
one's self up, to stand up; to
arise from sitting, but not from
lying.—diduhá, lift thyself, *i. e.,*
arise!

i dú ka, *n.;* meat of any kind,
particularly dried meat.

i du kśí ti, *n.;* fresh meat;
flesh.

i du kśí ti í mi di ti, *n.;* fry-
ing-pan. See imiditi.

i du pu pi, *n.,fr.* dupupi ; elastic band or web.

i dú ti, *n.,fr.* duti, *to bind;* any
thing used to bind, especially a
bridle, or a raw-hide or rope tied
around a horse's jaw as a bridle.
See uetsa iduti.

i dú tsi, *n.,fr.* dutsi; an instrument for taking up or lifting, as
a fork.

i hȧ, *v. i., adj.;* to differ, to be different; other, of another kind.

i hȧ di, *v. t.;* to set out food, to
put a feast before a guest; lately
applied to setting a table.

i hȧ du, *adv.,fr.* iha ; in another
place.

i hȧ ke, *v. t.,fr.* iha ; to cause to
be different, to change, to alter;
changed. ·

í"lio

i hȧ ko a, *adv.,fr.* iha ; in another direction or place.

i hȧ' ta ha, *v.;* take care, get
out of the way, make room.

i hé, *interj.;* there now! what do
you think of that ?

i hí śȧ dsi ke, *n.,fr.* hiśadsike;
material to dye reddish.

i hí śi ke, *n.,fr.* hiśike; red dye-
. stuff.

í lia, *n., ? fr.* lia, *rough, etc.;* dust,
solid dirt; the dirt on a floor or
dish, but not soils on clothing.

i lȧ tsą ki, *adj.,fr.* ilia ; to be
covered with dirt, dirty.

i lȧ tsą ki ke, *v. t.;* to cover
with dirt; to throw dirt on.

í li, *n.;* the forehead.

í lii, *n.;* braided hair; woven fab-
ric. See maśiilii.

í lii, *n.;* the *omentum,* the crop of
a fowl. This word and the one
immediately preceding are perhaps but different applications
of one term.

í lio, *n., fr. hypoth. word* lio ; a
body; his or her body; their
bodies.—malio, my body. dilio,
your body.

i lió a de, *v. i., comp. fr.* ilio *and*
ade; to be sick, to have general
disease.—malióadets, I am sick.

í lio ka, *n.;* a fox.

í lio ka da ka, *n.,fr.* ihoka *and*
daka; a fox-cub.

í lio ka ic ke, *n.,fr.* ihoka *and*
icke; the Fox Band, a secret
degree or order among the men
of this tribe.

i lio ka í ti pe, *n.,fr.* ilioka *and*
itipe; a little fall-trap such as
boys make for catching foxes.

í" lio ka mi a ic ke, *n.,fr.* ihoka, mia, *and* icke; the Fox-wo-
man Band, a secret degree or

ílio

'order among the females; its
members are usually from fifteen
to twenty years old.

í lio ka tạ ki, *n.*; *Artemisia
ludoviciana*, or small "sage" of
the northern plains. .

í lio ka tạ ki—a ku sí pi ša,
n.; *lit. black sage; Artemisia bi-
ennis.*

i lio ki, *n., fr.* lioki; an oar.

i lio tạ ká du i, *v. i., fr.* iliotạ-
ki; bleaching, becoming white.

i lio tạ ká dsi, *v. i., adj.*; whitish, having a white appearance.

i lio tạ ki, *adj., v.*; white; to be
white.

i lió tạ ki de, *adj.*; almost white.

i lió tạ ki he, *v. i. and t.*; to
whiten; to bleach.

i lió tạ ki ke, *v. t.*; to cause to
be white, to bleach, to wash
white, to change from dark to
white.

i liú a lia, *n., fr.* lualia; the
knee or knees; his or her knee
or knees.—maliúalia, my knee.
diliúalia, your knee.

í i ti pe, *n., fr.* i', *mouth, and* itipe; a lid, the lid of a pot or kettle.

i í pšạ ki, *n., fr.* ipšạki; a screen;
a covering.

i ka, *n.*; the chin.

i ka', *n.*; mother; my mother; a
mother's sisters. — ikạš is the
common form of address.

i' ká, *n., fr.* ka; his, her, or their
daughter.—maká, my daughter.
niká, your daughter.

í ka, *v. t.*; to see; he or she sees.—
ámaka, I see. ádaka, you see.

i ká li, *v. .t., reflex.*; to lean
against.

í ka ka, *v. t.*; *red. of* ika; look,
behold!

iki

í ka ki, *n., fr.* kaki; a wheel; a
rolling vehicle.

í ka ti pe, *n., fr.* katipe; a button. See maikatipe, which is
more commonly used.

í ka tsu ti, *v. reflex.*; to scarify
one's self; to cut the flesh in
mourning. Scarifying the flesh
is a common method of showing
sorrow for the dead.

í ki, *n.*; a whip.

i' ki, *n.*; beard.

í ki da ka pu ši, *n., fr.* kidaka-
puši; something used to inflate,
or fill out. See madạhapi—iki-
dakapuši.

í ki da ku di, *n., fr.* kidakudi;
a fan. maikidakudi is the more
common form.

í ki da tsó pe, *n., fr.* i', *mouth,
and* kidatsope; a kiss.

í ki da tsó pe, *v. t., comp.*; to
kiss the mouth, to kiss.—imaki-
datsope, I kiss. idakidatsope,
you kiss.

í ki du tá ta, *n.*; an open space
in a solid covering, as the fonta-
nels of an infant head. This
word and the word midiikiduta-
ta (which see) are apparently
from a verb "kidutata", which,
however, I have never heard except in these words.

i ki kí ški, *n., fr.* kikiški; an instrument for measuring or determining any quality.

í ki pa mi di [ikipawídi], *v.
reflex., fr.* kipamidi; to turn one's
self around, to look behind.

í ki pa tạ ki, *n., fr.* kipatạki; a
bolt or bar for a door; accent
also on penult.

í ki pa tó' ti, *v. reflex., fr.* kipato'ti; to shake one's self; said of
a bird shaking its plumage, of

an animal drying itself by shaking; also íkipato'ti.

í ki pi, *n.*; a pipe.

í ki pi hu pa, *n.*; a pipe-stem.

i ki pkí ti, *n.*, *fr.* kipkiti; a sad-iron.

i kí śi, *n.*; a nest, a bird's nest.

i ki tsá ti ke, *n.*, *fr.* kitsatike; polish, varnish, etc.

í ko ki, *v. t.*; to hang up on a peg or nail.

i kó' pa, *n.*, *fr.* ko'pa; her friend or comrade.—makó'pa, my friend.

í ko zi, *n.*, *fr.* kozi; a whistle.

í' ko zi, *v. i.*, *fr.* i' and kozi; to whistle with the mouth.

í kśi a, *v. i.*; stuck or stranded, as a vessel.

i kśú ki, *v.*; to dash or splash; to dash on.

i ktsá ti, *v. t.*, *? fr.* kitsati; to be-daub; to apply any soft sub-stance, as mud or molasses.

i kú, *n.*; a grandmother; a grand-mother's sisters.

i kú pa, *v. t.*; to accompany, to go with.

i kú'pa, *adv.*; with, along with.

i kú' pa, *v. t.*; to hate; he hates.—amaku'pa, I hate. adaku'pa, you hate.

i kú' pa dsi, *v. t.*, *fr.* ikú'pa *and* adsi; to dislike very much.

i kú ti, *n.*; the wrist; his or her wrist.

i kú ti a du śu ka, *n.*, *fr.* ikuti *and* aduśuka; the wrist, the wrist joint.

i kú tski, *n.*, *fr.* kutski; a meas-uring-stick; a pattern. See mai-kutski, which is more commonly used.

í má lipi [iwáḷipi], *v. i.* and *re-flex.*; to set; said of heavenly bodies.

í má lipi de, *v.*, *adv.*; almost setting; near the time of setting.

í má lipi du [iwáḷipiru], *adv.*; at the time of setting.

í má lipi duk [iwáḷipiruk], *adv.* of future time; when it will set.

í má lipi śe du, *adv.* of past time; when it did set, at last time of setting.

í mąk i [iwąki], *n.*, *? fr.* mąki; the chest, the sternal region.

í mąk i e ke, *n.*, *fr.* i and mąki; gaming materials; cards.

í mąk i du, *a contraction of* ima-kihidu, and more commonly used than the latter.

í mąk i hi″ du, *n.*, *fr.* imąki and hidu; the breastbone, the *ster-num.*

i mąk í ka ti pe, *n.*, *fr.* imąki, *the chest, and* ikatipe, *or fr.* i, mąki, *and* katipe; buttons which join a garment in front.

í mąk śi di, *n.*, *lit. tawny breast;* the western meadow-lark, *Stur-nella neglecta.*

í ma śi, *n.*; price, value.

í mi a [iwia], *v. i.*; to weep; to cry and weep.

í mi a ke, *v. t.*; to cause to cry.

í mi dí pi ke, *n.*, *fr.* midipi; a sponge.

i mi di ti, *n.*, *fr.* miditi; a fry-ing-pan.

i ó pe, *n.*, *fr.* ope; a receptacle, a box.

i ó ki, *n.*, *fr.* oki; a receptacle which closely surrounds or encir-cles, as a candlestick, a socket.

i ó ptsa ti, *n.*, *fr.* optsati; nearly synonymous with ioki. See śa-kioptsati.

i pa ka dĕ, *n.*, *fr.* i and pakade; a fork.

ípa

í pa ša ki, *n., fr.* i *and* pašaki; a belt; *same as* maipašaki.

í pa ta ki, *v. i., fr.* pataki; to come in contact; to lean against.

í pa tsa' ti, *n., fr.* patsa'ti; a skewer or fork.

i plio ki, *n.*; a species of eagle.

i pi, *v. t.*; to cohabit.

i pí ta, *n.*; behind, the rear, the back part of anything.

i pí ta ,du, *adv., fr.* ipita; in the rear, in the back part; after, following.

i pí ta lia, *adv.*; toward the rear, backward.

i pí ta ko a, *adv.*; at the rear, behind.

i pkí ti, *v. t.*; to smooth out; to spread smoothly; to coat or cover smoothly, as in spreading butter or mortar.

í·pša ki, *v. t.*; to conceal, screen, hide from view.

í ptsa, *n.*; an upright, a supporting-post or pillar.

í ptse, *v. t.*; to garnish, to embroider with beads.

í ša, *n.*; tooth; teeth.

i ša, *adv.*, suf. to verbs, etc.; alike, resembling; nearly resembling.

íša, *adv.*; thus, in this manner.

í ša, *conj.*; and, also.

i šá ki, *n., fr.* šaki; his or her hand. See šaki.—mašaki, my hand. dišaki, your hand.

i ša ki a du tsa mi he. See šakiadutsamihe.

i ša ki íc pu. See šakiícpu.

i šá mi [išáwi], *n.*; an aunt; his or her aunt; a father's but not a mother's sisters.—mašami, or mašawiš, my aunt. dišami, or nišawiš, your aunt.

i šá mi ke, *v. i.*; said of young sprouts growing from a stump.

ist

í ša tsa, *adv.*; gratuitously, without reward.

í šě, *same as* iša; alike, resembling.

í ši, *n.*; a vessel, box, sack, cover, or receptacle of any kind.

i ší a, *v., adj.*; bad.

i ši á du i, *v. i., fr.* išia *and* adui; deteriorating.

i ší a ke, *v. t.*; to make bad, to spoil, damage, ruin.

i ší a ke, damaged, ruined.

i ší ta, *n.*; the back; his or her back.—mašita, my back. dišita, your back.

i ši kí si, *n.*; a brother-in-law, a woman's husband's brother; his or her brother-in-law.—mišikiši, my brother-in-law. dišikiši, your brother-in-law.

í ši pi he, *n., fr.* i, *mouth, and* šipihe; Mouth Blackeners, an order or degree among the Hidatsa men.

i ší pi ša ke, *n., fr.* sipišake; dye-stuff for coloring black.

i ške', *v. t.*; to command or direct.—amaške, I direct.

i špá li, *n., ? fr.* palii; the elbow; his or her elbow.—mišpalii, my elbow. dišpálii, your elbow.

í sta or í sta, *n.*; an eye; eyes.

i šta dá lipi, *n., fr.* išta *and* dalipi; the eyelids.

i šta du i lió ta ki, *n., fr.* išta, adu, *and* iliotaki; the white of the eye.

i šta du ší pi ša, *n., fr.* išta, adu, *and* šipiša; the pupil.

i šta dú ta, *v., adj., prob. fr.* išta *and* duti, *to bind;* squint-eyed.

i šta liú lii, *v. i.*; to wink.

í šta mi di [-bidi], *n., fr.* išta *and* midi; tears.

i šta ó ze, *n., fr.* išta *and* oze; an eye-water.

i šta pé di, *n.*, *fr.* išta *and* pedi ; purulent or mucous matter adhering to the eyelids.

i štá pi, *n.* ; eyelashes.

í šu, *n.* ; quills ; primary feathers of wings of large birds, particularly of eagles' wings.

í šu a ti ší a, *n.*, *fr.* išu *and* atišia ; a bat.

í šu šĭ ša, *n.* ; a species of kingbird, *Tyrannus verticalis.*

i šú tĭ, *n.* ; the lap.

i šu tĭ pša ki, *n.*, *fr.* isuti *and* ipšaki ; an apron.

i tá, *n.*, *fr.* i *and* ta ; an arrow, *lit.*, an instrument of death. See maita.

í ta or í ta, *comp. pers. pron.*, 3d pers., sing. and plur., possessive, and used for all genders ; denotes principally acquired or transferable possession. ita (or its equivalents in the first and second person,—mata and dita) is prefixed to nouns, forming compounds which often differ so much from the original nouns in sense or sound that they are to be regarded as distinct words. A few examples follow. (¶ ¶ 58–61).

i tá da mi a [itarawia], *n.*, *fr.* mia ; a wife ; a betrothed wife ; a wife's sister.

í ta dé lipa, *n.* ; the navel.

í ta do lipá ka, *n.*, *fr.* ita *and* dolipaka ; one's own people, relations, kindred.

í ta dó ta du [-lotaru], *n.*, *adv.*, *fr.* ita *and* dotadu ; this side of it ; a place nearer than some given point ; used also in comparison of adjectives to denote a less degree, or inferiority. (¶ 233).

i ta dó ta ko a, *adv.*, *fr.* dotakoa ; "at this side of it", at a point nearer than some given point whose name is the antecedent of ita.

i tá du [-ru], *n.* ; a mother's brother, his or her mother's brother, uncles in the female line.—matádu or matáruš, my uncle. ditádu or nitáru, your uncle.

i ta dú lia, *n.*, *fr.* midulia ; one's own gun or bow.—matadulia, my own gun. ditadulia, your own gun.

i ta dú lia ke, *n.*, *fr.* miduliake ; one's own pop-gun.

i ta du liá pi, *n.*, *fr.* aduliapi ; one's own bed.—mataduliapi, my own bed.

i tá dsi, *n.* ; leggings ; his or her leggings.—matadsi, my leggings. ditadsi, your leggings.

i tá dsi—ó da ka pi li, *n.*, *fr.* itadsi *and* odakapili ; the flap or fringe worn on the outer seam of the legging.

i ta há tski, *n.*, *fr.* ita *and* hatski, *lit.*, *Long Arrows* ; the Dakota Indians.

i ta lí', *n.*, *fr.* ita *and* hi' ; an arrow-point.

í ta hu, *n.* ; a mouse.

i ta hu ic tí a, *n.*, *fr.* itahu *and* ictia ; a rat.

i tá ĭ šu, *n.*, *fr.* itá *and* išu ; the quills at the base of an arrow, arrow-directors.

i tá ka, *n.* ; an aged man ; a venerable person.

i tá ka lie or itákalie, *n.*, *fr.* itaka *and* lie ; a very old man.

i ta ka té taš, *prop. n.*, *fr.* itaka, te, *and* tá, *lit.*, *Old Man Immortal* ; one of the Hidatsa names for a Deity.

íta

í ta ki, *n., fr.* i, *hair, and* tạki, *white;* the jackass rabbit, or *Lepus campestris,* which turns white in winter.

í ta ki da ká he, *n., fr.* kidakabe; a span, the outstretch of the hand, the measure of a span: See šakiitakidakabe.

í ta kí ša, *n.;* a sister; a man's younger sister.—matakiša, my sister. nitakiša your sister.

i ta kši pi ša, *n., fr.* itạki *and* šipiša; the small rabbit, the "wood-rabbit", *Lepus sylvaticus* var. *nuttalli.*

i tá ku, *n.;* a woman's younger sister; her younger sister.—mataku, my sister. ditaku, your sister.

i ta kú pe, *n.;* an owl, particularly the great horned owl, *Bubo virginianus.*

i tá ma, *n., fr.* ita *and* ama; one's own country, the proper hunting-ground of any tribe.

i ta má e, *n., fr.* ita *and* mae; one's own property; his own property.—matamae, my own. ditamae, your own. (¶ 122).

i ta ma pI ša, *n.;* grandchild; his or her grandchild.

i ta má ši, *n.;* a servant; used when speaking of white men.

i ta ma šú ka, *n.;* his dog.

i tá ma ta, *adj., adv., fr.* ite, ama, *and* ta; face downward; with the face to the ground.

i ta mé tsa [-wetsa], *n., ? fr.* matse; a brother; brethren (in the widest sense); this is also the only term for a woman's elder brother.—matametsa, my brother.

i ta mí a [-wia], *n., fr.* ita *and* mia; a man's elder sister.—ma-

ité

tamia, my sister. ditamia, your sister.

i ta ó ka du, *adv., fr.* ita *and* okadu; the other side of it, on the other side of it, in a place further off than some object mentioned. This word and the next following are commonly used in comparison of qualities to denote superiority,—the antecedent of ita being the inferior. (¶233).

i ta ó ka ko a, *adv., fr.* ita *and* okakoa; at the other side of it, beyond some object mentioned.

i ta ó ki ko a, a rare pronunciation of the word immediately preceding.

i tá pa, *n., fr.* ita *and* hupa; moccasons; his or her moccasons.—matapa, my moccasons.

i tá ši, *n., fr.* ita *and* maši; his or her own robe or blanket.—mataši, my robe.

i tá ši i ptsi, *n., fr.* itasi *and* iptsi (*see* mašiiptsi); the garnishing of his or her robe.

i tá šu, *n., contraction of* itaišu.

i tá šu ka, *n., fr.* ita *and* itsuašuka *or* šuka; one's own horse.—matašuka, my horse.

i tá šu pu zi, *n., fr.* itašu *and* puzi, *lit., Spotted Arrow-quills;* the Cheyenne Indians.

i tá tsu, *n., fr.* ita *and* tsu; the half of anything.

i tá tsu he, *v. t., fr.* itátsu; to divide into its halves; also used as a noun or adjective, signifying half or halved.

i ta wĕ tsa, *n., same as* itametsa.

i ta wí a, *n., same as* itamia.

i té, *v. t.;* to admire; to be fond of.—amatets, I admire. adatets, you admire.

í te or **itĕ,** *n.* ; the face.

i tĕ á ka ta, *adv., same as* ita-kata.

i te á ma ta, *adv., same as* ita-mata.

í tĕ lia, *adv., fr.* ite ; toward the face or front, forward.

i te i śí a, *v. i., adj., fr.* ite *and* iśia ; to be ill-favored ; ugly.

i tĕ ko a, *adv., fr.* ite ; at or to the front or face, in front.

í tĕ ko a hi, *adv.* of time, *fr.* ite-koa ; soon, presently, at a future time not very distant.

í tĕ ko a hi duk, *adv. of time, fr.* itekoahi ; soon, in a little while ; when, or if, a future time not very distant arrives.

í te ma tse e″ tsiś, *n.* See Local Names.

í tĕ ta, *adv.* and *n.* ; on the face ; the cheek.

í tĕ ta a du ho pi, *n.* ; a dimple.

í tĕ tsą ki, *v. i., adj., fr.* ite *and* tsąki ; possessed of a handsome face, pretty.

i te ú i, *n., fr.* ite *and* ui ; vermilion or other pigment used in painting the face.

í ti pe, *n., fr.* i *and* tipe ; something which closes or covers, as a lid, a fall-trap, etc. See mai-tipe.

i tó di, *v. i., ? reflex.* ; to be ashamed of, to feel shame.

i tó di ke, *v. t.* ; to cause to be ashamed, to shame.

i tó hi ke, *n., fr.* tohike ; dyestuff for coloring blue.

i tó hi śi ke, *n., fr.* tohiśike ; material for dyeing bluish or green.

i tó pa, *ord. num., fr.* topa ; fourth.

11

i tó pa du, *adv., fr.* itopa ; fourthly, in the fourth place or order.

i tó pa du ke, *v. t., fr.* itopadu ; to put in the fourth place or order.

í tsą ki, *v. comp.,* often used as pronoun, *fr.* i *and* tsaki ; he, she, or it alone ; he by himself, unaided.—mitsąki, I alone. ditsąki, you alone.

i tsá ti, *n., fr.* i *and* tsati ; oil or other material used to render a surface smooth.

i tsá′ ti, *n.* ; the Isanti or Santee Dakotas. This word is simply the Hidatsa pronunciation of the Dakota word.

i tsa ú zi e, *v. t., fr.* uzie ; to meet another person face to face, to meet in coming from opposite directions.

i tsé, *v., ? reflex.* ; to waken up, to arouse one's self.

i tsí. See itsii.

i tsi, *v. i.* ; to be awake.

í tsi, *n.* ; the human foot ; the claws of a fowl ; the hind paws of a quadruped.—matsi, my foot. ditsi, your foot. Itsi, his foot. See tsi.

I tsi a du tsá mi he [-wihe], *n.* ; the toes.

I tsíe pu, *n., fr.* itsi *and* iepu ; the toe-nails.

i tsí di ke, *n., fr.* i *and* tsidike ; yellow dye-stuff, a lichen found by the Indians on dead pine-trees in the mountains. The name has been recently applied to turmeric and other yellow dyes obtained from the whites.

í tsi he, *v. t., fr.* itsi ; to arouse another person.

i tsí i, *v. i.* and *adj.* ; to be strong ;

its

physically strong; said of organized beings.

i tsí i ke, *v. t.*; to strengthen; strengthened.

í tsi ka, *adv.* and *adj.*; first, foremost.

í tsi ka ko a, *adv., fr.* itsika; formerly, in the beginning, very long ago; used in reference to very remote past time.

í tsi ka ma hi diś, *n., fr.* itsika, ma, *and* hídi ; one of the Hidatsa names for their Deity, or object of greatest veneration.

I tsi śí pi śa, *n., fr.* Itsi *and* śipiśa; the Blackfoot Indians.

I tsí ti, *n., fr.* Itsi ; a foot-print, a track; his, her, or its foot-print.

i tsí tsá du i, *v. i., fr.* itsitsi; becoming very bright.

i tsí tsi, *v. i., adj.*; very bright, gleaming, resplendent.

i tsí tsi ke, *v. t.*; to cause to brighten ; made bright.

í tski, *v. i.*; to be large enough for a purpose, to contain, to accommodate ; said if it is desired to cut a pair of moccasins out of a piece of buckskin, and, on laying on the pattern, the piece is found to be large enough, etc.— itskitats, it is not large enough.

i tskí ti, *n., fr.* i *and* tskiti; an instrument for shearing off, or cutting close, as a scissors. See maitskiti.

i tsú a śu ka, *n., fr.* śuka; a horse. The meaning of the first three syllables is not now known. Some of the tribe think that the word was originally itsímaśuka, the 'strong dog' or 'strong beast of burden'.

i tsú ka, *n.*; a man's or woman's younger brother.—matsuka, my

kad

brother. ditsuka, or nitsuka, your brother.

i tśú a śu ka. See itsuaśuka, which is sometimes pronounced thus.

i tú di, *v. i., adj.*; containing pus, purulent, suppurating.

i tú lii, *n.*; a dress, coat, or shirt; one's own dress. — matúlii, my coat. ditulii, your coat.

i tú ka, *same as* itekoa.

i tu pá, *n.*; any wild feline, particularly the Canada lynx, *Lynx canadensis.*

i tu pa ic tí a, *n., fr.* itupa *and* ictia; the puma, *Felis concolor.*

i tu pa pú zi, *n., fr.* itupa *and* puzi; the red lynx, *Lynx rufus.*

í wą ki, *same as* imąki.

k.

ka, *prep.*; at; in; suffixed to nouns, it forms adverbs of place.

ka, hypothetical word for daughter. See iká.

ka, an adjective, or qualifying suffix, denoting quantity.—tuaka, how much ? hídika (or hídikąts), this much, so much.

ka, *2d pers. of* ke, an auxiliary suffix; to make ; to cause.

ka', *v. i.*; to laugh.

ka dá, *v. i.*; to flee from, to run away.

ką́ da lia, *v. t., prob. fr.* ki *and* adalia; to kindle.

ką́ da mi [-wi], *v. t.*; to remember, to recollect.

ką́ da mi ke, *v. t.*; to cause to remember, to remind.

ka ką́ tsi, *v. i.*; to be willing.

ka ką́ tsi ke, *v. t.*; to cause to be willing, to persuade or induce.

ka dé [**karé**], *v.*; to vomit.

ka dé ti, *v. i.*; to have a desire to vomit, to feel nausea.

ka dé kśa, to vomit excessively or continuously.

ká di, *v. t.*; to ask for a gift, to beg.

ka díc ka [**-ric-**], *n.*; lightning.

ká di kśa, *v. t., fr.* kadi; to beg excessively, habitually, shamelessly.

ka dí śta [**-ri-**], *adj.*; small; refers to size, not quantity or number.

ka dí śtú du i, *v. i., fr.* kadíśta; decreasing gradually in size.

ka dí śta de, *adj.*; almost small; almost small enough.

ka dí śta di, *adj.*; very small.

ka dí śta ke, *v. t.*; to cause to be small; decreased, diminished.

ka dí śta kśa, *adj.*; constantly small.

ka dí tska [**-ri-**], *adj.*; to glisten, to shine brightly by reflected light.

ka dí tska pa [**-ri-**], *v. i.*; to stick; to adhere, as a glued or pasted surface.

ka dí tska pa he, *v. t.*; to stick, to place in contact with an adhesive surface.

ka dí tska pa ke, *v. t.*; to cause to adhere, to apply an adhesive substance.

ká dse, *v. i.* and *t.*; to blow with the mouth; to blow away.

ka dú, *n.*; a season of the year, a period of time marked by some natural phenomenon.

ka dú du, *adv.*; during the season.

ká du lie, *n.*; an old woman. lie is an adjective signifying *old*,

and kadu is, I doubt not, the original noun; but I have never heard it without the adjective suffixed. See itaka and itakalie.

ka é, *v. t.*; to scratch with the nails.

ká he, *v. t.*; synon. dakábe.

ka hé, *v. t.*; to set free, to liberate.

ká' ke, *v. t., fr.* ka'; to cause to laugh. — ka'ike, it makes him laugh.

ka ké' ki, *v. i.*; to make a loud rattling or stamping noise.

ká ki, *v. i.*; to roll, as a wheel.

ka kÏ lii, *adj.*; round, circular.

ka kÏ lii de, *adj.*; almost circular; irregularly circular.

ka kÏ lii ke, *v. t.*; to make circular; to cause to be circular.

kú kśa, *n.*; any large tuber, as the potato, wild artichoke, etc.

ká' ksa, *v. i., fr.* ka'; to laugh excessively.

ka kú i, *n.*; a squash.

ká mi [**-wi**], *same as* komi, which is more common.

ka míc ka, *adj.*; tough, hard, and elastic.

ka míc ki śu, *adj., fr.* kamicka *and* iśu; the name of a waterfowl, which sheds its quills on lakes. The quills are collected by the Indians on the leeward shores, split, dyed, and used in embroidery like porcupine quills. The name applies to both bird and quills.

ká mi he, *same as* komihe.

ka pe, or **kapi,** verbal root; scratch, lacerate. See adakapi, dukapi, etc.

ká ptsi, verbal root; nick, notch.

ka rá, *same as* kada.

ka rá tsi, *same as* kadatsi.

kar

ka rí sta. See kadista and its derivatives.

kạ́ ta ke, *v. t.*; to turn inside out; to roll up the sleeves.

kaí' ti, *adj.* and *adv.*; true, real; truly, really; exceedingly.

ka tí a, *adj.*; extended, as the arms in yawning, as the hands outspread.

ka tí he, *v. t.*; to extend, to stretch out.

ka tí ke, *v. t.*; to change, or pour, from one vessel to another. kạtika.

kạ́ tsi, *v.*; to make a buffalo-surround.

kạ́ tsi, *v. i., adj.*; to be extinguished, as a light or a fire; to be cooled by being blown on with the mouth, or by being taken from the fire and set aside to cool.

kạ́ tsi he, *v. i.*, 3d pers.; to cool by blowing, etc.; to extinguish a light or a fire.—kạtsimats, I extinguish. kạtsidats, you extinguish.

ka tsú ka, *adj.*; to be swollen and hardened, as a diseased joint, or a cicatrix on a tree.

ka ú sta, *adj.*; small in quantity or number.

ka ú sta—ali″ pi, *n., adj., fr.* kausta *and* alipi; a small part or portion; fractional.

ka ú sta de, *adj.*; almost too few.

ka ú sta di, *adj.*; very few; a very small quantity.

ka ú sta du i, *v. i.*; decreasing in number or quantity.

ka ú sta ke, *v. t.*; to cause to decrease in number or quantity; reduced in numbers.

ka wíc ka, *adj., same as* kamic-

kia

ka, and a more common pronunciation than the latter.

ka wíc ki su, *n., same as* kamic-kiṡu.

kaí za, a diminutive of limited use applied to about twenty words of the language.

kaí zi, *same as* kaza.

ke, *v. t.*; to give away, to present.

ke, *v. t.*; to scratch, as in relieving an itchy sensation; synon. with kae, of which it may be a contraction.

ke, a suffix to verbs, adjectives, etc., or a verb auxiliary; to make, to cause; to change condition; to use as. Where ke is suffixed, ki is commonly prefixed. In the sense of "to use as", it is added to nouns; and the words thus formed may be used as nouns; as, makadiṡtake, *a doll*, from makadiṡta, *a child;* miduliake, *a pop-gun*, from midulia, *a gun.*

ki, *v. t.*; to bear on the back; to carry a heavy load.

ki, an intensifying prefix to verbs denoting that the action is done forcibly, completely, frequently, under circumstances of difficulty, etc. ki often merely strengthens without altering the meaning—the intensified word requiring no separate definition; but in other cases it totally changes the significance.

ki, an interjection, used when something false or absurd is heard.

ki a á ti, *v. t., fr.* aati; to hit severely with a missile.

ki a dá du i, *v. i., fr.* adadui; becoming rapidly and exceedingly painful.

ki ă dă lia, *v. i., fr.* adalia; to be burned up, consumed by fire.

ki ă dă lia ke, *v. t.*; to cause to be consumed by fire; to burn up, to reduce to ashes.

ki ă dă liă pe, *v. t., fr.* adaliape; to kick severely.

ki ă dă lié lie, *v. t., fr.* adalielie; to hold securely.

ki ă dă lié se, *v. t., fr.* adaliese; to tear to pieces with the foot.

ki ă dă lió lii, *intensive form of* adaliolii.

ki a dắ lipi ke, synon. with adạlipike.

ki ă dă liŭ e, *v. t., fr.* adaliu; to overthrow completely, or by kicking violently.

ki ă dă kắ pe, *v. t., fr.* adakape; to scratch vigorously with the paws; said when an animal tears up the ground by scratching.

ki ă dă kI de, *v. t., fr.* adakide; to push completely away with the foot.

ki ă dă kí ti, *v. i., fr.* adakiti; said of a wide stretch of country, that has been thoroughly cleared by fire.

ki ă dă mí di, *v. t., intensive of* adamidi.

ki ă dă pa pă du i, *v. i., fr.* adapapi; becoming rapidly and extensively scorched.

ki ă dă pắ pi, *intensive of* adapapi.

ki ă dă pắ pi ke, *v. t.*; to cause to be extensively scorched or chapped.

ki ă dă pe, *v. t., fr.* adape; to kick angrily or repeatedly.

ki ă dă sŭ ki, *v. t., fr.* adasuki; to completely erase with the foot.

ki ă dă tắ pi, *v. t., fr.* adatạpi; to squeeze severely under foot.

ki ă dă te, *v. i., intensive form of* adate.

ki ă dă té he, *v. t., fr.* adatéhe; to kill a number by trampling, to kill a brood of young birds by accidentally stepping on them, to trample a number of insects to death.

ki ă dă tó' ti, *v. t., fr.* adató'ti; to shake vigorously or entirely with the foot.

ki ă dă tsắ ki, *v. t., fr.* adatsạki; to divide a thick body rapidly by fire.

ki ă da tskắ pi, *v. i., intensive form of* adatskapi.

ki a dạ tsku ă du i, *v. i., fr.* adạtsknadui; becoming wet throughout.

ki a dắ tsku i, *v. i., fr.* adạtskui; entirely wet, etc.

ki a dắ tsku i ke, *v. t.*; to moisten thoroughly or rapidly.

ki a dé, *v., fr.* ade; to pain exceedingly.

ki a dé a du i, *v. i.*; becoming very sultry.

ki a dé he, *v. t.*; to be very angry; to become suddenly very angry.

ki a dé ke, *v. t.*; to make exceedingly painful, etc.

kí a dĕ tsi, *adj.*; to be possessed of admirable qualities, to be brave, skilful, intelligent, ingenious, enduring, etc.; to be skilled in any particular art or calling.

kí a de tsi ke, *v. t.*; to cause to be brave, enduring, or skilful; to instruct thoroughly in any art.

kí ă di a sắ dsi ke, *v. t., fr.* adi-

kiă

'ašadsike; to impoverish greatly, to render destitute.

ki ă di i tă du i, *v. t.,fr.* adiiti; becoming ravenously hungry.

ki ă di í ti, *v., intensive of* adiiti.

ki ă di í ti ke, *v. t.*; to starve, to deprive of food.

ki a du ă du i, *v. i.,fr.* aduadui; becoming entirely or excessively bitter.

ki ă du i, *v. i.,fr.* adui; entirely bitter.

ki ă du i ke, *v. t.*; to render completely or exceedingly bitter or pungent.

ki a hú ke, *v. t.,fr.* ahuke; to multiply rapidly, to increase largely and rapidly; to increase every one of a number of objects.

ki a hó e, *v. t.,fr.* alioe; to conceal carefully or completely; to conceal all.

ki a kǎ lipi, *v. t.,fr.* akalipi; to step completely over a wide space; to cross a chasm successfully but with difficulty.

ki a kǎ ma he, *v. t., intensive form of* akamahe.

ki a kǎ ma he ke, *v. t.*; to divide completely into six equal parts.

ki a kǎ ma ke, divided into six equal parts.

ki ǎ ka pe, *v. t.,fr.* akape; to court assiduously.

ki ak' de, *v. t.,fr.* akde; to seize and bear off; to carry to a distance; to carry the entire of anything away.

ki ak' hu, *v. t.,fr.* akhu; to bring with difficulty, or from a distance; to bring all.

ki ǎ ki ka he, *v. t.,fr.* akikahe; said when something is captured

kia

and brought from a distance; as when a war-party brings home a prize in haste and danger, but in triumph.

ki ǎ ki tsa, *v. t.,fr.* akitsa; to miss widely; to miss at every trial.

ki ak' ši e, *v. t.,fr.* akšie; to hold firmly.

ki ak' šu e, *v. t.,fr.* akšue; to spit on repeatedly.

ki ak' tsi še, *v. t.,fr.* aktsišě; to look l o n g or scrutinizingly through a door or window.

ki a ma hó ka, *v. i.,fr.* amahoka; to be far within; deep under ground.

ki a ma hó ka ke, *v. t.*; to place far within; to put all in.

ki a má ki, *v. i.*; to remain sitting long or steadily.

ki a má ki ke, *v. t.,fr.* amakike.

ki a má tsa ki, *v. i., intensive form of* amatsaki.

ki a má tsa ki ke, *v. t.*; to soil entirely with earth; to soil all of a number of objects with earth.

ki a pá di, *v. i.,fr.* apadi; to grow vigorously.

ki a pá di ke, *v. t.*; to cause to grow vigorously; to cause all to grow.

ki ǎ pi ke, *v. t.,fr.* apike; to place together closely or continuously.

ki a tá di, *v. i.,fr.* atadi; to go out and remain out; said, too, when a number of individuals go out from a house.

ki a tá di ke, *v. t.*; to cause to go out, etc.

ki a tǎ ki ke, *v. t.,fr.* atakike, to render completely white.

kia

ki a tá zi ko a, *v. i., intensive of* atazikoa.

ki a té, *v. i., fr.* ate; to come into full view; to come suddenly into full view.

ki a té he, *v. t.*; to present immediately to full view.

ki a té he ke, *v. t.*; to cause to appear entirely; to exhibit all of a number of objects.

ki ä tskä, *intensive form of* ätskä.

ki ä tskä du i, *v. i., fr.* ätskädui; becoming rapidly very fierce.

ki ä tskä ke, *v. t.*; to persistently aggravate to fierceness.

ki dá, *n.*; a husband.

kí da he, *v. t., fr.* kida *and* he; to marry; said of the woman, if the marriage is informal or against parental consent.

ki da hé, *v., same as* kiduhe, which is more common.

ki da he ká' ti ke, *v. t., intensive form of* daheká'tike.

ki da hiá pe si, *v. i., fr.* daliapesi; to rise perpendicularly to a great height; to extend perpendicularly to a great length.

ki da hiá pe si ke, *v. t.*; to cause to be perpendicular to a great height or length.

ki da hiá pi, *v. t., fr.* daliapi; to peel entirely, to strip a tree bare.

ki da hié si, *v. i., fr.* daliési; torn to shreds with teeth.

ki da hié si ke, *v. t.*; to cause to be torn to shreds with teeth.

ki dä lii se, *v. t., prob. fr.* ki *and* adälliše; to forget.—makidälliišets, I forget. dakidälliišets, you forget. kidalliišets, it is forgotten.

ki da li pi, *v. i., intensive form of* daliipi.

kid

ki dá lipa, *v. t., fr.* dalipa; to embrace, to hug.

ki da hiú e, *v. t., fr.* daliue; to spill or overset completely and forcibly.

ki da hiú pi, *v. t., fr.* daliupi; to drink or absorb a large amount completely and rapidly.

ki da ká he, *v. t., fr.* dakahe; to stretch completely out.

ki da ká hi si, *v. t., fr.* dakahisi; to carry in the arms; to hold long in the arms.

ki däk a hió hi, *v. t., fr.* dakaliolii; to break completely across with a blow; to break something large, or to break a number of objects across with a blow.

ki däk a kí ti, *v. t., fr.* dakakiti; to scrape the hair entirely away.

ki däk a mí di, *v. t., fr.* dakamidi; to turn completely by force; to twill tightly by sudden force.

ki däk a mí di ke, *v. t.*; to cause to turn completely by sudden force.

ki däk a mï tsi, *v. t., fr.* dakamitsi; to mince completely, to chop fine all that is given to be chopped.

ki däk a pá ki, *v. i., fr.* dakapaki; to bloom fully; to expand numerous blossoms.

ki da ká pe, *v. t., intensive form of* dakape.

ki da ká pi, *v. t.*; to pick out, to cull, to separate; to pick grain from chaff, stones from coffee, etc.

ki da ka pï lii, *v., fr.* dakapilii; to float well or continuously.

ki da ka pï lii ke, *v. t.*; to

kid

cause to float continuously; to cause all to float.

ki da ká ptsi, *v. i., fr.* dakaptsi; covered with nicks or tallies.

ki da ka pú si, *v. i., fr.* dakapuši; greatly inflated; permanently inflated.

ki da ka pú si ke, *v. i.*; to inflate extensively or permanently.

ki dăk' a ta, *v. t., fr.* dăkata; to smash completely; to smash and resmash.

ki dăk a tá lii, *v. i., intensive form of* dăkatạlii.

ki dă-ka' ti, *n., fr.* kida *and* ka'ti; a first husband.

ki dăk a tó' ti, *v. t., fr.* dăkato'ti; to shake repeatedly or continuously with force suddenly applied.

ki dăk a wí di, *same as* kidăkamidi.

ki dăk a wĭ tsi, *same as* kidăkamitsi.

ki da kí ti, *v. i., fr.* dakiti and nearly synonymous with it, but more commonly used.

ki dăk sạ́ ki, *v. t., fr.* dăkṣạki; to wound repeatedly or severely by throwing missiles.

ki dăk' si, *v. t.*; to bundle securely or completely.

ki dăk sí pi, *v. i., intensive form of* dăkṣipi.

ki dăk sí pi ke, *v. t.*; to cause to be much later.

ki dăk tá de, *v. t., fr.* dăktáde; to drive hard; to nail securely or completely.

ki dăk tsá da ke, *v. t.*; synon. with dăktsadake.

ki dăk tsạ́ ki, *v. t., fr.* dăktsạki; to chop all up; to chop into numerous pieces.

ki dăk tsă ti, *v. t., fr.* dăktsa-

kid

ti; to impale securely or frequently.

ki dăk tsi, *v. i., ? fr.* dăktsia; to settle as water; also kidaktsio.

ki dăk tsi ắ du i, *v. i.*; increasing rapidly and greatly in weight.

ki dăk tsí a ke, *v. t., intensive form of* dăktsiake.

ki dăk tsí ke, *v., fr.* dăktsike; to continue, remain, or follow one another, in single file; said of the motion of a flock of wildgeese, or of a band of antelope running after their leader.

ki dăk tsú ti, *v. t., fr.* dăktsuti; to braid completely.

ki dăk ú di, *v. t., fr.* dăkudi; to fan; a form more commonly employed than dăkudi.

ki dăk ú dsi, *v. t., fr.* dăkudsi; to swing vigorously or continuously.

ki dăk ú dsi ke, *v. t.*; to cause to oscillate continuously.

ki dăk ú liti, *intensive form of* dakuliti.

ki dăk ú liti ke, *v. t.*; to decrease greatly or rapidly in weight.

ki da mi hé ke [+ kinawi-heke], *v. t., fr.* damiheke; to divide completely into three equal parts; divided equally in three.

ki dá mi ke, *same as* kidamiheke.

ki da mĭ tsi, *v. t., intensive form of* damitsi.

ki da mó ki, *v. i.*; to ebb away, to sink down, to fall as a river.

ki dá mu ke [ki ná wuke], *v., fr.* damuke; to deepen greatly, rapidly, or throughout.

ki dá pe, *v. t., fr.* dape; to de-

kid

vour by tearing, to tear meat with the teeth and devour it.

ki da psŭ ti, *v. t., intensive form of* dapšuti.

ki dá ša, *v. t., fr.* daša; to cut extensively or **severely** with the teeth.

ki da ší pi, *v. t., fr.* dašipi; to untie completely with the teeth.

ki dá šku, *v. t., fr.* dašku; to take out with the teeth something difficult to extract.

ki dá šte, *v. t., fr.* dašte; to comminute completely.

ki da' ta dé ša, *v. i., fr.* da'ta-deša; to be completely inconsiderate, etc.

ki da' ta dé ša ke, *v. t.;* to cause to be inconsiderate, etc.

ki da' ta hé pi, *v. i., fr.* da'taliepi; to be thoroughly lazy, or always lazy.

ki da' ta hé pi ke, *v. t.;* to cause to be lazy.

ki da' ta i ší a, *v. i., fr.* da'taiša; to be miserable or despondent; to be continually unhappy, **sorry** or ill-tempered; said too of a number of individuals who are unhappy.

ki da' ta i si ŭ du i, *v. i.;* becoming very unhappy, miserable, etc.

ki da' ta i ší a ke, *v. t.;* to make constantly unhappy, etc.

ki da tá pi, *v. t., intensive form of* datapi.

ki da' ta tsá ki, *v. i., fr.* da'tatsaki; to be very happy; constantly happy.

ki da' ta tsa kí ki, *v. t.;* to render very happy; to make all happy.

ki da' ta tsó ki, *v. i., intensive form of* da'tatsoki.

kid

ki da' ta tsó ki ke, *v. t.;* to render very resolute; to inspire all with resolution.

ki da tó' ti, *v. t., fr* dato'ti; to skake vigorously in the mouth; to **worry** to death by shaking in the mouth.

ki dá tsa, *v. t., fr.* da'tsa; to bite severely or repeatedly.

ki da tsŭ ti, *v. t., fr.* datsati, and nearly or quite synonymous.

ki da tsí pi, *v. t., fr.* datsipi; to lick repeatedly and **continuously**; to lick all over.

ki da tskŭ pi, *v. t., intensive of* datskapi.

ki da tskŭ ti, *v. t., fr.* datskati; to leak through a large orifice; to leak rapidly or entirely away.

ki da tsó pe, *v., fr.* datsope; to kiss.—makidatsope, I kiss. dakidatsope, you kiss. See ikidatsope.

ki da tsŭ ki, *v. t., intensive form of* datsuki.

ki da wó ki, *same as* kidamoki.

kĭ de, verbal root; push; transfix, impale.

ki dé, *v. i., ? fr.* de; to fly.

ki dé ak de, *v. t., comp. of* kide *and* nkde; to fly off with; to bear off flying, as an eagle with its prey.

ki dé e, *v. i., same as* kide; to fly.

ki dé ša, *v. i., intensive form of* deša.

ki dĕ šá dsi, *v. t., fr.* kidéši *and* adsi; to like very much; to love, but not dearly.

ki dé ša ke [kinešake], *v. t., fr.* dešake; to destroy, exterminate, banish, annul, abrogate; to cure a disease completely, etc.

ki dĕ ši, *v. t.;* to love; said of the affection existing between

kid

.parent and child, husband and wife.

ki dĕ ta, *v. t.*; to fancy, to admire.

ki dĕ tá dsi, *v. t.*, to admire, but not greatly.

kí di, *v. t.*, *? fr.* di; to search for any person or thing, to go for game, to pursue, to seek. kikidi is more commonly used.

kí di e, *v.*; to mount a horse; to ride on horseback.

kĭ di é, *v. i.*; to be greatly terrified.

ki dĭ ki, *v. t.*, *fr.* diki; to strike repeatedly.

ki dĭ si, *v. i.*, *fr.* diši; to dance.

ki do pa hé ke, *v. t.*, *fr.* dopaheke; to divide completely into two equal parts; divided equally in two.

ki dó pa ke, *v. t.*, *synon.* kidopaheke.

ki du é tsa pi ke, *v. t.*, *fr.* duetsapike; to divide into nine equal parts.

ki du hǎ, *imperative of* kiduhe; arise; said if the person is recumbent, not sitting. See duha and duhe.

ki du ha ku té, *n.*, *adv.*, *fr.* kiduha; early morning, time to rise.

ki du ha ku té du, *adv.*, *fr.* kiduhakute; during the early morning.

ki dŭ he, *v. t.*; to arise from a recumbent posture; to lift out of.

ki dŭ hi, *v. i.*; arisen; standing.

ki dŭ hi ke, *v. t.*; to cause or assist to arise from a recumbent posture.

ki dŭ lia, *v. t.*; to spread out on the ground; to spread to dry; to spread bedding.

kid

ki du liǎ dĕ, *v. t.*; to rake; to clean thoroughly by raking.

ki du liǎ de, *v. t.*, *intensive form of* duliǎde.

ki du lié mi, *v. i.*, to settle down, as a river; to dry up; to become shallow.

ki du lié še, *v. t.*, *fr.* dulieše; to tear to pieces.

ki du lié wi, *same as* kiduliemi.

ki du lió lii, *v.*, *fr.* duliolii; to break, or to be broken completely across.

ki du lió lii ke, *v. t.*; to cause to be completely broken.

ki du lió ki, *v. t.*, *fr.* dulioki; to comb out, to comb completely or thoroughly.

ki dú lipi, *v. t.*, *fr.* dulipi; to take down something that is hanging high.

ki du ká pi, *v. t.*, *fr.* dukapi; to lacerate extensively or severely.

ki du kĭ ti, *v. t.*, *intensive of* dukiti.

ki du kŭ ti, *v. t.*; pluck out extensively.

ki du mǎ lii ta, *v. i.*, *fr.* dumaliita; to ride or move repeatedly and rapidly back and forth.

ki du mǎ lii ta-ti di é, *v.*; to run or ride back and forth, as is done when one man alone makes a war-signal.

kí du mi [+ -wi], *v. t.*; to count.

ki du mí di, *v. t.*, *fr.* dumidi; to twill thoroughly.

ki du mí lia [-wilia], *intensive form of* dumilia.

ki du sǎ, *v. t.*, *fr.* duša; to place in security, to store or put away with care.

ki du sĭ pi, *v. t.*, *fr.* dušipi; to open widely or completely.

ki dú śke, *v. t., fr.* duśke; to open a door or lid widely.

ki du śú ki, *v. t., fr.* duśuki; to wash entirely or thoroughly by rubbing.

ki du tá, *v., fr.* duta; to burst violently, to fly to pieces.

ki du tá̧ pi, *v. t., fr.* dutá̧pi; to squeeze long and hard.

ki du tá̧ ti, *v. t., intensive of* dutati.

ki dú ti, *v. t., fr.* duti; to eat up; to devour, to eat all; said also if you speak of eating an animal still living, conveying the idea that you will both kill and eat.

ki du tó' ti, *v. t., fr.* duto'ti; to cover by sprinkling; to exhaust by dredging or sprinkling.

ki du tsá da, *v., fr.* dutsada; to slide far or rapidly.

ki du tsá̧ ki, *v. t., fr.* dutsa̧ki; to dissever completely and repeatedly.

ki du tsá ti, *fr.* dutsati; to impale securely.

ki dú tse, *v. t., fr.* dutse; to take off under difficulties; to take and hold securely.

ki du tsí pi, *v. t., fr.* dutsipi; to completely untie anything secured by hard and numerous knots.

ki du tsĭ́ śi, *v. t., fr.* dutsiśi; to sprink back, to regain suddenly and completely the original position when released from a bending pressure.

ki du tsĭ́ ti, *v. t., fr.* dutsiti; to raze to the ground, to completely destroy a building.

ki du tská̧ pi, *v. t., fr.* dutska̧pi; to pinch severely or repeatedly.

ki du tskĭ́ śi, *v. t., fr.* dutskiśi;

---

to wash thoroughly, to wash clean; to wash all that is given to be washed.

ki du tskí ti, *v. t., intensive form of* dutskiti.

ki du tskú pi, *v. t., fr.* dutskupi; to bend in several places; to fold repeatedly.

ki du tsú ki, *v. t., fr.* dutsuki; to knead the abdomen long and vigorously.

ki du wá li ta, *v. i., same as* kidumalita.

ki du wí di, *v. t., same as* kidumidi.

kí e, *v. t.*; to fear.

ki ha hé ta, *v. t., intensive of* haheta.

ki hă lipi, *v. i., fr.* halipi; to sneeze repeatedly.

ki hă lipi ke, *v. t.*; to cause to sneeze hard or repeatedly.

ki ha ká' ti ke, *v. t., fr.* haka'tike; to completely and suddenly arrest progress.

ki há ka̧ tsi, *v. t., fr.* haka̧tsi; to butcher completely, to cut up all the meat killed.

ki ha pá ke, *v. t., fr.* hapake; to render very cold, or cold throughout; chilled, frozen.

ki ha̧' pé śa du i, *v. i., intensive form of* ha̧'peśadui.

ki ha̧' pé śe, *v. i., fr.* ha̧'peśe; completely dark.

ki ha̧' pé śe ke, *v. t.*; to completely exclude light.

ki ha śĭ́ śi, *v. i., fr.* haśiśi; to smart severely.

ki ha śĭ́ śi ke, *v. t.*; to cause to smart extensively or severely.

ki ha tsí te, *v. t., intensive form of* hatsite.

ki hă tská du i, *v. i., fr.* hatskadui; increasing rapidly in length.

kih

ki hǎ tski ke, *v. t.*; to lengthen rapidly a n d greatly; greatly lengthened.

ki hí ke, *r.,fr.* híke; entirely drunk up.

ki hi sǎ dsi, *v. i., fr.* hišadsi; to be completely reddish.

ki hi sǎ dsi ke, *v. t.*; to dye throughout of a dull red color.

ki hǐ si ke, *v. t.,fr.* dišike; to dye red; to dye the entire of anything red.

ki hi si sǎ du i, *v. t., intensive of* bišišadui.

ki hi sǐ si ke, *v. t.*; to cause to assume a reddish hue rapidly or throughout.

ki hi tǎ du i, *v. i.,fr.* hitadui; rapidly increasing in speed.

ki hí ta ke, *v. t.,fr.* hitake; to accelerate motion greatly; to increase the speed of a number of objects.

ki ho' pá du i, *v. i., intensive form of* ho'padui; more commonly used than the simple form.

ki ho pá se, *v. t.,fr.* hopaṣe; to horrify; to horrify all.

ki hó' pi ke, *v. t.,fr.* ho'pike; to riddle, to perforate in many places.

ki hú, *v. t., comp. of* ki *and* hu; to come with a load; to come bearing on the back.

ki hú a, *v. i.,fr.* hua; to cough repeatedly or severely.

ki hú a ke, *v. t.*; to cause to cough repeatedly.

kí lia, *n.*; the paunch, the stomach or stomachs of an animal.

ki lia a du pi dǎ lipa, *n.,fr.* kilia, adu, *and* pidalipa; the rumen or first stomach of a ruminant.

ki lǎ da li ke, *v. t.,fr.* liada-

kili

liike; to starve completely, to make very lean; to make a number lean.

ki lǎ da lí kša ke, *v. t., intensive form of* hǎdalikšake.

ki lia lǎ du i, *v. i., fr.* lialiadui; becoming completely rough.

ki lǎ lii, *v. i.,fr.* lialii; to be entirely or completely striped.

ki lǎ li ke, *v. t.*; to cover with parallel b a n d s; completely striped.

ki lia lú a ke, *v. t., intensive of* lialiuake.

ki lia kǎ du i, *v. t.*; used the same as liakadui, but more commonly; said of a healing sore, etc.

ki lǎ ka hé ta, *v. i., intensive form of* liakaheta.

ki lǎ ka ke, *v. t.,fr.* liakake; to render a large surface itchy.

ki lia kú pa du i, *v. i.*; becoming extensively furrowed.

ki lia kú pi, *v. i.,fr.* liakupi; extensively furrowed, furrowed over the entire surface.

ki lia kú pi ke, *v. t.*; to mark the entire surface with furrows; completely furrowed.

ki lǎ ma dsi ke, *v. t.,fr.* liamadsi; to cause to appear much branched; to depict as very branching.

ki lǎ mi ke, *v. t.,fr.* liamike; to make entirely diverging or scattering.

ki lǎ pa dui, *v. i.,fr.* liapadui; wearing thin throughout, or in numerous places.

ki lia pá ti, *v. i., intensive of* liapati.

ki lia pá ti he, *v. i.*; to eat to complete satiety.

ki lia pa ti kša, *v. i.*; synon. with liapatikša.

ki lia pa ti kša ke, *v. t.*; to gorge, to glut; to feed a number of persons to excess.

ki liá pi he, *v. t.. fr.* liapihe; to lose hopelessly; to lose all.

ki há pi ke, *v. t., fr.* liapike; to scrape or wear thin throughout.

ki lia' pi ke, *v. t.*; hopelessly lost; all lost.

ki lia' pi kša. See liapikša.

ki liá pi kša, synon. with liapikša.

ki liá pi kša ke, *v. t.*; to scrape, wear, or rub to thinness the entire of a skin or other such article.

ki liä tæta ki, *fr.* liatataki, and nearly or quite synonymous.

ki liä ta ta ki ke, *intensive form of* liatatakike.

ki liä tsa, *n., fr.* kilia *and* itsa, *lit., They Refused the Paunch;* the Crow Indians. Lewis and Clarke spell this " kee-heet-sas" on their map, and speak of a portion of the Crows as " Paunch Indians". (See Lewis and Clarke, p. 96). For the origin of this name see a preceding page of this work.

ki liä wi ke, *same as* kiliamike.

ki lié mi ke, *v. t., intensive of* liemike, but more commonly used.

ki lié mi kša ke, *v. t., fr.* liemikša; to cause to be constantly very lonesome or melancholy; to make a number lonesome.

ki lié pi, *v. i., fr.* liepi; entirely shallow.

ki lié pi ke, *v. t.*; to make entirely shallow, to leave no deep part; dried or drained to shallowness.

ki lié wi ke, *same as* kiliemike.

ki lii di ä du i, *v. i., fr.* liidia; becoming rapidly or extensively itchy or sensitive.

ki lii di a ke, *v. t.*; to cause to be entirely or extensively sensitive or itchy.

ki lii di a kša, *v. i.*; denoting itching, constant or excessive, over the entire surface or afflicting a number.

ki lii di a kša ke, *v. t.*; to cause constant extensive itching, etc.

ki lii é ke, *v. t., intensive of* liieke.

ki lii pi, *v. i., fr.* liipi; entirely wrinkled.

ki lii pi ke, *v. t.*; to make entirely wrinkled.

ki lió ka di ti, *intensive* (and common) *form of* liokaditi.

ki lio pa še, *v. t., fr.* liopáše; to occasion general terror.

ki lio pa si ke, *v. t.*; to cause general or continued alarm.

ki lio ta ká dsi ke, *v. t., fr.* iliotakadsi; to change to a whitish color.

ki lio ta ká du i, *v. i., fr.* iliotakadui; whitening throughout.

ki lio tá ki ke, *v. t., fr.* iliotakike; to bleach uniformly throughout; to paint entirely white; whitened, bleached.

ki liu, *num. adj.*; five.

ki liú a he, *v. t.*; to make five; made into five.

ki liú a he ke, *v. t.*; to divide into five parts; divided into five parts.

ki liú a ke, *v. t.*, synon. with kiliuabeke.

ki ic tí a, *v. i., fr.* ictia (*intensive form*).

kii

ki̇̀ ic ti á du i, *v. i.*; increasing rapidly or greatly.

ki̇̀ ic tí a ke, *v. t.*; to cause to be enlarged greatly or through-out; to increase several objects.

ki i dá mi ke [-nawi-], *v. t., fr.* idamike, and of similar mean-ing.

ki i dí a ḣi, *v. i., fr.* idiaḣi; to sigh repeatedly.

ki i di pá du i, *v. i., fr.* idipa-dui, and used synonymously.

ki i dᴵ pi, *v. i., intensive form of* idipi.

ki i dᴵ pi ke, *v. t., fr.* idipike; to fatten rapidly; to fatten a number.

ki i di pᴵ kṡa ke, *v. t.*; to make constantly fat.

ki i di tsi i ṡí a ke, *v. t.* See iditsiiṡiake.

ki i dᴵ tsi ke, *v. t., intensive of* iditsike; nearly or quite similar in meaning to the simple form.

ki i di tsi tsạ ḱi ke, *v. t.* See iditsitsakike.

ki i dó pa du ke, *v. t., fr.* ido-paduke; to change to the second order or position, to change from some other position and place second.

ki i dó pa ke, *v. t.*; to make sec-ond; to change to second.

ki i há ke, *v. t., fr.* ihake; to make entirely different, to change all attributes.

ki i ḣá tsa ḱi, *v. i., fr.* iḣiatsaki; stained extensively with dirt.

ki i ḣá tsa ḱi ke, *v. t.*; to stain completely or extensively with dirt.

ki i ḣó a de, *v. i., fr.* iḣoade; to be severely sick; said, too, of a number suffering from an epi-demic.

kii

ki i ḣó a de ke, *v. t.*; to make sick; sickened.

ki i ko ki, *v. t., fr.* ikoki; to hang up high or securely.

ki i kú pa, *v. t., fr.* ikupa; to accompany closely or continu-ally.

ki i kú' pa, *v. t., intensive form of* ikú'pa.

ki i kú' pa dsi, *v. t., intensive of* ikú'padsi.

ki i ku' pá dsi ke, *v. t.*; to cause to dislike.

ki i kú' pa ke, *v. t.*; to cause to hate.

ki̇̀ i má ḣipi, *v. i., fr.* imaḣipi; set completely.

ki í mi a, *v. i., fr.* imia; to cry long or frequently; to mourn by crying.

ki í mi a ke, *v. t.*; to cause to cry long, etc.

ki ᴵ psạ ki, *v. t., fr.* ipsạki; to conceal or screen completely.

ki i ṡí a, *v. i., intensive form of* iṡia.

ki i ṡi á du i, *v. i.*; deteriorat-ing greatly.

ki i si á du i ke, *v. t.*; to cause a rapid progressive deteriora-tion.

ki i ṡí a ke, *v. t.*; to make bad, to change from good to bad; greatly damaged; all damaged.

ki i tó di ke, *intensive of* ito-dike.

ki i tó pa du ke, } *v. t.*; to place
ki i tó pa ke, } fourth; to cause to be fourth. See itopake.

ki i tsí i ke, *v. t., fr.* itsiike; to strengthen completely.

ki í tsi ka ke, *v. t., fr.* itsika; to cause to be first; placed first.

ki i tsí tsi, *v. i., intensive of* itsi-tsi; gleaming continuously.

ki i tsí tsi ke, *v. t.*; to cause to gleam.

ki í tski ke, *v. t., fr.* itski; to make large enough.

ki i tú di, *v. i., fr.* itudi; suppurating extensively; said of large or numerous abscesses.

kí i tú di ke, *v. t.*; to cause extensive suppuration.

ki ką́ da mi, *v. t., fr.* kądami; to remember after having long forgotten; to remember completely.

ki ka dą́ tsi ke, *v. t., fr.* kadątsi; to cause to be willing.

ki ka dé, *v. t., intensive of* kade; to vomit all up.

ki ka dé ke, *v. t.*; to cause to vomit.

ki ká di, *v. t., fr.* kadi; to beg repeatedly, to importune; to beg all away.

ki ka dí śta, *v. i., intensive of* kadiśta.

ki ka di śtá du i, *v. i.*; dwindling rapidly.

ki ka dí śta ke, *v. t.*; synon. with kadiśtake, and more commonly used.

ki ka dï tska, *v. i., fr.* kaditska; to glisten continuously or over an extensive surface.

ki ka dï tska ke, *v. t.*; to cause to glisten; made to glisten.

ki ka dï tska pa, *v. i., fr.* kaditskapa; to adhere firmly over a large surface.

ki ka dï tska pa ke, *v. t.*; to cause to adhere, etc.

ki ká dse, *intensive of* kadse.

ki ka ké' ki, *v. i., fr.* kake'ki; to make a continuous rattling noise.

ki ká ki, *v. t.*; to sew; to join by sewing.

ki ka kĭ há du i, *v. i., fr.* kakilii; assuming a circular form.

ki ka kĭ lii ke, *v. t.*; to cause to be entirely or permanently circular.

ki ką́ ta ki, *v. t.*; to turn com pletely inside out.

ki ka tí he, *v. t., intensive of* katibe.

ki ka tí ke, *v. i., fr.* katike; to pour all from one vessel to another, to empty one vessel into another or others.

ki ką́ tsi, *v. i., fr.* kątsi; completely cooled; said, too, of a number of objects which have been cooled or extinguished.

ki ką́ tsi ke, *v. t.*; to cool completely; to cool a number.

ki ka tsú ka, *v. i., intensive of* katsuka.

ki ka tsú ka ke, *v. t.*; to cause to be swelled and hardened.

ki ka ú śta du i, *v. i., fr.* kauśtadui; decreasing greatly and rapidly in number or quantity.

ki ka ú śta ke, nearly synonymous with kauśtake, but more commonly used.

ki kĕ́, *v. t.*; to resemble.

ki ké, *v. t., fr.* ke; to scratch back and forth; to scratch repeatedly or severely.

ki kí di, *v. t., fr.* kidi; to hunt, to seek and pursue.

ki ki liú a he ke, *v. t., fr.* kiliuaheke; to divide completely into five equal parts; divided into five.

ki ki liú a ke, *v. t.*; to cause to be divided into five parts; divided by five.

ki kĭ śki, *v. t.*; to determine quantity or quality in any way; to taste, measure, or gauge with a view to determining quality or quantity; to sound a person's feelings or opinions.

ki kó mi [wi], *synon.* with komi.

ki kó mi he, *v. t., fr.* komihe; to complete or finish perfectly; to finish all.

ki kó mi ke, *v. t.*; to cause to be concluded, terminated, or exhausted; concluded, finished, etc.

ki kó wi he, *same as* kikomihe.

ki kó wi ke, *same as* kikomike.

ki kša, *imperative of* kikše.

ki kše, *v. t.*; to arrange; to repair, to mend, to "fix".

ki kú, *v. t., fr.* ku; to give back, to restore.

ki kú a, *v. t.*; to listen; to hear; to pay attention to.

ki ku há, *v. t.*; to send for a person, to invite.

ki ma á zi, *v. i., fr.* maazi; to be full to overflowing; to be all full—if a number of vessels are referred to.

ki ma á zi ke, *v. t.*; to cause to be filled.

ki má di he, *v. t., fr.* madihe; to cook all the food on hand; to complete the cooking.

ki ma du há pa ke, *v. t., fr.* maduliapake; to set beastly drunk; to set all drunk.

ki ma du litá du i, *v. i., fr.* madulitadui; becoming very foolish.

ki ma dú lita ke, *v. t.*; to make quite foolish.

ki mąk' i a, *v. t., fr.* mąkia; to fight; to battle.

ki mąk i ma ká da ha ti di e", *v. i.*; synonymous with mąkimakadahatidie, but more commonly used.

ki mąk še sá du i, *v. i.*, used in nearly or quite the same sense as mąkšešadui.

ki mąk šé še ke, *v. t., fr.* mąkšešeke; to cause two things to resemble each other in every respect; to cause several things to resemble one another.

ki mąk ší a ka, *v. i., fr.* mąkšiaka; to be of the same size in all dimensions.

ki mąk ší a ka ke, *v. t.*; to cause two or more things to be of the same size in all their dimensions.

ki má ku ke, *v. t.*, *intensive of* makuke, and more commonly used.

ki mé [-we], *v. t.*; to tell, to relate; to disclose a secret.

ki mi á ti ke, *v. t.*; synonymous with miatike.

ki mi dé di, *v. t., fr.* midedi; to come in and sit down; to pay a long visit; to visit frequently.

ki mí di ke, *v. t., fr.* midike; to liquefy completely.

ki mi dú e, *v. i., fr.* midue; to boil vigorously.

ki mi dú e ke, *v. t.*, synonymous with midueke.

ki ó da pí, *v. t., fr.* odapi; to find all, to make a complete discovery.

ki ó hi, *v. t.*, *intensive of* ohi.

ki ó hi ke, *v. t.*; to cause to be attached, to treat with kindness and foster attachment.

ki ó lia ta du i, *v. i., fr.* oliatadui; becoming white throughout.

ki ó lia ti, *v. i., fr.* oliati; to be entirely white or pale.

ki ó lia ti ke, *v. t.*; to render entirely pale.

ki ó ka ta, v. t., fr. okata; to put all on, to dress completely.

ki ó ki, v. t., fr. oki; to hold firmly; to hold all.

ki ó ti, v. t., fr. oti; to be cooked or ripened throughout; all ripened.

ki ó ti ke, v. t.; to cause to be entirely ripened.

ki ó tsha mi [-wi], v. i., intensive of otsliami.

ki ó ze, v. t., fr. oze; to plant all the seed or all of a field, to finish planting.

ki pá, v. t., fr. pa; to powder or grind completely.

ki pa dó pa du i, v. i., fr. padopadui; becoming rapidly low in stature.

ki pa dó pi ke, v. t.; to shorten in stature.

ki pä du i ke, v. t., fr. paduike; to diminish in length; shortened.

ki pá hi, v. i., fr. pabi; to sing loudly or continuously; to sing a song.

ki pá lia du i, v. i., fr. paliadui; becoming extensively chafed.

ki pä litu e, v. t.; to scratch or rub with the finger-tips or knuckles; to rub the hair loose with the fingers; to rub the eyes in sleepiness.

ki pá liu e, v. t., fr. paliue; to spill all out, to empty.

ki pá ka de, v. t., fr. pakade; to stick in numerous places.

ki pa ká pi, v. i., fr. pakapi; to be torn extensively or severely.

ki pá ki di, v. t., fr. pakidi; to push hard; to shove completely away.

ki pá ki si, v. t., fr. pakiši; to rub back and forth as in scouring, or as in drying with a towel; to dry by rubbing.

ki pa mi tsi [-wi-], v. t., fr. pamitsi; to cut all up finely.

ki pa mú dsi [-wu-], v. t., fr. pamudsi; to roll up completely, to make au entire piece into a roll.

ki pa šá ki, v. t., fr. pašaki; to engirdle completely; to put on a belt outside of the robe and all the clothing.

ki pa škú, v. t., fr. pašku; to shove completely through.

ki pa tá ki, v. t., fr. pataki; to shut as a door or a box-lid, to close up as a book, etc.—mide kipaták, shut the door.

ki pä té, v. t., fr. pate; to turn completely over.

ki pá ti, v. i., fr. pati; to fall from a great height.

ki pá ti he, v. t.; to throw down from a great height.

ki pá ti ke, v. t.; to cause to fall from a great height; to shoot a bird sitting iu a tree-top and, thereby, cause it to fall to the ground.

ki pa tó' ti, v. t., fr. pato'ti; to shake repeatedly or vigorously.

ki pa tsä ti, v. t., fr. patsati; to puncture repeatedly.

ki pa tskú pi, v. t., fr. patskupi; to fold several times; to fold into a small bundle.

ki pa tskú pi ke, v. t.; to cause to fold up.

ki pé, v. t., fr. pe; to swallow all, to devour completely.

ki pě, v. t., fr. pe; to triturate finely; same as kipa.

ki pliú ti, v. t., fr. pliuti; to squeeze completely out; to pro-

12

kip

'trude by squeezing or pressing; to eject metallic cartridges.

ki pí, *v. t., fr.* pi ; to deck or tattoo the body extensively.

ki pī di e ke, *v. t., fr.* pidie ; to flute or ruffle, to ornament with ruffles.

ki pkī di, *v. t., intensive of* pakidi.

ki pkí ti, *v. t., fr.* pkiti ; to iron clothes ; to **smooth** completely out.

ki pó a du i, *v. t., fr.* poadui ; to make completely globular.

ki pó pi, *v. i.* ; worn out, as old clothing.

ki pšú ki, *v. i., fr.* pšuki; to belch ; to **b e l c h** repeatedly ; much less used than the simple form.

ki pšú ti, *v. t., fr.* pšuti ; to dislocate, to put out of joint.

ki ptsú ti, *v. t., fr.* ptsuti ; to thrust forward.—deši [neši] kiptsuti, to stick out the tongue.

ki pu á du i, *v. i., fr.* puadui ; becoming rapidly or extensively swollen.

ki pú a ke, *v. t., fr.* puake ; to cause to be greatly or extensively swollen.

ki pú dsi, *v. t., fr.* pudsi ; to mark, sew or wrap extensively or completely.

ki pú dsi ke, *v. t.* ; to cause to be finely marked or wrapped.

ki pú lii, *v. i., intensive of* pulii ; to foam.

ki pú lii ke, *v. t.* ; to cause to **f o a m** greatly ; to cover with foam.

ki pú zi ke, *v. t., fr.* puzike ; to cover with spots or figures.

ki ša pu a hé ke, *v. t., fr.* šapuaheke; to divide into seven equal parts.

kit

ki šá pu a ke, divided into seven parts.

ki ša šú ki ke, *v. t.*; to cause to be completely dull; dulled throughout.

ki ši di ke, *v. t., fr.* šidike ; to render tawny; to smoke a skin until it assumes a tawny hue.

ki ši dī ši, *v. i., intensive of* šidisi.

ki ši dī ši ke, *v. t.* ; to cause to hasten.

ki ši kí a ke, *v. t., fr.* šikia ; to cause to curl or tangle ; tangled.

ki šī ki he, *v. t., intensive of* šikihe.

ki ši pi šá dsi ke, *v. t.* ; to dye blackish.

ki ši pi šá du i, *v. i.* ; darkening throughout.

ki šī pi ša ke, *v. t., fr.* šipišake; to dye black uniformly throughout.

kī ški, *v. t.* ; synonymous with kikiški, but rarely used.

ki šó ki ke, *v. t., fr.* šoki; to widen, to make broad or blunt.

ki šu á du i, *v. i., fr.* šua; decreasing in speed.

ki šú a ke, *v. t.* ; to cause to be slow, to change from a rapid to a slow motion.

ki tá, *intensive of* ta ; killed.

ki tá di, *v. t., fr.* tadi ; to cross completely, as **w h e n** a large party with all its effects crosses a stream.

ki ta hé, *v. t., fr.* tahe; to murder, to slaughter.

ki ta mú e, *v. t., fr.* tamue; to ring long and loudly.

ki ta mú hi ke, *v. t., fr.* tamulii; to cause to be minute, to change from coarse to fine.

ki ta tsá du i, *v. i., fr.* tatsadui ; thickening throughout.

ki tą tsi ke, *v. t.*; to make thick in every part; to thicken all.

ki té, *v. i., fr.* te; to be all dead; said if a number of individuals are referred to.

ki te, verbal root; clear off, make smooth (shave, pluck, etc.).

ki ti, verbal root; *same as* kite.

ki tí di e, *v. i., fr.* tidie; to run far or long; to run away.

ki ti di é ke, *v. t.*; to cause to run far.

ki ti pi ä tsa ki, *v. i., fr.* tipiatsaki; completely soiled with mud.

ki ti pi ä tsa ki ke, *v. t.*; to soil completely with mud.

ki tí sa ke, *v. t., fr.* tiša; to cause to be distant, to remove far away.

ki tí tsä du i, *v. i., fr.* titsadui; thickening rapidly or along the entire length.

ki tí tsi ke, *v. i., fr.* titsike; to thicken throughout.

ki to ha dsä du i, *v. i., fr.* tohadsadui; becoming bluish throughout.

ki to há dsi ke, *v. t., fr.* tohadsike; to dye or color bluish throughout.

ki to há du i, *v. i.*; assuming a pure blue color throughout.

ki tó hi ke, *v. t., fr.* tohike; to dye or color all a pure blue.

ki tó ki si ke, *v. t., intensive of* tohišike.

ki tó pa he, *v. t., fr.* topahe; to divide into four completely.

ki to pa hé ke, *v. t., fr.* topaheke; to divide completely into four equal parts; divided into four equal parts.

ki tó pa ke, *v. t.*; synonymous with kitopaheke.

ki tsä da ke, *v. t., intensive of* tsadake.

ki tsa dá tsa ki ke, *v. t., fr.* tsadatsakike; to soil all over with grease.

ki tsa ká dsi ke, *v. t., fr.* tsakadsi; to improve all moderately.

ki tsą kí ke, *v. t., fr.* tsąkike; to completely cure, improve, or mend; mended, restored, perfected.

ki tsa mé a te, *v. i., fr.* tsameate; to perspire freely, or from the whole surface.

ki tsa mé he, *v. t., fr.* tsamehe; to heat thoroughly.

ki tsa mé ke, heated throughout; changed from very cold to very hot.

ki tsa mú tsa du i, *v. i.*; straightening along the entire length.

ki tsa mú tsi ke, *v. t., fr.* tsamutsike; to straighten completely.

ki tsä ti ke, *v. t., fr.* tsati; to render smooth and glossy; to oil, polish, or varnish.

ki tsa tsú ki ke, *v. t., fr.* tsatsukike; to render completely hard by drying, baking, or otherwise.

ki tsi dá dsi ke, *v. t., fr.* tsidadsi; to dye of a color allied to yellow.

ki tsi dá du i, *v. i.*; becoming yellow throughout.

ki tsi di e ke, *v. t., fr.* tsidie; to cause to be cold; reduced in temperature.

ki tsí di ke, *v. t., fr.* tsidike; dyed all yellow.

ki tsi kó a, *v. i., fr.* tsikoa; thoroughly sweet.

kit

ki·tsi ko ú du i, *v. i.*; becoming sweet throughout.

ki tsi kó a ke, *v. t.*; to make entirely or thoroughly sweet.

ki tsĭ pi, *v. i., fr.* tsipi; to sink entirely, to be lost completely in the water.

ki tsĭ pi ke, *v. t., fr.* tsipike; to cause to sink totally.

ki tsĭ pĭ ti, *v. i., intensive form of* tsipiti.

ki tsi pĭ ti ke, *v. t.*; to place the whole in a condition to sink; to upset all on the water.

ki tso kú du i, *v. i., fr.* tsokadui; becoming entirely hard.

ki tsó ki, *v. i., intensive of* tsoki.

ki tsó ki ke, *v. t.*; to make entirely or permanently hard.

ki tsu tsú ki, *v. i., fr.* tsutsuki; to make a continuous rattling or stamping noise.

ki tsú tsu ti, *v. i., fr.* tsutsuti; to be entirely smooth; uniformly soft.

ki tsú tsu ti ke, *v. t.*; to make entirely or uniformly smooth.

ki u á, *v. t., fr.* uá; to envy continually or maliciously.

ki ú a he, *v. t., intensive of* uahe.

ki u ă lipi, *v. t., fr.* ualipi; to smash to pieces by shooting.

ki u ă ti, *v. t., fr.* uati; to ridicule continuously or severely.

ki u dsá du i, *v. i., fr.* udsadui; becoming uniformly dry.

ki ú dsi, *v. i., fr.* ndsi; to be dried completely.

ki ú dsi ke, *v. t.*; to dry completely.

ki ú zi a, *v. t., intensive of* uzia.

ki wé, *v. t.*; to tell; *same as* kime.

kó a, *prep.*; at; in; suffixed to nouns to form adverbs.

kúa

kó e, *v. i.*; to leave, depart, go from.—makóemits, I will leave—a common equivalent for *good-bye.*

kó ha ti, *n.*; corn, maize.

kó ha ti a, *n.*; a corn-stalk, the stalk or the entire plant.

kó ha ti i śi, *n., fr.* kohati *and* iśi; a bag for containing corn. *Caches* are sometimes called kohatiiśi.

kó ha ti pi, *n.*; coarse corn-meal, such as is made in a wooden mortar.

kó ha ti ta pa, *n.* (tapa, *soft*); flour.

ko ká, *v. t.*; to cease to act, to stop, to discontinue; commonly used imperatively.—kokáts, it is done.

kó mi, *v. i.*; to be finished, exhausted, expended, or completed.

kó mi he, *v. t.*; to finish, to exhaust, to complete.

kó wi, a common pronunciation of komi.

kó wi he, *same as* komihe.

kó zi, *v. i.*; to make a whistling sound.

kśa, an adverbial suffix, denoting that an action or quality is constant, habitual, or excessive. See ¶ ¶ 163 and 231.

kta dé, *v. t.*; to secure or join with nails or rivets.

ku, *v. t.*; to give, to present.

ku, *demonst. pronoun,* referring to something pointed out, obvious or previously described; that, that one. Most of the following words beginning with 'ku' are more or less directly derived from this pronoun.

kú a, *adv.*; in that way or place, just so.

kú a du, *adv., fr.* ku *and* adu; in that very place, right there.

kú a ru, *same as* kuadu.

kú dsi, *v. t.*; to take back something given.

kú i ša, *adj., adv., fr.* ku *and* iša; like that, just like that.

ku i šá dsi, *adj., adv., fr.* kuiša *and* adsi; much like that, resembling that closely.

ku i šá dsi ke, *v. t.*; to cause to resemble imperfectly something previously mentioned or pointed out.

kú i ša ke, *v. t., fr.* kuiša; to cause to resemble something previously demonstated or defined.

kú plie da, *adv.*; opposite or facing something previously named or pointed out.

kú pi, *v. i., adj.*; to smell like, to have the same odor as something previously mentioned and compared.

kú ta, *adv., fr.* ku *and* ta; thereat, therein.

kú ta pa, *interrog. pron.* or sentence, *fr.* ku *and* tapa; what is that, what is the nature of the thing named or pointed out.

kú ti, *adj.*; dirty, seedy, shabby; said of old clothes, etc.

kuts, v.; here, take it. This word is perhaps a form of the verb ku, and may mean "it is given to you"; but is used when commanding a person to accept something offered.

kú tsa ki, *pron.* (?), *fr.* ku *and* tsaki; that one alone, that by itself.

kú tski, *v. i.*; to be like, to accord; to be measured, regulated, or shaped according to a standard or pattern.

l.

l. Words heard to begin with the sound of l may be found under d. See ¶ ¶ 6, 20, and 22.

m.

m, a common contracted form of the simple personal pronouns of the first person. (¶ ¶ 105, 112).

ma, *pers. pron.*, 1st pers., sing. and plur., simple, incorporated, nominative and possessive; I; we; my; our. (¶ ¶ **58,** 81, and 105–108, inclusive.)

ma, a prefix to verbs of all classes forming nouns; a prefix to nouns slightly limiting their meanings; to be carefully distinguished from the pronoun 'ma', which is often used as the first syllable of a word. (¶ ¶ 53–56).

ma', n.; snow.

ma á, *n., fr.* a; the entire plant; the body or chief portion of a plant or tree as distinguished from any of its parts.

ma á da lia, *n., fr.* adalia; coffee in the grain; parched coffee; but *not* the infusion or decoction. See midišipiša.

ma a dá lipi, *n., fr.* adalipi; a single part or portion.

ma á da í du ti, synonymous with ádaiduti.

ma á da í ki du lio ki, *n., fr.* áda *and* ikidulioki; a comb.

ma a dé, *n., fr.* ade; a warm season, a sultry time.

ma a du á dá pa pi, n., fr.

maă

'adapapi; a scorched or sunburnt spot.

ma ă du hi da, *n.*, *fr.* aduhida; anything new or recently made; an unworn garment.

ma a du hó' pi, *same as* aduhopi.

ma a du lia kú pi, *n.*, *fr.* aduliakupi; a crease or groove in anything.

ma a du liá pi, *n.*, *fr.* aduliapi; a bed, any one's bed; commonly applied to a permanent bed with bedstead.

ma a du lié pi, *n.*, *fr.* aduliepi; a shallow spot.

ma a du i dă ki śa, *n.*, *fr.* aduidakiśa; a left-handed person.

ma a du i dĭ tsi, *n.*, *fr.* aduiditsi; a particular odor.

ma a du i dĭ tsi i śi″ a. See aduiditsiiśia.

ma a du i dĭ tsi tsą″ ki. See aduiditsitsąki.

ma a du i śí a, *n.*, *fr.* aduiśia; a worthless person; an inferior thing.

ma a du í ti pe, *n.*; a fall-trap.

ma a du kí a de tsi, *fr.* adukíadetsi; a brave man.

ma a du ki du śá, *n.*, *fr.* adukiduśa; a place where anything may be stored, or where only certain things are stored which it is not necessary to specify.

ma a du ó ki pa di, *n.*, *fr.* okipadi; a scion, a sapling.

ma a lii dú lia, *n.*; large beads, such as are used in necklaces; a necklace of such beads.

ma ą ka ką śi, *n.*, *fr.* ąkakąśi; a writing, an inscription.

ma a ku kĭ kśe, *n.*, *fr.* akukikśe; one who arranges or mends

mád

something understood or not specified.

ma a ku má di he, *n.*, *fr.* akumadihe; a cook, one who cooks anything.

ma á pi, *n.*; a necklace.

ma á po kśa, *n.*; a house-fly.

ma á pu zi, *n.*, *fr.* puzi; a meat-fly.

ma a śá di, *n.*, *fr.* aśadi; a stolen article; a theft.

ma á tsi, *n.*, *lit.*, *yellow tree;* pine.

ma á zi, *v. i.*; to be full.

ma á zi he, *v. t.*; to fill full.

ma á zi ke, *v. t.*; to cause to be full; filled.

ma bú a, *same as* mamua.

má da [-ra], *n.*; winter; a year.

má da da ka, *n.*, *fr.* mada *and* daka; snow-bird, Lapland bunting (*Plectrophanes* sp.).

má da du [-ru], *adv.*, *fr.* mada; during the winter.

má da duk [-ruk], *n.*, *adv.*, *fr.* mada; next winter; during next winter.

ma dą lia pi, *n.*; bread.

ma dą lia pi hó' pi, *n.*, *fr.* ho'pi; light bread.

ma dą lia pi-i ki da ka pú śi, *n.*; saleratus or other leavening material. See kidakapuśi.

ma dą lia pi tso″ ki, *n.*, *fr.* tsoki; hard-bread, crackers.

ma da ka pĭ lii, *n.*, *fr.* dăkapilii; a flag, a banner.

ma dá ki, *v.*; to paint, to draw; to ornament with drawings.

ma da kó ĕ [malakoe, balakoe, barakoe], *n.*, *fr.* dakoe *or* idakoe; my friend, my comrade.

má da śe du, *n.*, *adv.*, *fr.* mada

and šedu; last winter; during last winter.

ma dá̧ ški he [-la-], *n.*; unripe corn prepared for keeping.

ma dá' ti, *n.*; my brother-in-law. See idá'ti.

má di, *adj.*; cooked.

ma dí di, *n.*; meat dried in broad thin layers.

ma di é [badiets], *v. t.*; I think, I suppose, I believe. See idie.

má di he, *v. t.*; to cook, to prepare food.

ma dí ši, *n., fr.* diši; a dance; synonymous with makidiši.

ma dí ši, *n.*; my son. See idiši.

ma dó lia, *n.*; gypsum. These Indians burn gypsum and use it as a pigment.

ma dó ka, *n.*; an elk.

ma dó ka o dä″ lipi, *n.*; an elk-skin.

ma dó ti ka de, *n.*; a gall or swelling on a plant caused by an insect laying its egg.

ma du li̧á pa, *adj.*; crazy, insane; drunk.

ma du li̧á pa dši, *adj.*; appearing as if drunk; acting crazily.

ma du li̧a pá du i, *v. i.*; becoming drunk.

ma du li̧á pa ke, *v. t.*; to cause to be crazy; to set drunk.

ma dú lii, *n.*; ice.

ma du lii ic′ pu, *n., fr.* madulii *and* icpu; an icicle.

ma dú lita, *n.*; a foolish or silly person, a fool; a harlot.

ma dú lita, *adj.*; foolish, silly.

ma du litá du i, *n.*; becoming foolish.

ma dú lita, ke, *v. t.*; to cause to be foolish.

ma du šká̧ pi, *n.*; urethritis.

ma dú ti [maruti], *n., fr.* du-ti; food, particularly solid food.

ma du″ ti a du ki du sá, *n*; a place for storing food.

ma du ti ki dí ti, *v. i.*; to be surfeited, to be sick from eating.

má e, *n., fr.* e; private property, anything retained in possession. See itamae.

ma é pa ka, *n., fr.* maepe *and* aka; the club or pestle used with the wooden mortar for grinding corn, meat, etc.; more commonly pronounced mĕpaka.

ma é pe, *n., fr.* ĕpe; a wooden mortar used by these Indians for pounding corn, dried meat, and other articles of food.

ma é tsi [baetsi], *n.*; a knife.

ma é tsi-a du ki da kí ti, *n.*; a pocket-knife.

ma é tsi a zis, *n.* See Local Names.

ma é tsi ha″ tski, *n., lit., Long Knives;* synonymous with maetsiictia, which is the more common expression.

ma é tsi ic ti″ a, *n., lit., Big Knives;* the inhabitants of the United States. This word is probably translated from the language of some tribe farther east.

ma é tsi í ši, *n., fr.* maetsi *and* iši; a knife-case.

má ha, *n.*; a swamp; a spring. The springs of the Hidatsa country are swampy, not clear and bubbling; hence, the double meaning of this word.

ma ha ka kí ški, *n.*; meat cut in long strips and dried.

má he, *v. t.* See maihe.

ma hĭ́ ši, *n., fr.* hiši; the bull-berry or buffalo-berry.

ma hĭ́ ši a, *n.*; the bull-berry tree, *Shepherdia argentea.*

ma hó pa, *n., same as* mahupa, which is more common.

ma ho pá, *n., fr.* hopa; medicine; a charm, a spell.

ma ho pá mi a, *n., same as* mahopamiiš.

ma ho pá mi a i ta ma" tsu, *n.* (matsu, *cherry*); the fruit of the Virginia creeper. See dóki-daliitamatsu.

ma ho pá mi a i ta ma" tsu a, *n.*; the Virginia creeper, *Ampelopsis.*

ma ho pa mí iš [-wiiš], *n.*; a fabulous old woman (some think there are more than one), who dwells in the woods and delights in doing evil. She is supposed to strangle such children as, through parental ignorance or carelessness, are smothered in bed.

ma hŭ́ pa, *n.*; the stem or handle of anything; a corn-cob.

ma liá lia, *n., fr.* lialia; *Cynoglossum Morrisonii.*

ma liá ka, *n., fr.* liaka; small-pox.

má lio, *n., fr.* lio *or* ilio; my body.

ma lió ki, *v. t.*; I row. See dalioki.

ma lĭ́ŭ a lia, *n., fr.* iliualia; my knee.

ma lĭ́ŭ li ša, *n*; tree-willow, *Salix lucida.*

ma í a ka ką ši, *n., fr.* ąkaką-ši; a pen or pencil.

ma í ą pą ti, *n.. same as* iąpąti.

ma ic tí a, *n., fr.* ictia; a boy or girl nearly or quite full grown;

said in contradistinction to ma-kadišta.

ma i dăk tsá da ke, *n.. fr.* daktsadake; skates.

ma í dăk u dsi, *n., fr.* dakudsi; a swing; a swinging cradle, such as these Indians use to rock their children.

ma í da tska ti, *n., fr.* datskati; a syringe.

ma i di ké di kša, *n.*; straps or bands for supporting the leggings; garters.

ma i dĭ́ tsi, *n., fr.* iditsi; material for scenting.

ma í du tsa da, *n.. fr.* dutsada; a sled.

ma í dŭ tsi, *n.*; synonymous with idutsi; a fork of any description.

ma í du tska pi, *n., fr.* dutską-pi; a pincers; a clothes-pin. In the latter sense, maitulii-idutską-pi is preferable.

ma í du tsku pi, *n.* See mua-idutskupi.

ma i há, *n., fr.* iha; an enemy, an inimical tribe.

ma i há di, *n., fr.* ihadi; food set out, a meal, a feast.

ma i há lipi, *n., fr.* halipi; an errhine, a plant obtained by these Indians on the prairies, powdered and used as snuff in cases of catarrh; name recently applied to snuff.

ma i há mi a, *n., fr.* maiha *and* mia; a member of the Enemy-woman Band.

ma i há mi a ic ke, *n.*; the Enemy-woman Band, one of the orders or degrees among the Hidatsa women.

ma í he, *v. t.*; to try, to endeavor.—maihe, he tries. ma-

maí

dahe, you try. mamabe [wawabets], I try. Possibly **mabe** is the true radical form, but it is never heard. (¶ 199).

ma í hu [**ba—**, **wa-**], to trade, to buy. (¶ 199).

ma í ha ka, n., fr. hiaka—alluding to effects upon the skin; poison vines, *Rhus toxicodendron* and *Rhus radicans*.

ma i ka dí tska pa, n., fr. kaditskapa; adhesive material, paste, mucilage.

ma í ka ti pe, n., fr. ikatipe; a button of any kind.

ma í ki da ku di, n., fr. kidakudi; a fan. The Hidatsa commonly make fans from wings of birds.

ma í ki da ku dsi, n., fr. kidakudsi; *same as* maidakudsi.

ma í ki di ki. See makidiki, which is more commonly used.

ma í ki du lia di, n., fr. kiduliadi; a rake.

ma í ki du lio ki, n.; synonymous with maadaikidulioki.

ma i ki ka, n., fr. ika; glass; a window.

ma í ki ka ki, n., fr. kikaki; thread.

ma í ki ki ski, n., fr. kikiski; a weight; a measuring vessel.

ma i kí ku, n.; a spring-trap.

ma í ki pa ki si, n., fr. kipakisi; a cloth for wiping or rubbing, a towel.

ma í ki pa sa ki, n., fr. kipasaki; a belt worn outside of all the clothing, around the robe or blanket.

ma í ki pki ti, n., fr. kipkiti; a sad-iron.

ma í ki tsa ti ke, n., fr. kitsa-

maí

tike; any material used in polishing.

ma í ki tso ki, n., fr. kitsoki; material used to render anything hard, as starch.

ma í kta de, n.; a nail, peg, or spike, anything driven in for the purpose of securing.

ma i kú tski, n., fr. ikutski; anything copied or taken from some model or used as a model, a pattern for a garment, a model of an instrument or utensil; sometimes applied to a measuring tape or stick.

ma i kú tski ksa, n., fr. kutski; an imitator, a mimic, one who frequently imitates the manners of others for the amusement of spectators.

ma í ma da ki, n., fr. madaki; a pencil, brush, or prepared stick used in painting pictures.

ma í mak i e ke, n.; playing-cards. See imakieke.

ma í mi dí ti. See iduksitii-miditi.

ma í pa ka de, n., fr. ipakade; a fork, a table-fork.

ma í pa sa ki, n., fr. ipasaki; the belt worn around the waist, outside of the dress or shirt; the girdle.

ma í pa tsa ti, n.; synonymous with ipatsati.

ma í ptsa, n., ? fr. iptsa; an axe.

ma í ptsa da ka, n., *diminutive of* maiptsa; a hatchet.

ma í si, n., fr. iši; a covering; corn-husks.

ma i ské, n., fr. iške; one commanded, one obeying.

ma í spa du mi di, n.; a snail.

ma í su, n., ? fr. išu; the war-eagle, *Aquila chrysaëtus*.

ma ɪ śu i ki".śiś, *n.* See Local Names.

ma i śu tɪ pśą ki, *n., fr.* iśuti *and* ipśąki; an apron.

ma i tá, *n.*; an arrow; syn. itá.

ma i tá hi, *n.* See itahi.

ma i tá i śu, *n., fr.* itaiśu, and of similar meaning.

ma i ta mú a; *n., fr.* tamua; a bell; also maítamua.

ma i te í du śu ki, *n., lit.,* material for washing the face; soap.

ma i te í ki pą ki śi, *n., fr.* ite, i, and kipąkiśi; a towel. (¶ 44).

ma i tɪ du śu ki, *n., a con-tracted form of* maiteiduśuki com-monly used.

ma í ti pe, *n., fr.* itipe; a fall-trap.

ma i tsi mú a, *n., fr.* tsimua; ornamental metallic pendants.

ma i tskí ti, *n., fr.* itskiti; a scissors.

ma i tu ki í ki pki ti, *fr.* itu-lii *and* maikipkiti, aud synony-mous with the latter.

mąk [wąk], a prefix to verbs denoting opposition, reciprocity, etc. See mąki and ¶ 153.

ma ku, *n.*; my daughter (form of address).

ma ka dɪ śta [-ri-], *n., fr.* ka-diśta; a child, a young persou.

ma ka dɪ śta i" dăk u dsi, *n., fr.* makadiśta *and* dakudsi; a child's swing, or swinging cradle; au arrangement, for rocking chil-dren, made of ropes and blankets and suspended from a beam. See maidakudsi.

ma ka dɪ śta ke, *n.*; a doll. See ke.

ma ka dɪ śta ma tse, *n.* (ma-tse, *a man*); a young boy.

ma ka dɪ śta mi a, *n.* (mia, *a woman*); a young girl.

ma ka dɪ śta ti, *n.* See Local Names.

ma' ką lipɪ ta mi [-wi], *n.*; hail.

ma ką ptsi, *v. t.,* 1st *pers. of* da-kąptsi.

mą ka ta, *n.*; large fruit, par-ticularly plums.

mąk i, *v. i.,* and adverbial pre-fix, *same as* mąk.

mąk i a, *v. i., fr.* mąki; to con-test, to oppose, to struggle with one another; to play a game in which opposite sides are taken.

mąk i a pé, *adj.*; checkered, cross-barred.

mąk i a pé ke, *v. t.*; to checker, to ornameut with intersecting lines.

mąk i á ti di e", *v. i., fr.* tidic; to run a contested race.

mąk i á ti di e" ke; *v. t., fr.* tidieke; to cause to run in con-test, *i. e.,* to race horses, to have a horse-race.

mak i dá kśi, *n., fr.* kidakśi; a very young child, one tied up in a bundle (as these Indians usual-ly carry children until they are about six months old); the bun-dle and child together.

ma ki dé kśa, *n., fr.* kidekśa; au excessive vomiting; a sick-ness characterized by prolonged or excessive vomiting.

ma ki dɪ ki, *n., fr.* kidiki; a hammer.

ma ki dɪ śi, *n., fr.* kidiśi; a dance.

ma kí du mi [+-wi], *n., fr.* kídumi; a numeral.

ma ki du tskɪ śi, *n., fr.* kidu-tskiśi; a lot of washed clothes.

mąk i é ke, *r. i.* and *t.*; to contest, or cause to contest ; used in much the same sense as mąkia.

mąk i hi, *r. i.*; to stand mutually in contact, as two sticks placed so as to support one another.

mąk i hi ta, *negative of* mąkihi; to be separated mutually.

mąk i i dé, *v. i., fr.* maki *and* ide ; to interchange speech, to hold a dialogue.

mąk i i kú' pa, *v. t., fr.* mąki *and* iku'pa ; to hate one another.

mąk i Y ši, *n., fr.* mąki *and* iši,—so called because the covers or flaps close from opposite directions ; a meat-case or *parflèche* case, which is an arrangement made of decorated raw-hide for holding dried meat and other articles.

mąk i ki dé ši, *v. t., fr.* mąki *and* kideši ; to love one another.

ma ki kú a, *n., fr.* kikua ; a soldier ; one of the Soldier Band of the tribe.

mąk i ma kå da ha, *r.*; to pass and repass one another coming from opposite directions.

mąk i ma kå da ha ti di é, *v.* (tidie, *to run*); to run or ride rapidly, passing and repassing one another, coming from opposite directions; as when two persons, on foot or mounted, make a war-signal.

mak i mąk i a [bakiwąkia], *n., fr.* kimąkia ; a battle, a fight.

ma ki pá, *n., fr.* kipa ; hominy.

ma ki pá hi, *n., fr.* kipahi ; a song.—makipahi mąk, give (us) a song—a common mode of asking a person to sing.

mąk i pa tá ki, *v. t., fr.* mąki *and* pataki ; to shut together, to

close together ; to shut anything when two sides are moved in the act, as in closing a book or a covered mirror.

ma kó' pa, *n.*; my comrade ; said by one female to another. See iko'pa.

mak sá ki, *v. t.*; *1st person of* dáksaki.

mąk sé ša, *same as* mąkšeše.

mąk sé ša dsi, *adj., fr.* mąkšeše ; seeming to resemble one another.

mąk sé ša du i, *v. i.*; becoming more and more alike.

mąk sé še [+ wąk-], *v. i., adj., fr.* šeše ; mutually resembling one another, alike.

mąk sé še de, *adj.*: closely but not exactly resembling one another.

mąk sé še ke, *v. t.*; to cause to resemble one another, to make alike.

mąk sí a, *adj., fr.* mąk *and* šia ; nearly the same as mąkšeše.

mąk sí a de, *adj.*; much alike.

mąk sí a ka, *adj., fr.* mąkšia *and* ka ; of the same size or length as one another ; nearly synonymous with šiaka and šeka.—mąkšiakąts, they are of equal size.

mąk sí a ka dsi, *adj.*; apparently alike in size or length.

mąk sí a ka ke, *v. t.*; to increase or reduce in size so as to make two things of equal length or size.

mak tsá ki, *v. t., 1st person of* dáktsąki.

má ku, *n.*; the cottonwood tree; perhaps so called in allusion to its height.

má ku, *n.*; night. The word is also used to denote the astro-

mák

, nomical day or cycle of twenty-four hours, and sometimes to denote a year.

má ku, *adj.*; tall, lofty.

má ku a du o″ ki pa di, *n.*; young cottonwood shrubs growing at the base of a tree. See aduokipadi.

má ku du, *adv., fr.* maku; during the night.

má ku duk, *adv.*; during the coming night.

má ku ka za, *n., same as next word,* but less in use.

má ku ka zi, *n., diminutive of* maku; a young cottonwood tree.

má ku ke, *v. t., fr.* maku; to make tall; made tall.

má ku mi di [-bidi], *n., fr.* maku, *night, and* midi; the moon.

má ma, *v.*; a word used imperatively when trying to get an infant to drink or nurse.

má ma da ki, *n., fr.* mądaki; a picture, a painting; a book.

ma mak i é ke, *n., fr.* mąkieke; a game in which opposite sides are taken.

ma mú a, *n.*; haw; haws.

ma mú a a, *n.*; haw-tree; a species of *Cratægus* growing in Northern Dakota.

ma o dé ša [-neša], *n., fr.* deša, *? lit., a thing which is not;* a thing of imaginary existence, a groundless story, etc.

ma o dé ša a ziš, *n.* See Local Names.

ma pa ší pi ša, *n.*; sunflower seeds,—used as food by these Indians.

ma pą́ tska ki di ti, *n.*; a wasp.

ma pé *or* **má pe,** *n*; day, day-

maš

time; a period of twenty-four hours.—hidi-mapé, to-day.

má pe du, *adv., fr.* mape; during the day.

ma pe ho pá, *n., fr.* mape *and* hopa; any day observed as sacred by white men, as Sunday and Christmas.

ma pé mi di [-bidi], *n., fr.* mape *and* midi; the sun.

ma pi dą́ lipa, *n., fr.* pidalipa; ribbon.

ma pó kša, *n.*; any animal or animals offensive to the sight of these Indians or unfit for food, as insects, worms, snakes, etc.

ma pó ša, *n.*; a term applied to flies and insects less offensive to the sight than the mapokša.

ma po ša ki dí ti, *n.*; an ant.

ma pú dsi ke, *n., fr.* pudsike; a cord of buckskin or other material having porcupine quills or other ornamental trimming wrapped around it.

ma ró ka, *n., same as* madoka.

ma rú lita, *n., same as* madulita.

ma šá mi, } *n.*; my aunt. See
ma šá wiš, } išami and dišami.

ma ší, *n.*; a buffalo-robe; a blanket worn as a robe.

ma ší, *n.*; a white man. The word was originally applied only to the French and Canadians, who are now sometimes designated as mašika'ti, the true whites.

ma ší a de, *v.*; to dream.—mamašíade, I dream. madašíade, you dream.

ma ší a lia, *v.*; to sweep out dirt, to clean by sweeping with a broom.

ma ší a í lia, *n., fr.* mašialia; a

broom. The position of the particle ' i ' in this word is unique.

ma śi dá lia mi, *n.*, *fr.* maśi *and* daliami; a shawl.

ma śi í li, *n.*, *fr.* maśi *and* ilii; dry-goods of any description.

ma śi i li lá pi, *n.* (liapi, *thin*); light cotton goods; muslin.

ma śi i li pú zi, *n.* (puzi, *spotted*); calico prints.

ma śi i li tá tsi, *n.* (tatsi, *thick*); cloth; woolen goods.

ma śi í ptse, *n.*, *fr.* maśi *and* iptse; a wide, embroidered band in the centre of a robe or blanket.

ma śi″ i ta dá lipĭ tsi, *n.*, *lit.*, *white man's bear;* a hog.

ma śi″ i ta dá lipĭ tsi śu i, *n.* (śui, *fat*); bacon.

ma śi i ta í mạk i e ke, *n.*, *lit.*, *white man's gaming materials;* cards.

ma śi i ta mi te [-wite], *n.*, *lit.*, *white man's buffalo, or cow;* domestic cattle.

ma śi″ i ta tsa ká ka, *n.*, *lit.*, *white man's bird;* the domestic cock.

ma śi ka, *n.*; chewing-gum.

ma śi pi śa, *n.*, *fr.* śipiśa; grapes; raisins.

ma śi pi śa a ku du″ ti, *n.*, *lit.*, *grape-eater;* the cedar-bird, *Ampelis cedrorum*. (¶ 51).

ma śi śi pi śa, *n.*, *fr.* maśi *and* śipiśa; the negro.

ma śi ta, *n.*; my back; from iśita or the hypothetical word śita.

ma śi ta ká kśu, *n.*, *lit.*, *white man's tuber;* the potato.

ma śi ta rá lipĭ″ tsi, *same as* maśiitadalipitsi.

ma śú a ka za, *n.*, *diminutive*

of maśuka; a puppy; willow catkins are also so called.

ma śú ka, *n.*, *fr.* śuka; a dog.

ma śu ka ák śu, *n.*, *fr.* maśuka *and* ʔakśue; the coral-berry or wolf-berry, *Symphoricarpus*.

ma śu ka ák śu a ma śiś″, *n.* See Local Names.

ma śu ka íc ke, *n.*, *lit.*, *Dog Band;* one of the orders or societies among the men of the tribe.

ma śu ka ka dĬ śta, *n.*, *lit.*, *Little Dogs;* an order or society of the men.

ma śu ka ma dá ki, *n.*; another of the bands or orders of the Hidatsa men.

ma tá, *n.*, *prob. fr.* ta, *to kill;* autumn.

ma tá du, *adv.*, *fr.* mata; during the autumn.

ma tá duk, *n.*, *adv.*, *fr.* mata; next autumn; during next autumn.

ma tá li, *n.*; a turtle.

ma tá li i śa, *lit.*, *resembling a turtle;* a padlock.

ma tá lipi, *n.*; a heavy cord, a rope; a lariat.

ma tá ki, *n*; a plate; a shallow dish.

ma tá ki a du ki du śa, *n.*; a cup-board. See adukiduśa.

ma tá ki a zi, *n.* See Local Names.

ma tá ko a, *adv.*, *same as* matekoa.

ma tá śi, *n.*; my robe or blanket. See itaśi.

ma ta tsi dá lio ke, *n.*, *fr.* tatsi *and* dalioke; an Indian pad-saddle.

ma ta tsi ná lio ke, *same as last word.*

mat

ma té, *n., adv., fr.* te *or* tie; long ago; a long time; the last vowel is often lengthened to indicate very distant past time.

ma té ko a, *adv., fr.* mate; at a distant time in the past.

má ti, *n.;* a boat.—hutsi-mati (*wind-boat*), a sail-boat. mida-mati, a wooden boat.

má ti si sa, *n.;* a steam-boat.

ma tó ke, *n.;* a clam.

má tsa mi di [-bidi], *n.;* a bowl or basin.

má tsa mi di ka zi, *n., diminutive of* matsamidi; a small bowl or basin.

ma tsé [watse, batse], *n.;* a man.

ma tsé di di, *n., fr.* matse *and* didi; a war-party.

ma tse é tsi, *n.;* a chief; a person of prominence.

ma tshó ki, *n.;* eagle tail-feathers.

má tsi, *n., contraction of* maatsi.

má tsi, *n.;* my foot. See itsi.

ma tsi kó a, *n., fr.* tsikoa; sugar; a sweetened drink.

ma tsi kó a a ku ti″ du e, *n.;* molasses.

ma tsi kó a ha″ tski, *n.* (hatski, *long*); candy.

ma tsi kó a pu″ zi, *n.* (puzi, *striped*); candy.

ma tsí ta hi du, *n., fr.* tsita *and* hidu; the coccyx.

ma tsi tó, *n.;* a needle or awl.

má tsi to ic ti″ a, *n.* (ictia, *large*); an awl.

má tsi to-u″ ti po a du i, *n.* (uti *and* poadui); a pin.

má tsu, *n.;* small fruit, particularly cherries.

má tsu a, *n.;* a cherry-tree.

ma tsú a, *n.;* fibrous tissue from

me

the back of the buffalo, elk, deer, etc. It is dried and split into fine threads for sewing, and is commonly called *sinew* by the whites.

ma tsu a pá ki si, *n., fr.* matsua *and* pakisi; "sinew" twilled by rubbing, as it is fixed preparatory to being used in sewing.

ma tsu á tsa, *n.;* fragrant grass.

má tsu a zis, *n.* See Local Names.

ma tsú ka, *n.;* my younger brother. See itsuka.

má tsu o tąk a, *n.;* the smaller dogwood, *Cornus stolonifera.*

má tsu o tąk i, *n., fr.* matsu *and* tąki; the berries of *Cornus stolonifera.*

má tsu tą pa, *n., fr.* matsu *and* tąpa; the service-berry, *Amelanchier canadensis.*

ma tsu tą pá a, *n.;* the service-berry tree, shad-bush.

ma tú, *v.;* there are; there is; he has; they have, etc.; opposite of deśa.

ma tú a, *n.;* green corn, roasting ears.

ma tú lii, *n.;* my dress or shirt. See itulii.

ma ú pą ki, *n.;* a mallet.

ma ú pą kihu″ pa i sis. See Local Names.

má u tą pi, *n., ? fr.* tapa; a ball of buck-skin or elk-skin stuffed with hair, and used by women in their games; a game played with such a ball.

má wa da ki, *same as* mamadaki.

má zi, *n.;* a legend, a tale.

me, *n.;* a louse.

mĕ pa ka, *n., contraction of* mae-paka, but more common.

mĕ pi, *n., contraction of* maepi, much used.

mi' [bi'], *n.* ; a rock.

mi [wi, wits], prob. auxiliary verb, suffixed to denote 1st person, future. (¶ 167).

mi, simple pers. pron., 1st pers., used independently or incorporated, nominative and objective, usually singular, but when incorporated may refer to more than one. (¶ ¶ 109, 110, 172, 205).

mi [wi, wits], a suffix indicating number. See tuami and hidimi.

mi, a syllable or prefix of uncertain significance, beginning many nouns in the language; often pronounced bi, sometimes wi.

mí a [wia, bia], *n.* ; a woman.

mi a dó ka ta [-no-], *n.* ; a harlot. This is the proper word; but m a d u l i t a, *fool,* is often used.

mí a ka za, *n., fr.* mia *and* kaza ; a young woman.

mi á ti, *n., fr.* mia ; a man who dresses in woman's clothes and performs the duties usually allotted to females in an Indian camp. Such are called by the French Canadians "berdaches"; and by most whites are incorrectly supposed to be hermaphrodites.

mi á ti he, *v. t.* ; to become a miati ; said of a man who assumes the dress and tasks of a woman.

mi á ti ke, *v. t.* ; to cause to be a miati.

míc ki, *comp. pers. pron.,* 1st person ; I, myself. (¶ 117).

mí da [wi-, bi-], *n.* ; a wild-goose.

mi dá [+bida], *n.* ; wood ; a tree ; a forest.

mi da a ku dú ti, *n., lit., wood-eaters;* caterpillars which live on trees.

mi da á pa, *n., fr.* mida *and* apa ; leaves of any kind ; tea.

mi da du é tsa, *n., fr.* mida *and* duetsa; a wooden canoe, a "dug-out".

mí da ha, *n.* ; fire.

mi da há dsi, *n.* ; willows; a name applied to all shrub willows.

mi da há dsi hí ši, *n.* ; red willow.

mí da ha í du kạ pi, *n.* ; a friction-match.

mi da ha pó kša, *n.* ; embers.

mi da ha tíc ke, *v. i.* ; to play as young children play ; to play at any amusement in which opposite sides are not taken.

mi da ho pá, *n., fr.* mida *and* hopa ; red cedar.

mi da ho pá-o kạ́ tsa du, *n.*; trailing cedar.

mi da hú pa, *n., fr.* mida *and* hupa; boots and shoes, such as are used by the whites. The Hidatsa probably originally supposed them to be made of wood.

mi da hú pa i ki tsaⁿ ti ke, *n.*; blacking.

mí dạ lia, *n.* ; a pot or kettle.

mi dạ́ lia ši, *n.* ; a basket.

mi da í, *n.* ; elm.

mi da í a ka ki, *n.* ; a chair.

mi da i á ma lia ti, *n., fr.* mida *and* amaliati ; a torch; a candle.

mi da i á ma lia ti-i o" ki,
mi da i á ma lia ti-i o" pe,
mi da i á ma lia ti-i o" ptsa ti, *n.*; a candlestick. See oki, ope, and optsati.

mi da i á pi, *n.*; a spool.

mi da íc ke, *n.,fr.* mida *and* icke; the Goose Band, one of the orders among the women of the tribe.

mi da íc pa ti, *n.*; sunken tree or snag in a river.

mi da í ka ki, *n.* (kaki, *roll*); a wagon.

mi da i ó pë, *n.,fr.* mida *and* iope; a box of any kind, particularly a wooden box.

mi da Y si, *n.,fr.* mida *and* iši; bark.

mi da ka míc ka, *n.* (kamicka, *tough*); oak.

mí da ka za, *n., diminutive of* mida; a stick, a switch.

mi dá ki, *n.*; a shield.

mi dá kši, *n.*; a palisade or stockade; a skillet or pan; so called perhaps because like a palisaded enclosure.

mi da lu é tsa, *same as* midadu-etsa.

mi da ma í du tsa da, *n.*; a wooden sled. See maidutsada.

mi da má ti, *n.,fr.* mida *and* mati; a yawl or skiff.

mi dá pa, *a contraction of* mida-apa, often heard.

mí da pa, *n.*; beaver.

mi da tsa pi, *n.*; ashes; gun-powder; dust.

mi da tsa pi a zis, *n.* See Local Names.

mi dá tsa pi i si, *n.*; a powder-horn.

mi da tsú ka, *n.,fr.* mida *and* tsuka; boards; a floor.

mi dé, *n.*; a door; a door-way.

mi dé di, *v. t.*; to come through a door-way, to enter a house; to pay a visit.

mi dé ko a, *n.*; at or near the door; the seat around the fire nearest to the door.

mí di [bidi, mini], *n.*; water. The latter pronunciation, corresponding with the Dakota, is most commonly used in compound words.

mi di, *n.*; a name given to both sun and moon; it may be translated *luminary* or *great luminary*. When there is danger of ambiguity they are distinguished as mape-midi (day luminary) and oktsi-midi or maku-midi (night luminary).

mi di [widi], verbal root; turn, twist. See pamidi, dumidi, etc.

mi di a pó ka, *n., lit., water head-dress;* a rainbow.

mi di a té, *adv., n.,fr.* midi *and* ate; when the sun (or moon) rises; sunrise.

mi di a té de, *adv.*; near sun-rise, just before sunrise.

mi di a té du, *adv.*; at sunrise, during the time the sun is rising.

mi di a té duk, *adv.*; when the sun shall next rise.

mi di a te ó dak si pi, *adv.*; after sunrise. See dakšipi.

mi di dá ki si, *n.,fr.* midi *and* dahiše; a wave, a billow.

mi di dé ta, *n.,fr.* midi, *water,* and deta; the bank of a river; the shore of a lake.

mi di dí di [-niri], *v.,fr.* midi *and* didi; to swim.

mi di ho pá, *n.* See Local Names.

mi di í a pa ti, *n.*; a saw.

mid

mi di í da liu pi, *n., fr.* midi, i, *and* daliupi ; a sponge.

mi di i hí' ke, *n., fr.* midi, i, *and* hike ; a drinking-vessel, a cup.

mi di i ki ki ški, *n., fr.* midi *and* ikikiški ; a watch or clock.

mi di í mă lipi [-wă-], *n., adv., fr.* midi *and* imalipi ; sunset.

mi di í mă lipi de, *adv.* ; near sunset.

mi di í mă lipi du, *adv.* ; at sunset.

mi di í mă lipi duk, *adv.* ; when the sun shall next set.

mi di í mă lipi še du, *adv.* ; when the sun did last set.

mi di i tá tsu, *n., fr.* midi *and* itatsu ; the half-moon.

mí di ka, *adv., fr.* midi, *water;* in or by the water.

mi di ka kí hi, *n., fr.* midi, *moon,* and kakihi ; the full-moon.

mí di ka kí hi de, *n.* ; the gibbous moon.

mi di ka ó ze [mini-], *n., fr.* midika *and* oze, *lit., They Plant by, or in, the Water;* a band of the Teton Dakotas.

mi di ke, *v. t., fr.* mide *and* ke ; to liquefy, melt.

mi di kí da he, *fr.* midi, *moon, and* kidahe ; the new moon, the crescent.

mi di ki dạk tsí e, *n.* ; clear water, water allowed to settle.

mí di ó pe, *contraction of* midaiope.

mi di ma pé du pa hi [bidi-wapérupahi], *n., fr.* midi, mape, *and* dopahe, *lit., the sun divides the day in two;* noon.

mi di ma pé du pa hi-dăk a-mí di, *n.* ; afternoon.

13

mih

mi di ma pé du pa hi-dak sí pi, *n.* ; synonymous with last word.

mi di ma pé du pa hi de, *n.* ; nearly noon.

mi di mí tạ lia he, *n.* ; the Mandan medicine-ark.

mi dí pi, *v.* ; to enter the water, *i. e.,* to bathe one's self.

mi dí ša, *v., adj.* ; turbid ; said of water.

mi dí ša a ziš. See Local Names.

mi dí ša ke, *v. t., fr.* midiša ; to make turbid ; roiled.

mi dí ši, *n., contraction of* midaiši.

mi di ší pi ša, *n., fr.* midi *and* šipiša ; coffee, the infusion or decoction.

mi di tá di [minitari], *n., comp. v., fr.* midi *and* tadi ; to cross water, to go across a stream. The Hidatsa Indians ; so called by the Mandans.

mi dí ti, *v. t.* ; to cook by frying.

mi dí tsi, *adj.* ; of a watery consistency.

mí do, *pers. pron.,* plural ; we ; us.

mí do ki, *pers. pron.,* compound, plural ; we, ourselves.

mi dú e, *v. i., fr.* midi *and* ue ; to bubble ; to boil as water.

mi dú e he, *v. t.* ; to boil water.

mi dú e ke, *v. t.* ; to cause to boil, to set to boil ; boiled.

mi dú lia [bi-], *n.* ; a gun or bow.

mi dú lia ke, *n., fr.* midulia ; a pop-gun.

mí e, *n.* ; woman, *same as* mia.

mí lia ka, *n.* ; a generic name for ducks.

mí'

mí' i, *n.*; a stone or rock, *same as* mí'.

mí' i da' ta, *n., lit., stone heart;* a geode.

mi Ý ptsa, *n., fr.* mí' *and* iptsa; an axe, particularly a stone axe. See maiptsa.

mi Ý ptsa da' ka, *n., diminutive of* miiptsa; a tomahawk or hatchet, particularly a stone hatchet. See maiptsadaka.

mi ká, *n.*; a mare; as a suffix it indicates the female of all lower animals except buffalo.

mi ká', *n.*; grass; sedge; all grass-like plants.

mi ka' í du tsi, *n., fr.* mika' *and* dutsi; a pitchfork.

mi ka' kÝ ksa, *n., lit., Grass-fixers;* an order or degree among women.

mi ka' tó hi ša, *adj., fr.* mika' *and* tohiša; green.

mi ka' tsá ki, *n.*; a name sometimes applied to fragrant grass.

mi ka' ú dsi, *n., lit., dry grass;* hay.

mi ka' ú ta ku du ti, *n., fr.* mika'uti *and* akuduti; a caterpillar that eats onions.

mi ka' ú ti, *n., fr.* mika' *and* uti; onions; wild garlic.

mí' ka za, *n., diminutive of* mí'; gravel, pebbles.

mi ktá [wi-], *n.*; the bottom, the lower part or surface of anything.

mi ktá ka [wi-], *adv., fr.* mikta; at the lower part; below.

mi ktá ko a, *adv., fr.* mikta; near or at the bottom; under.

mi ktá ta, *adv., fr.* mikta; downward, in the direction of the bottom.

mit

mí' ma ú pa ki, *n., fr.* mí' *and* maupaki; a stone-headed mallet, such as is ordinarily made by these Indians.

mi špá [bišpa], *n.*; the ash-tree.

mi ta pa [witapa, wita-pats], *v. i.*; to lie, to deceive.

mi ta pá dsi, *v. i., fr.* mitapa; to equivocate.

mi ta pá kša, *v. i., fr.* mitapa; to lie frequently or habitually.

mi té, *n.*; a buffalo-cow; the word is also used generically.

mi té a ka zi, *n., diminutive of* mite; a buffalo-calf.

mí té a tä di ke [biteatäri-ke], *n.*; the box-elder, *Negundo aceroides.*

mi té a ta ki, *n., fr.* mite *and* ataki; an albino buffalo, white buffalo.

mi té a ta ki ic ke, *n.*; the White Buffalo Band, a secret degree or order among women of the tribe.

mi té ktsa tsa, *n*; the black currant.

mi té ktsa tsa a, *n.*; the currant-bush.

mi té o dä lipi, *n.*; a buffalo-hide.

mí' ti, *v. i.*; to creep, as a hunter approaching game.

mí tsa ki, *v.*; I alone; I unaided.

mí tsi, *n.*; a wedge for splitting wood.

mí' tsi, verbal root; mince; comminute finely.

mí' tsi a da zi. See Local Names.

mi tsí i ta mi da kši. See Local Names.

mit

mi tska pá, *n.*; the fruit of the rose; it is eaten by Indians.

mi tska pa á, *n.*; a rose-bush.

mi tska pa ó dák a pą ki, *n*; rose-blossom. **See** odaka-pąki.

mó tsa, *n.*; a coyoté (*Canis latrans*).

mó tsa i ta ma ka ta, *n.*, *lit.*, coyote's *plum*; the fruit of *Astragalus caryocarpus.*

mú, verbal root. See mna.

mú a, *v.* or verbal root; to sound, to make a noise. See hiamua, tamua, tsimua, etc.

múa [bua], *n.*; generic name for fish.

mu a dá ki, *v. i.*; to bark as a wolf or dog; to imitate the howl of a wolf, as Indian hunters commonly do when calling to each other in the woods.

mu a í du tsku pi, *n.*; a fish-hook.

mu á pä dé ki, *n.*, *fr.* mua, ápä, *and* delii; sturgeon.

mu á pä há tski, *fr.* mua, ápä, *and* batski; gar-pike (?).

mu a tsú ka, *n.* (tsuka, *flat*); sun-fish.

mú dsi [wudsi], verbal root; roll up, fold by rolling.

mú pi [wupi], *v. t.*; to smell.

mú ti, *v. t.*, *1st pers. of* duti; I eat.

n.

n. Words heard to begin with the sound of n may be found under d; n and d being interchangeable letters. (¶ ¶ 20 and 21.)

óda

o.

o, *adv.*; much; used in compounds; synonymous with ahu, which may be derived from o.

o, a prefix to verbs forming nouns which are names of places and actions; often synonymous with adu. (¶ ¶ 49, 50).

o, a prefix of undetermined meaning to verbal roots. In the 1st and 2d persons, it commonly takes m and d as pronouns, preceded by a. (¶ 197).

ó da [-ra], *v. t.*; to pass another person on the road either by overtaking or meeting him.

o dä lipi [-nälipi, -rälipi], *n.*, *fr.* dalipi; the hide of an animal, the entire hide.

ó dák a pą ki, *n.*, *fr.* dakapąki; a flower, a blossom; sometimes accented on penultimate.

ó dák a pi lii, *n.*, *fr.* dakapilii; an ornamental flap on a garment; also odakapilii.

ó da ki, *v. i.*; to chirp, to make a stridulous sound.

ó dák sa ki, *n.*, *fr.* daksaki; a contused wound; the act of giving a contused wound.

ó dák si pi, *n.*, *fr.* dakśipi; a subsequent time, a time after some other time mentioned.

o dä mu, *n.*, *fr.* damu; a deep spot in a stream; the channel of a river.

ó da pi [-ra-], *v. t.*; to find, to make an original discovery; *not* to recover something lost.

ó da ša' ti [ona-], *n.*; a name, a designation; *not* a proper name.

óda

ó da ša' ti, *v. t.*; to name, to speak of or call by name. In the conjugation of this word, o is not preceded by a, as in other verbs beginning with ' o'.—omadaša'ti, I name. odadaša'ti [olanaša'ti], you name.

o dí di, *n., fr.* didi; gait, walk.— odidi išia, said of a lame person.

o dú še, *n., fr.* duše; a place of deposit.

o du ška šką́ pka, *n.*; spruce gum, such as the Indians themselves gather. That obtained from the traders is called mašíka.

o dú tsi, *n., fr.* dutsi; a mine; a place where anything may be obtained with certainty.

ó hi, *v. t.*; to be fond of; said of the affection of pets for their owners.

ó lia ta dui, *v. i.*; becoming pale.

ó lia ti, *adj., fr.* liati; white, bright, clear, or pale; often used synonymously with iliotąki.

ó lia ti ke, *v. t.*; to make pale, to bleach or whiten.

ó lia ti kša, *adj.*; continually or habitually pale.

ó ka, *n., adv.*; yonder, over there.

ó ka du, *adv.*; in a distant place (pointed to), yonder; beyond.

ó ka ko a, *adv.*; at a distant place, at yon place; at the other side.

ó ką ta, *v. t.*; to put on an article of clothing, to dress.

ó ki, *v. t.*; to surround the base, to surround one end of an object; to maintain in position or support by thus surrounding,—

opă

as a candle is held in a candlestick, as the teeth are held in the gums.

ó ki, *n.*; a plume, a feather, something plumose.

o ki íc pu, *n., fr.* oki *and* iepu; a tassel.

ó ki pa di, *v. t., fr.* oki *and* apadi; to grow up around; said of young saplings or twigs growing around a parent tree.

ó ki pa pi, *v. t.*; to find, to recover something lost. See ¶ 197.

ó ktsi, *n., ? fr.* kątsi; darkness; hence, one of the names for night.—hidi oktsi, this night.

ó ktsi a de, *n., adv.*; almost night; almost dark; after sunset.

o ktsí a du [-ru], *adv.*; during the night.

o ktsí a duk [-ruk], *n., adv.*; next night; during the approaching night.

o ktsí še du, *n., adv.*; last night; during last night (¶ ¶ 256, 257).— oktsišedu itaokakoa, before last night.

o ktsí še ru, *same as last word.*

o ná wu, *same as* odamu.

ó' pa, *n.*; evening, near sunset.

ó' pa de, *n., adv.*; near evening, late in the afternoon.

ó' pa du, *adv.*; during the evening.

ó' pa duk, *adv.*; during the coming evening.

ó pă pe, *v. t.*; to bedaub slightly, to bespatter, to stick on in small quantities.

ó pă ša, *? n.*; a tucking.

o pă šá ku, *n., fr.* opaša *and* ku; to give a tucking, *i. e.*, to tuck in the edges of bedding.

ó pa śe, *v. t.*; to tuck bedding.

ó pe, *v. t.*; to contain to hold, as a box or vessel.

ó pĕ, *n.*; tobacco. This name is often applied to articles mixed with, or used in place of, tobacco, as bark of *Cornus* or leaves of *uva ursi.*

ó pĕ ha śa *or* **opéhaśa,** *n.*; the bark of *Cornus stolonifera,* or *Cornus sericea,* dried and prepared for smoking, "kinnekenick".

ó pe hi, *v. t., comp. of* ope *and* hi; to smoke tobacco or any substitute for tobacco.

ó pe i śi, *n., fr.* ope *and* iśi; a tobacco-bag.

ó pe pa mi tsi, *n., fr.* ope *and* pamitsi; a board on which tobacco is cut. This word is not formed according to ordinary etymological rules: it was probably originally opeipamitsi.

ó pśa śa, *v. t.*; to stop, to jar, to arrest motion; said of an object against which a person stumbles in walking.

ó ptsa ti, *v. t.,* to encircle or surround closely; to hold by surrounding closely; often used synonymously with oki.

ó ti, *v. i., adj.*; cooked; ripened; scalded.

ó ti he, *v. t.*; to scald or cook.

ó ti ke, *v. t.*; to cause to cook or ripen; to put fruit away to ripen.

ó tslia mi [-wi], *v. i., adj.*; numb; paralyzed; said of the feeling in the limbs produced by pressure, and commonly called "sleepiness",—matsi otsliawits, my foot is asleep.

ó tslia mi ke, *v. t.*; to make numb, or "sleepy".

o ze, *n., fr. the verb;* a drink, a cup of water or other fluid.

ó ze, *v. t.*; to pour into, to fill or partly fill a vessel; also to plant or sow seed.

p.

pa, *v. t.*; to reduce to powder by grinding or pounding.

pa, a prefix to verbs, commonly signifying that the action is performed by the hands or is capable of being performed by the hands. (¶ 154).

pa dó pi, *adj., ? fr.* padui; short in stature, low-sized.

pa dó pi di, *adj.*; very short.

pa du á du i, *v., fr.* padui; shortening; decreasing in length.

pă du i, *adj.*; short.

pă du i di di, *n., fr.* padui *and* didi; ceremonial processions performed by bands or secret orders of the tribe, in which the performers follow one another in a circle, taking very short steps and singing as they move. These processions are commonly called "medicine dances" by the whites; but the Hidatsa apply a different term to a dance.

pă du i ke, *v. t.*; to shorten; shortened.

pă du i kśa, *v., adj.*; constantly and excessively short.

pá hi, *v.*; to sing.

pá lia du i, *v. i.*; becoming chafed or blistered.

pa lió hi, *v. t., ? fr.* liolii; said of ice when it begins to break in the spring.

pá liu, *v. t.*; to spill; imperative form.

páli

pá liu e, *v. t., fr.* liu *or* line; to spill out, to pour; to empty by pouring.

pa ka dé, *v. t.*; to stick into or thrust through, to impale.

pa ká pi, *v. i., fr.* kapi; to be torn, as in walking through rose-bushes.

pá ki di, *v. t.*; to push, to shove away with the hand.

pá ki ši, *v. t.*; to rub gently in one direction with the hand, as in smoothing the hair or stroking a cat.

pa ki ti, *v. t., fr.* kiti; to press to smoothness, to make smooth by pressure with the hands.

pa mí di, *v. t., fr.* midi; to twist with the hand.

pa mí tsi [-witsi], *v. t., fr.* mitsi; to cut fine by pressing on with a knife held in the hand, as in cutting up tobacco or other material on a board preparatory to smoking.

pa mú dsi [-wudsi], *v. t.*; to roll up with the hands, to roll as a long strip of cloth or carpet or bandage is rolled; to fold or pack by rolling.

pa šá ki, *v. t.*; to engirdle or cover, as with a belt.

pa šá ki, *v. t.*; to love or like; possibly a figurative application of pašaki, to engirdle.

pa škú, *v. t., fr.* šku; to extract by pushing with the hand, to shove a cork into a bottle, to push a bullet out of a wound.

pä' tä, *imperative of* pä'te.

pa tá ki, *v. t.*; to place in contact. See ipataki, kipataki, and makipataki.

pä' te, *v. t.*; to turn over; to tumble over.

pat

pá ti, *v. i.*; to fall down off of, to drop from a height.

pá ti he, *v. t.*; to throw or knock down; to throw down from.

pa ti ke, *v. t.*; to cause to fall, to throw down, to remove a support and allow to fall.

pa tó' ti, *v. t., fr.* to'ti; to wave or agitate back and forth; to wave with the hand; to make a signal by waving.

pa tsa ki, *v. t., fr.* tsake; to cut; to cut with a knife or instrument held in the hand.—patsak, imperative.

pa tsá' ti, *v. t., fr.* tsati; to puncture.

pä tsa ti, *n.*; the west, the land to the west of the Hidatsa.

pä tsa ti lia, *adv.*; westward.

pä tsa ti koa, *adv.*; at or in the west.

pá tska, *adj.*; flattened, having one or more plane surfaces.

pa tská pi, *v. t., fr.* tskapi; to prick with a pin; to stick with an instrument held in the hand.

pa tskaš, *n.* proper. See Local Names.

pa tskí di a, *n., fr.* patska; cactus, particularly the different species of *Opuntia* or prickly pear.

pa tskí di a ó ka, *n., fr.* patskidiaoki *and* a; the round cactus of the Upper Missouri, which bears a pleasant edible fruit.

pa tskí di a ó ki, *n., fr.* patskidia *and* oki (alluding to the way in which the fruit grows on the plant); the fruit of the round cactus or *Mammillaria*. The name has recently been applied to figs.

pąt

pą tskú pi, *v. t.,fr.* tskupi ; to fold up as a blanket or robe is folded.

pa wí di, *same as* pamidi.

pe, *v. t.* ; to swallow ; to take a meal in which both liquid and solid food are served.

pe, *v. t.* ; to grind, as coffee in a mill.

pe da ku dú ti, *n.,fr.* pedi, aku, *and* duti ; a vulgar name sometimes applied to dogs ; offensive epithet applied to persons whom they wish to liken to dogs.

pe da ku pá' te, *n.,fr.* pedi, aku, *and* pá'te ; a species of beetle.

pé de tska, *n.* ; the large crow or raven.

pé de tska i ta hii″ pi sa, *n.* ; *Phlox aristata.*

pe de tski sta pé di, *n.,fr.* pedetska *and* istapedi ; a sort of soft hail or snow falling in globular flakes, " mountain snow ".

pé di, *n.* ; any offensive matter or excretion, dregs, ordure.

phié ta, *n.* ; nasal mucus.

phié ta i si, *n.* ; a pocket-handkerchief.

pliu, verbal root, or *?fr.* liu ; squeeze out and let fall.

pliu ti, *v.* or verbal root *?fr.* pliu *or* liu ; squeeze forward, squeeze out. See kipliuti.

pi, *v. t.* ; to tattoo.

pi, verbal root ; penetrate. As a verb, often used synonymously with ipi.—mapi, dapi.

pí a, *v. i.* ; crepitate.

pi á ti, *v. i.,fr.* pia ; denoting desire or readiness.

pi dá lipa, *v., adj.* ; light and thin, as silken goods.

púa

pí di e, *v., adj.* ; ruffled or frilled, ornamented with a ruffled border.

pi é, *v., adj.* ; smoky ; said of atmosphere rendered disagreeable by smoke.

pi é ksa, *adj.* ; constantly and disagreeably smoky.

pi ta kic tí a, *adj.* See pitikietia.

pí ti ka, *num. adj.* ; ten.

pi ti kic tí a, *num. adj., fr.* pitika *and* ictia ; one hundred.

pi ti kic tí a-á ka ko di, *num. adj.* ; one thousand.

pkí ti, *v. t.,fr.* kiti *or* pakiti ; to smooth out ; to iron clothes.—mapkiti, I smooth. dapkiti [na], you smooth. The word pkiti alone is rarely heard ; for in the third person the intensive form, kipkiti, is used.

pó a du a dsi, *adj.,fr.* poadui ; of a hemispherical or somewhat spherical appearance.

pó a du i, *adj.* ; globular, hemispherical, or nodular.

pó a du i ke, *v. t.* ; to make globular.

psu, verbal root ; dislocate ; knock out of line.

psu ki, *v. i.* ; to belch.—mapsuki, I belch. dapsuki, you belch.

psu kic ti, *v. i., fr.* psuki ; denoting desire or readiness.

psú ti, *v. t.,fr.* psu ; to dislocate.—kipsuti is the more common form.

ptsú ti, *v. t.* ; to shove or thrust forward, to protrude. See kiptsuti, which is the form most commonly used.

pú a, *v. i., adj.* ; to swell ; to be swollen, as a bruise ; also to rot or become putrid.

púa

pú a de, *v. i., adj.*; to be tainted or sour, but not decidedly rotten.

pu á du i, *v. i.*; becoming swollen, swelling gradually and constantly.

pú a ke, *v. t.*; to cause to swell, to inflict an injury which produces swelling; swollen.

pu á kša, *v. i.*; constantly swollen.

pú dsi, *v. t.*; to mark with fine indentations closely set; to sew with fine stitches; to wrap fine thread closely around; to wind colored horsehairs or porcupine quills closely around a buckskin string for ornament. The object of this verb is the name of the material used in wrapping or marking.

pú dsi ke, *v. t.*; to cause to be finely sewed, indented, or enwrapped. The object of this verb is the name of the article on which the marking or wrapping is done.

pu é, *n.*; visible vapor from warm water; mist, fog.

pu é, *v. i.*; to steam (said of water); misty.

pú lia ki, *n.*; sand.

pu″ lia ki a té, *n., fr.* puliaki *and* ate; a sand-bar appearing above the surface of the water; a sandy island.

pú lii, *n.*; foam or lather.

pú lii, *adj.*; freckled, blotched.

pú lii, *v. i.*; to foam.

pú lii ke, *v. t.*; to cause to foam, to agitate until a foam is produced.

pú pu, *n.*; a tall species of grass, the Dakota *cedi.*

pú zi, *adj.*; spotted, figured, or striped.

šah

pú zi ke, *v. t.* to mark or ornament with spots or figures; spotted.

pú zi ke, *n.*; the domestic cat, an animal not long known to this tribe. The name is said to come from puzi; but it was probably, to some extent, suggested by the English term pussy-cat.—puzike sounds just as the Hidatsa would be most likely to corrupt or mispronounce pussy-cat.

pú zi ke da ka, *n.*; a kitten.

r.

r. Words heard to begin with the sound of r may be found under d, these letters being interchangeable. See ¶¶ 19, 20, 22.

s.

s. Words heard to begin with the sound of s may be found in this dictionary with ts for their first letters. See ¶ 17.

š.

ša, *n.*; *same as* šada.

ša á ka, *n.*; a frog.

šá da, *n.*; pudendum muliebre.

ša hĕ, *n.*; the Cree or Knistineaux Indians. Assineboine "sha-i-yé". Other tribes of this region call the Crees by names which sound much like šahe or shaiye. There are various explanations of the derivations, but they are all doubtful.

šák

šá ka, *n., same as* šaaka; a frog. In the first syllable, the vowel is prolonged or pronounced as if doubled.

ša ka du šú ki, *n., fr.* šaki *and* adušuki; the knuckles.

ša ká pi, *adj.*; tepid, lukewarm.

ša ká pi he, *v. t.*; to make tepid.

šá ki, *n.*; the human hand; sometimes applied to the forepaws of brutes.—šaki, alone and in derivatives beginning with it, is commonly preceded by the pronouns. See išaki.

ša ki a du tsá mi he, *n.*; fingers.

ša ki du má ta du, *n., fr.* šaki *and* dumatadu; the middle finger.

ša ki i ó ptsa ti, *n., fr.* šaki *and* ioptsati; a finger-ring.

šá ki i ta ki da ka" he, *n., fr.* šaki *and* itakidakahe; a span; a span measure.

šá ki ka zi, *n., diminutive of* šaki; the little finger.

ša ki ka zi ú ti du, *n.*; the third finger. See utidu.

ša ki ó ptsa ti, *a contraction of* šakiioptsati.

šá ki ta, *n.*; the thumb.

ša kú pa du i, *v. i.*; becoming crooked, warping.

ša kú pi, *adj.*; crooked.

ša kú pi he, *v. t.*; to distort; to bend.

ša kú pi ke, *v. t.*; to make crooked.

šá mi, hypothetical word; aunt. See išami.

šá pu a, *num. adj.*; seven.

šá pu a he, *v. t.*; to make into seven forms or parts.

šá pu a he ke, *v. t.*; to cause to

šét

make into seven; nearly synonymous with šapuake.

šá pu a ke, *v. t.*; to separate into seven parts, to divide into sevenths; divided into sevenths.

ša pú a pi ti ka, *num. adj.*; seventy.

šá ša, *v., adj.*; to fork or divide; forked, branched.

ša šú ka du i, *v. i.*; becoming dull or blunt.

ša šú ki, *adj.*; dull, as an edge-tool.

ša šú ki he, *v. t.*; to tickle.—nišašukimáwits, I will tickle you.

ša šú ki ke, *v. t.*; to cause to be dull.

še, *demonst. pron.*; that one, that thing.—šets, that is he, that is the very one.

šé du, *adv., fr.* še *and* du; there; then; at that very time or place. As a suffix, this word is used to denote time, as the English *last* or *ago*. (¶ 255).

šé i ške, *adv., fr.* še *and* iške; just as directed, just as ordered.

šé ka, *adj., fr.* še *and* ka; of the same size as something previously described.

šé ko a, *adv., fr.* še *and* koa; there, at that very place.

šé ru, *adv., same as* šedu.

šé ša, *adj., adv., fr.* še *and* iša *or* iše; *same as* šeše.

šé še, *adj., adv.*; resembling something previously described, "just like that".

šé šets, a form of the last word used when it is desired to agree with some particular version of a story; "it is just as you say".

šé tá, *adv.*; "not the same as that", "not just that".—šetáts.

šé tsa ki, verb or phrase used as

šía

a pronoun; that alone; he or she unaided or unaccompanied.

ší a, synonymous with še. Possibly the latter is a contraction.

ší a ka. See šeka, šiakats.

ší di, *adj.*; tawny, dull yellow.

ší di ke, *v. t.*; to make tawny, to color a dull yellow.

ši dí ši, *v. i., fr.* diši; to hasten, to be in a hurry.—dišidiši, hurry thou.

ši dí ši ke, *v. t.*; to cause to hurry, to make hasten.

ši ká ka, *n.*; a young man.

ši kí a, *adj.*; curly, as the hair of a buffalo; said also of tangled underwood.

ší ki he, *v. t.*; to curl.

ší pa, *n.*; the bowels.

ší pe, *adv.*; tangled, hard to penetrate; said of bad-lands, dense woods, etc.

ší pi, *adj.*; black, pure black.

ší pi he, *v. t.*; to blacken; to apply powdered charcoal.

ší pi ša, *adj., fr.* šipi *and* iša; blackish; of a very dark blue, brown, or other color scarcely distinguishable from black; often applied to pure black.

ší pi ša de, *adj.*; almost black, distinguishable from black, but approaching it.

ši pi ša dsá du i, *v. i.*; becoming dark, as the face from exposure to weather.

ši pi šá dsi, *adj.*; resembling black, seeming to be blackish.

ši pi šá dsi he, *v. t.*; to darken, to deepen or darken the color.

ši pi šá dsi ke, *v. t.*; to dye of a darkish color.

ši pi šá du i, *v. i.*; darkening, becoming blackish (as iron allowed to cool); said when re-

ta

porting the progress of an operation for dyeing of a blackish color.

ší pi ša ke, *v. t.*; to make very dark; to dye anything of a black or blackish color.

ší ta, hypothetical. See išita.

ške, *v.*; command; direct.

šku, verbal root; force through, extract.

só ki, *adj.*; broad; often used for dull. See šašuki.

šú a, *adj., adv.*; slow; slowly.

šú a ha, *adv.*; slowly.

šú a ke, *v. t.*; to cause to move slowly, to retard motion.

šú e, *v. t.*; to spit.

šú i, *n.*; unmelted fat, adipose tissue.

šú ka, perhaps hypothetical; a dog, a beast of burden; *same as Dakota,* šunka; found in the words itsuašuka, itašuka, mašuka, etc.

šú ki, *adj.; same as* šoki.

t.

ta, *adv.*; only, but; commonly pronounced as if suffixed.

tǎ *or* **ta',** an adverb and adverbial suffix denoting negation; not. As it commonly terminates a sentence, it is often heard pronounced tǎts. Ex.—itskits, *it is large enough.* itskitǎts, *it is not large enough.* (¶ 260).

ta, a suffix to nouns and pronouns denoting possession, particularly acquired or transferable possession. (¶ 85).

ta, *prep.*; toward, in the direction of, etc.; suffixed to nouns, it forms adverbs. (¶ 261).

ta, *v. i.* and *t.*; to kill; to be killed.

tá da to di [-la-], to discharge a gun.

ta dé, *v. i.*; almost killed; nearly dead.

tá di [-ri], *v. t.*; to cross over, to go from one side to the other; to row or swim across a stream.

tá du, hypothetical. See itadu.

ta hé, *v. t., fr.* ta; to kill; he kills.—tamats, I kill. tadats, you kill. tahets, he kills.

ta hú', *n., v.*; thunder; to thunder. Like most other tribes of the plains the Hidatsa attribute thunder to the movements of a great bird.

ta hú i da ka, *n., fr.* tahu' *and* idaka; low rumblings of thunder following a loud peal.

ta hú i ki šiš, *n.* See Local Names.

tá ka, *interrog. pron.*; what; which.

ta ka dá [-ra], what do you say?

tá ka ta, *inter. adv., fr.* taka; in what direction, whither.—tápata and tóta are synonyms more commonly employed.

tá ki, *adj.*; white. See ataki and iliótaki.

ta mú a [tabua], *v., fr.* mua; to make a loud ringing sound, to be ringing, to ring.

ta mú li, *adj.*; very fine, minute.

ta mú li di, *adj.*; exceedingly fine, very minute.

tá pa, *interrog. pron.*; what? what is it?

ta pá, *adj.*; soft, easily broken or yielding.

ta pá i, *adj., same as* tapa.

tá pa ta, *adv.*; in what direction, whither.—tapata dade, where are you going?

ta pé, *interrog. pron.*; who.

ta pé i ta, *interrog. poss. pron.*; whose.

ta pé ta, *same as* tapeita.

ta pi, verbal root; press, squeeze. See dutapi, etc.

tá ta, *adv.*; referring to past time not very distant; a short time ago, some time ago.

tá ta ko a, *adv.*; at or during a past period not very distant.

ta tsá dsi, *adj., fr.* tatsi; thickish, appearing to be thick.

ta tsá du i, *v.*; thickening.

tá tsi, *adj.*; thick, as cloth, etc.; also used to express total obscurity of the sky. See apalitatsi.

tá tsi ke, *v. t.*; to thicken; thickened.

ta wú li, *same as* tamuli.

te, *v., adj.*; dead.—tets, he is dead.

te dú ti [-ruti], *n.*; a prairie terrace; a low open plain.

té he, *v.*; to die.—temats, I am dying. temamits, I will die.

ti, a suffix to verbs denoting readiness or desire to perform an action; to be about to —.

ti a, *adv., same as* tie.

ti di a, *v. i.*; to run.

ti di é ke, *v. t.*; to cause to run; to race a horse.

ti e, *n., adv.*; a long time; long continuing.

ti e duk [-ruk], *adv.*; referring to distant futurity.

ti e hi duk, *adv.*; when a distant future time shall arrive.

ti pi a, *n.*; mud.

ti pi a da zi. See Local Names.

ti pi á tsa ki, *v., adj., fr.* tipia

tip

· *and* tsaki; soiled with mud, bespattered with mud.

ti pi á tsa ki ke, *v. t.*; to cause to be soiled with mud.

ti śa *or* **ti śe,** *adj., adv.*; far, distant; to a distance.

ti tsá du i, *v. i., fr.* titsi; thickening, increasing in diameter.

tí tsi, *adj.*; thick, as a fat or swollen limb or the trunk of a large tree; refers to diameters of cylindrical bodies.

tí tsi ke, *v. t.*; to thicken, to increase in diameter; thickened.

tí tsi ksa, *adj.*; thick excessively and habitually, as a permanently swollen limb.

to, *interrog. adv.* and *pron.*; what place? what person? what kind or color?

tó du [-ru], *adv., fr.* to *and* du; in what place? wherein? whereat?

to ha dsá du i, *v. i., fr.* tohadsi; assuming a bluish hue.

tó ha dsi, *adj.*; having a bluish or impure blue color.

tó ha dsi ke, *v. t.*; to dye an impure blue color.

tó ha du i, *v. i.*; assuming a blue color.

tó hi, *adj.*; blue; denotes pure or positive blues, sky-blue, ultramarine.

tó hi ke, *v. t.*; to dye anything a pure blue.

tó hi śa, *adj., fr.* tohi *and* iśa; of a color allied to blue; green. See mika'tohiśa.

tó hi śa ke, *v. t.*; to dye anything green or other color allied to blue.

tok, *adv.*; it is used after sentences and verbs to denote prob-

tsa

ability or uncertainty; hence, it is often used interrogatively and is frequently followed by madiets, *I suppose.*

tó ka, *adv., fr.* to *and* ka; whereto? where? whither?

tó ka ta *or* **tó kta,** synonymous with toka.—tókatadade [toktarade, toktalale], where are you going?

tó pa, *num. adj.*; four.

tó pa he, *v. i.* and *t.*; to part in four.

to pa hé ke, *v. t.*; to cause to part in four.

tó pa ke, *v. t.*; to divide into four parts; divided into four parts.

to pá pi ti ka, *n., adj., fr.* topa *and* pitika; forty.

tó śa, *interrog. adv., fr.* to; how? in what manner?

to śé, *interrog. adv.*; why? wherefore?

tó ta, *interrog adv., fr.* to; in what direction? toward what place?—tótadade [totarade, totalale], in what direction are you going?

to' ti, verbal root; implying sudden, repeated reversion of motion. See dato'ti, duto'ti, pato'ti, etc.

tsa, *adj.*; raw, uncooked.

tsa, verbal root; separate, divide.

tsá da, *n.*; grease, oil.

tsá da, *v.* or verbal root; slide, move smoothly.

tsá da ke, *v. t.*; to make slide, to cause to assist to slide.

tsa dá tsa ki, *adj., fr.* tsada, *grease, and* tsaki; soiled with grease.

tsa hí du mi di, *v. i., fr.* dumidi; to suffer from vertigo.

tsa kȧ dsi, *adj.*, *fr.* tsȧki ; moderately good ; rather pretty.

tsa kȧ dsi ke, *v. t.* ; to make moderately good.

tsa kȧ du i, *v. i.* ; improving, becoming good.

tsa kȧk', *interj.* ; an expression of contempt or disapprobation.

tsa kȧ ka, *n.* ; a bird.

tsa kȧ ka da ka, *n.* ; an egg ; eggs.

tsa kȧ ka hi, *n.*, *fr.* tsakaka *and* hi ; feathers, any portion of a bird's plumage.

tsa kȧ ka i kȋ śi, *n.* ; a bird's nest.

tsȧ ke *or* **tsȧki**, modified verbal root ; to cause to be divided.

tsȧ ki, *v. i.*, *adj.* ; to be stained with — ; to be rendered offensive ; suffixed to nouns it forms adjectives ; as amatsaki, tsadatsaki, *et al.*

tsȧ ki *or* **tsȧkits** *or* **sȧkits**, *adj.* ; good ; pretty ; often accented on last syllable.

tsȧ ki, *v.* ; alone, by itself ; used only with pronouns. See ítsȧki, mítsȧki, and śetsȧki.

tsȧ kíc ti, *adj.*, *fr.* tsȧki ; very good ; very beautiful.—tsȧkictidi denotes a still higher degree of excellence than tsȧkicti.

tsȧ ki hȧ, *adv.* ; quiet, quietly.

tsȧ ki hȧ mak, *v. comp.*, *imperative*, *fr.* tsȧkiha *and* amak ; sit quietly, stay quiet.

tsȧ ki he, *v.*, *adv.*, *fr.* tsȧki ; well, in a satisfactory manner ; to act well.

tsȧ ki ke, *v. t.*, *fr.* tsȧki ; to improve, to make good, to cure a disease ; improved, cured, restored.—kitsȧkike is more frequently employed.

tsa kȋś, *n.* ; something inferior or worthless, a nuisance.

tsa mȧk, a form of tsame, used in the sense of a noun.—tsamak iśiats, its being hot is bad, *i. e.*, the heat is oppressive.

tsa mé [-we], *adj.* ; hot, very warm.—tsawéts, it is hot.

tsa mé a te [-we-], *v. i.*, *fr.* tsame *and* ate ; to perspire.

tsa mé he, *v. t.* ; to heat.

tsa mé ke, *v. t.*, to make hot, to change from hot to cold ; heated.

tsa mé kśa, *adj.* ; constantly warm ; very warm.

tsa mȧ tsa dśi [-wu-], *adj.*, *fr.* tsamutsi ; straightish, nearly straight or appearing to be straight.

tsa mȧ tsa du i, *v. i.* ; straightening.

tsa mȧ tsi [-wu-], *adj.* ; straight.

tsa mȧ tsi de, *adj.* ; almost straight.

tsa mȧ tsi he, *v. t.* ; to straighten.

tsa mȧ tsi ke, *v. t.* ; to straighten ; straightened.

tsȧ pi, *adj.* ; puckered, wrinkled.

tsȧ ti, *v.*, *adj.* ; smoothed ; oiled ; polished.

tsa' ti, verbal root, or *fr.* tsa ; stick, impale.

tsȧ ti ke, *v. t.*, *fr.* tsati ; to polish.

tsȧ tse *or* **tsȧtsi** *or* **sȧtsi**, *n.* ; a species of goshawk or falcon, known on the Upper Missouri as the " spotted eagle ".

tsa tsȧ i ta ma pa, *n.* ; the pasque flower or pulsatilla.

tsa tsȧ ki, *adj.*, *fr.* tsuki *and* ?tsa ; hard to break, not brittle.

tsa tsȧ ki ke, *v. t.* ; to render hard ; hardened.

tsi

tsi, *n.,* hypothetical word; foot; hind paw. See itsi, ditsi, and matsi.

tsi, a prefix to verbs denoting a low or jingling sound. See tsimua and tsitside.

tsi. See tsídi.

tsi dä dsi, *adj., fr.* tsidi; yellowish; orange-colored.

tsi dä du i, *v. i.;* becoming yellow.

tsí di, *adj.;* yellow. In compound words, this is often represented by its first syllable 'tsi', which may be a word wherefrom tsidi is derived.

tsi dí a, *same as* tsidie.

tsi di á du i, *v. i.;* becoming cold.

tsi dí e *or* **tsí di ets,** *adj.;* cold; refers chiefly to reduction of temperature in inorganic bodies.

tsi dí e, *n;* cold weather; winter is sometimes so called.

tsi dí e ke, *v. t.;* to cause to be cold; chilled.

tsí di ke, *v. t., fr.* tsidi; to dye of a yellow color.

tsí di šĕ pi, *adj., fr.* tsidi *and* šipi; bay; said in describing horses.

tsi kó a, *adj.;* having a marked but not unpleasant taste, sweet, salty, savory.

tsi kó a de, *adj.;* almost salty, having a slight saline taste; said of such "alkali springs" and creeks as have water not very strong or unpalatable.

tsi ko á dsi, *adj.;* sweetish.

tsi ko á du i, *v. i.;* becoming sweet; said of coffee which is being alternately sweetened and tasted.

tsí

tsi kó a ke, *v. t.;* to sweeten; sweetened.

tsi mú a [-bua], *v. i.* and *t., fr.* mua; to jingle, as metallic pendants, steel chains, etc.

tsí pa, *n.;* a marmot; a prairie-dog.

tsi pa ku šú ti, *n.;* the burrowing owl, which dwells along with the prairie-dog.

tsí pa tso pe, *n., fr.* tsipa *and* ?tsope; the striped marmot, *Spermophilus tridecem-lineatus.*

tsí pi, *v. i.;* to sink, to sink in water.

tsí pi de, *v. i.;* almost sunken, sinking but rescued in time.

tsí pi ke, *v. t.;* to cause to sink; to scuttle, overload, or upset a boat and make it sink.

tsí pĭ ti, *v. i., fr.* tsĭpi; to be in a condition to sink, or ready to sink; said if something falls on the surface of the water, and it is yet uncertain whether it will sink or not; said of a river-bank which is being gradually washed away.

tsi pĭ ti de, *v., adj.;* nearly in a position to fall upon water; said of portions of a river bluff that are cracked off and ready to topple, or of anything in danger of falling on water.

tsi pĭ ti ke, *v. t.;* to cause to fall upon water; to place in a condition favorable to sinking.

tsí ta, *n.;* the tail of a quadruped.

tsí ta ši pi ša, *n., fr.* tsita *and* šipiša; the black-tailed deer, *Cervus macrotis.*

tsí ta tạ ki, *n., fr.* tsita *and* tạki; the white-tailed deer, *Cervus virginianus.*

tsí tsi de, *v. i., fr.* tsi *and* ide; to whisper.

tsí tska, *n.*; the " prairie-hen " of Western Dakota—the sharp-tailed grouse, *Pediœcetes phasianellus* var. *columbianus.*

tsí tska do lipa ka, *n., fr.* tsitska *and* dolipaka; the Prairie-hen People, one of the hereditary bands or totems of the Hidatsa tribe.

tsí tska ic tí a, *n., fr.* tsitska *and* i tia; the sage-hen, *Centrocercus urophasianus.*

tsi tú ki, *adj.*; turned up, pugged.

tská pi, verbal root; denotes pressure on a small surface; pinch, squeeze, poke.

tská ti, verbal root; pass or force through an aperture.

tskí ti, verbal root; denotes pressure on a small surface from different **directions**; strangle, shear, etc.

tskú pi, verbal root; bend, fold, double. See datskupi and patskupi.

tsó hi, *adj.*; pointed, tapering.

tsó hi ke, *v. t.*; to point, to taper.

tsó ka du i, *v. i., fr.* tsoki; becoming hard, solidifying, congealing.

tsó ki, *adj.*; hard; resisting pressure, but not necessarily hard to break.

tsó ki he, *v. i.* and *t.*; to harden.

tsó ki ke, *v. t.*; to harden by baking or otherwise; hardened by any obvious cause or process.

tsó pe, *v. i.*; to make a chirping or smacking sound.

tsu, *n.*; half; side; division; compartment.

tsu, *adj.* (radicle); smooth, flat.

tsú a, *adj.*; narrow.

tsú a de, *adj.*; almost narrow enough.

tsu á dsi, *adj.*; narrowish, seemingly narrow.

tsú a he, *adj.*, *? fr.* tsua; synonymous with tsohi, which may be a contraction of tsuahe.

tsú a ke, *v. t.*; to make narrow.

tsu á ta, *n.*; brains.

tsú he, *v. t., fr.* tsu; to divide into two parts; to halve.

tsu i ta dó ta du, *n., adv., fr.* itadotadu; bottom-land on the near side of a river; in the bottom-land, etc.

tsu i ta dó ta ko a [-lota-], *adv.*; at or on the portion of bottom-land or flood-plain on the near side of the river, " on the point this side ".

tsu i ta ó ka du [-ru], *n., adv., fr.* itaokadu; the part of the bottom-land beyond a river; on the opposite side of the river in the bottom.

tsu i ta ó ka ko a, *adv.*; at or in the bottom on the opposite side of a river.

tsú ka, *adj.*; flat, as low ground.

tsú ka, *adv.*; at or in the bottom-land.

tsú ki, *adj.*, *same as* tsoki.

tsú ta, *n., adv.*; a half; the side of a house; an apartment; in an apartment.

tsú ta he, *v. t.*; to break into halves.

tsú ta ka, *adv.*; within a half or portion; in one side.

tsú ta ta, *adv.*; toward one side; toward one half or portion.

tsu tsú hi, *v. i.*; to rattle or stamp loudly.

tsú tsu te, *adj.*; smooth to the touch, soft; also tsutsuti.

tsé

tsé se, *n.*; the large wolf.

tsé sa do lipa ka [-no-], *n.*, *lit.*, *Wolf People;* the Pawnee Indians.

tsé sa ma si, *n.*, *fr.* tsesa *and* masi; a gray blanket.

tú a, *interrog. adv.*; nearly synonymous with to.

tú a ka, *interrog. adj.*, *fr.* tua; how much? how many?

tú a ka duk, *adv.*, *fr.* tuaka *and* duk; how long hence? how many days or nights hence?

tú a ka ruk, *adv.*, same *as* tuakaduk.

tú a ka se du [-ru], *interrog. adv.*, *fr.* tuaka *and* sedu; how long ago? how many days ago?

tú a kạts, when tuaka stands alone as an interrogative it takes this form.

tú a mi, *interrog. adv.*, *fr.* tua *and* mi; how many?

tú a wits, same *as* tuami, with terminal 'ts'.

u.

u, *v.*; to wound; to be wounded.

u á, *v. t.*; to envy; he envies.— amáts, I envy. adáts, you envy. uáts, he envies.

ú a, *n.*; a wife, a wife by actual marriage; not perfectly synonymous with itadamia.

ú a he, *v. t.*; to marry. (¶ 203).

u a hé ke, *v. t.*; to cause to marry, to give or take in marriage; said usually of the female.

ú a ke, *v. t.*; to cause to be a wife; married.

u ä lipi, *v. t.*; to smash by shooting.

úhi

ú a ka, *n.*, *? fr.* ua *and* ika; a man's brother's wife.

ú ạ ki, *n.*; anything used as bedding, except a pillow; a mattress, sheet, blanket, robe, or skin used as bedding.

ú ạ ki tạ tsi, *n.*, *fr.* uạki *and* tạtsi; a mattress; a tick.

u ä ksa, *v. i.* and *t.*, *fr.* ná; to envy habitually, to be of an envious disposition.

u á ti, *v. t.*; to ridicule.

u á ti ksa, *v. t.*; to ridicule unreasonably or habitually.

ú dsa du i, *v. i.*; drying, becoming dry.

ú dsi, *adj.*; dry, devoid of moisture; thirsty.

ú dsi de, *adj.*; nearly dry.

ú dsi ke, to cause to dry, to place before a fire to dry; dried.

ú e, *v. i.*; to boil. See midue.

ú e he, *v. t.*; to boil; he boils.

ú e tsa, *n.*; metal of any kind; coin; recently applied to money of any description and to the unit of our money, a dollar.— uetsa duetsa [luetsa], one dollar. uetsa topa, four dollars. uetsa itatsuhe, half a dollar.

ú e tsa hi sí" si, *n.* (hisisi, *reddish*); copper.

u e tsa í du ti, *n.*, *fr.* uetsa *and* iduti; a bridle-bit.

u e tsa ká' ti, *n.* (ká'ti, *true*); gold.

ú e tsa ma i kta de", *n.*, *fr.* uetsa *and* maiktade; a nail.

u e tsa sí di, *n.* (sidi, *tawny*); brass.

u e tsa sí pi sa, *n.* (sipisa, *black*); iron.

ú hi, *n.*; American antelope.

ú hi ma du ti, *n.*, *lit.*, antelope food; the prairie sage, *Artemisia.*

úi

ú i, *n.*; paint for the face, rouge, vermilion.

ú i l si, *n., fr.* ui *and* isi; a paint-bag, a small embroidered bag for holding vermilion or other paint for the face.

ú ka ki, *v. i., ? fr.* kaki; to roll, as a horse rolls himself on the ground.

ú ka ta ka zi, *n.* See Local Names.

ú ka ta ki, *n., fr.* uki *and* ataki; a white earth which these Indians use in decorating their bodies.

ú ki, *n.*; indurated clay, compact earth of uniform appearance.

ú ki a ta ki, *same as* ukataki.

ú ma ta, *n.*; the south, land south of the Hidatsa hunting-grounds.

ú ma ta lia, *adv.*; toward the south.

ú ma ta ko a, *adv.*; at the south.

ú ma ta ta, *adv.*; southward, looking or moving south.

ú sa ti, *n.*; east, land east of the Hidatsa country.

ú sa ti lia, *adv.*; eastward, toward the east.

ú sa ti ko a, *adv.*; at the east, in the east.

14

z

ú sa ti ta, *adv.*; facing the east.

ú si, *n.*; the anal region.

ú ti, *n.*; base, bottom; root or larger extremity.

ú ti lia, *adv.*; toward the base or bottom; qualifies verbs denoting motion.

ú ti du, *adv.*; in the base, bottom, or root.

ú ti ko a, *adv.*; at the base. utikoa and utidu are often used in the sense of *near, beside,* or *ad-joining.*

ú tsi tsa, *n.*; a variety of change-able weasel, or so-called "er-mine".

ú zi a, *v. t.*; to pay a visit; to meet, to encounter.

W.

w. Words heard to begin with the sound of w may be found under m. (¶ ¶ 5, 20, 21).

Z.

z. No words have been noted as beginning with z.

LOCAL NAMES.

The names of some localities known to the tribe are here given together for convenience of reference. The translations are in *italics*.

á di ša I ta pa" hiš, *fr.* adiša, ita, *and* pahi ; *Song of the Ravens* or *Singing-place of the Ravens;* a high butte situated between the Missouri and Little Missouri Rivers, west of Fort Berthold.

a ma dé ta ku ši" diš, *fr.* amadeta, a k u, *and* šidiš ; *Tawny Bluff;* a prominent river bluff on the south side of the Missouri, about fifteen miles below the mouth of the Yellowstone.

a ma de ta ma pa" hiš, *fr.* amadeta *and* mapahi ; *Song Bluff;* a prominent point on the Missouri, below the last.

a ma ic pu ša šaš, *fr.* amaicpu *and* šaša ; *Forked Hill-top;* a high butte south of the Missouri in the neighborhood of the upper Great Bend.

a ma mąk i má ka da, *Lands Crossing One Another;* the lower Great Bend of the Missouri, near Fort Thompson. The derivation is indicated in the word mąki-makadaha, which see.

a má ti, The Missouri River. Some of the tribe say that the name comes from ama, *earth,* and alludes to its muddiness ; others think it is from mati, *a boat,* and alludes to its navigability.

a ma" ti a du ša šaš, *fr.* amati *and* adušaša ; *Fork of the Missouri ;* Milk River is sometimes so called.

a má ti ka za, *fr.* amati *and* kaza ; *Little Missouri River.* The English name is a literal translation of the Hidatsa.

a má ti pa" du iš, *fr.* amati *and* padui ; *Short Missouri;* a small stream entering the Missouri from the south, above Fort Berthold.

a ma tsí di o du tsi [-tsiš], *fr.* amatsidi *and* odutsi ; *Ochre Mine;* a place southeast of the mouth of the Yellowstone, where a yellow mineral pigment is obtained.

a pá di a ziš, *fr.* apadi *and* azi ; *Porcupine River;* a stream entering the Missouri in Montana Territory.

dă lipi tsa" tu a du a má kiš [nă-], *fr.* dalipitsi, atu, adu, *and* amaki ; *Place Where the Bear's Head Sits;* a high hill rising from the plateau, southeast of Fort Buford and north of the Little Missouri.

dă lipí tsi a du a ma" kiš, *fr.* dalipitsi, adu, *and* amaki ; *Place Where the Bear Sits;* the termination of a mountainous ridge, immediately opposite the mouth of Milk River, Montana.

dă lipí tsi a ziš; *Bear River;* Milk River, Montana.

dă' ta a zi [-ziš], *fr.* da'ta *and* azi ; *Heart River;* the Heart River, which enters the Mis-

210

souri from the west, above Fort Rice.

dé zi a zi [neziazis], *fr.* dezi and azi; *Tongue River;* the Tongue River, a branch of the Yellowstone.

do ki dá hi ta pa hiš [no-], *fr.* dokidalii, ita, and pahi; *Singing of the Ghosts,* or *Where the Ghosts Sing;* a high pinnacle of red rocks about mid-way between the Little Missouri and Yellowstone Rivers near the point of greatest proximity of the two streams.

hi dá tsa, formerly the principal village of this tribe when they dwelt on Knife River.

hi dá tsa ti, *fr.* hidatsa and ati; *Dwelling of the Hidatsa Indians;* the present village of the tribe at Fort Berthold.

lia lia" tu a a du ta hés, *fr.* lialiatua, adu, and tahe; *Where the Chippeway was Killed;* a locality near the foot of the upper Great Bend of the Missouri.

i hic ti" a a du ta hés, *Where Big Forehead was Killed;* the Tobacco Garden bottom, at the mouth of Tobacco Garden Creek.

i té ma tse e tsiš, *fr.* ite and matseetsi; *Face of the Chief;* the Black Hills of Dakota.

ma é tsi a zis, *fr.* maetsi and azi; *Knife River;* a name applied to two streams, one of which enters the Missouri from the north, above Fort Berthold, and the other from the south, below that place.

ma ka dí sta ti, *fr.* makadišta and ati; *House of the Infants;* a cavern near the old villages on Knife River, supposed to be inhabited by mysterious infants.

ma o dé ša a zi [-ne-], *fr.* maodeša and azi; *Nothing River* or *Nameless River;* an affluent of the Little Missouri, entering the latter about one hundred miles above its mouth.

ma pó kša a ti, *fr.* mapokša and ati; *Snake House;* a cave near the Missouri River, on the north or left bank, close to Snake Creek. It is said, at some seasons, to swarm with serpents.

ma pó kša a ti a zi [-zis], *Snake House River.* So called by these Indians; but Lewis and Clarke have given the name as "Snake Creek," and it has been thus known to the whites ever since. It enters the Missouri five miles east of Fort Stevenson, Dakota Territory.

ma šu" ka ak šu a ma šiš, *fr.* mašnkaakšu and amaši; *Earth-trap,* or *Eagle-trap,* of *Coral Berry;* a point on the left bank of the Missouri, immediately below the upper Great Bend.

má ta ki a ziš, *Dish River;* Platte River, Nebraska.

má tsu a zi [-zis], *fr.* matsu and azi; *Cherry River;* a stream which enters the Little Missouri from the east, above the maodešaaziš.

ma u" pa ki hú pa i šiš, *fr.* maupaki, hupa, and išiš; *Like the Handle of a Mallet;* a prominent bluff on the south side of the Missouri, nearly opposite the mouth of upper Knife River.

mi da I ši a ziš, *fr.* midaiši and azi; *Bark River;* a stream which enters the Missouri from the south above the Yellowstone.

mi dá tsa pi a ziš, *fr.* midatsapi and azi; *Powder River* or

Dust River; the branch of the Yellowstone now known as Powder River.

mi di ho pá [bidi-], *fr.* midi and hopa; *Sacred, Medicine,* or *Mysterious Water;* the Minnewakan or Devil's Lake, in northern Dakota.

mi di o dá mu a zis [bidionawuazi], *fr.* midi, odamu, and azi; '*River with Deep Spot* or *Channel.* Some say that this name signifies the *River that Rises,* or *River that Deepens,* and such may be liberal translations of the word; hence the English names of Rising-water and Tidewater Creek, and the French *L'eau-qui-mont.* This stream enters the Missouri from the north, about twenty-five miles west of the Grosventre village.

mi di si a zis, *fr.* midi, isia, and azi; *Bad Water River;* the Muddy, a stream flowing from the north and entering the Missouri about twenty-five miles east of Fort Buford.

mi di tó hi a zis, *fr.* midi, tohi, and azi; *Blue Water River;* a creek near Fort Berthold to the west.

mi te a tă di ke a zis, *fr.* miteatadike and azi; *Box Elder River;* a stream entering the Missouri from the south, about thirty miles below the mouth of the Yellowstone.

mi tsí a da zi [mitsianazi], *prob. fr.* mi', tsi or tsidi, and azi; the Yellowstone River.

mi tsí í ta mi dạ ksis, *fr.* mitsi, ita, and midaksi; *Palisade of the Wedge;* a high conical hill in the valley of the Little Missouri, some eighty miles southeast of the mouth of the Yellowstone; a prominent landmark.

pạ tskás, *fr.* pạtskə; the Coteau of the Missouri.

pe de tski" hi i ta a ma sís, *Eagle-trap of Crow-(Crop) Breast;* the bottom-land in the neighborhood of Dry Fork, on the road between Forts Buford and Stevenson.

ta hú i ki sis, *fr.* tahu and ikisi; *Nest of the Thunder;* a prominent flat-topped hill lying south of the Missouri, near the amaiepušašas.

ti pí a a zis, *or* **tipíanazis,** *Mud River;* the Big Muddy River, a stream flowing from the north and entering the Missouri about twenty miles west of Fort Buford.

ú ka tạ ka zis, *fr* ukiatạki and azi; *White-earth River.* The White Earth River enters the Missouri from the north in W. long. 102° 30' (nearly); it was formerly the extreme western boundary of Minnesota Territory.

ENGLISH-HIDATSA VOCABULARY.

ENGLISH-HIDATSA VOCABULARY.

A.

ABASE, v. t., išiake.
ABASH, v. t., itodike, kiitodike.
ABATING, par., kadištadui.
ABDOMEN, n., edi.
ABED, adv., maaduliápikoa.
ABJECT, adj., adiašadsi ka'ti.
ABOARD, adv., mátikoa, mati amahoka.
ABODE, n., ati, atike.
ABOLISH, v. t., kidešake.
ABOVE, pr., adv., aka, akoka.
ABRIDGE, v. t., kipaduike.
ABSORB, v. t., daliupi, liupi, kidaliupe.
ACCELERATE, v. t., kihitake.
ACCELERATING, par., hitadui.
ACCEPT, v. t., dutše.
ACCOMPANY, v. t., ikupa, ikupa de.
ACCOMPLISHED, par., komi, kikomike.
ACETABULUM, n., idikiutioki.
ACHE, v. i., ade, kiadó.
ADD, v. t., ikupake.
ADHERE, v. i., kaditskapa.
ADJUST, v. t., kikša.
ADMIRE, v. t., kideta, kidetadsi, ite.
ADULT, n., maietia.
ADVANCE, v. t., kiitsikake.
AFLOAT, adv., dakapilii.

AFRAID, adv., kie, kiets.
AFTER, adj., ipita, ipitakoa.
AFTERNOON, n., midimapedupahidakšipi.
AFTERWARDS, adv., ipitadu.
AGITATE, v. t., liakahe.
AGO, adv., šedu, tata, tatakoa. See HOW and LONG.
AHEAD, adv., itekoa, itsika.
ALIKE, adv., makšeše, makšešadsi, makšia. See EQUAL.
ALIVE, adj., tétats, hidakatsa.
ALL, adj., etsa, liakaheta.
ALOFT, adv., hakoka.
ALONE, adv., itsaki, mitsaki, šetsaki, etc.
ALSO, adv., iša.
ALTER, v. t., kiihake, ihake.
AMERICAN, n., maetsiietia.
AMIDST, prep., dumatadu [nuwataru].
AMPLE, adj., itski, itskits.
ANECDOTE, n., mazi.
ANGER, v. t., adeheke, da'ta išiake.
ANGLE, n., adupalii.
ANGLE, v. i., muakikidi, muadutsi.
ANGRY, adj., adehe, kiadehe.
ANNIHILATE, v. t., kidešake.
ANOTHER, n., iha, aduihá.
ANT, n., maпošakiditi.
ANTELOPE, n., ulii.
ANTIQUATE, v. t., liieke, kiliieke.
ANTLER, n., aziliami.
ANUS, n., uzi.

NOTE.—There are some Hidatsa words in this section which are not contained in the Dictionary proper. In such words, the accent is indicated; in the others, as a rule, it is not.

APART.

'BEAR.

APART, *adj.*, ihadu, ihakoa, mąkibita.

APEX, *n.*, icpu, aduícpu.

APPEAR, *v. i.*, ate, kiate.

APPROACH, *v. t.*, kiãtseke.

APRON, *n.*, išutipšąki, maišutipšaki.

AQUEOUS, *adj.*, miditsi.

ARE, *v.*, matu.

ARICKAREE INDIANS, *n.*, adakądaho.

ARISE, *v. i.*, iduhi, kiduba, kiduhe.

ARISEN, *part.*, kiduhi.

ARM, *n.*, ada, adaaduictia.

AROUND, *adv.*, ialialia.

AROUSE, *v. t.*, itsihe.

ARRANGE, *v. t.*, kikša.

ARROW, *n.*, ita, maita.

ARROW-CASE, *n.*, maitáiši.

ARROW-HEAD, *n.*, itahi', maitahi'.

ARROW-QUILLS, *n.*, itaišu, maitaišu.

ARTEMISIA, *n.*, iliokatąki-akušipiša. *See* SAGE.

ARTICHOKE, *n.*, kakša.

ASH, *n.*, mišpa.

ASHAMED, *adj.*, itodi, itodike.

ASHES, *n.*, midątsapi.

ASLEEP, *adj.*, hidami.

ASSINNEBOINE INDIANS, *n.*, hidušidi.

AT, *prep.*, ka, koa.

ATTEMPT, *v. t.*, maihe waihe.

AUGER, *n.*, mída-ikihópike.

AUNT, *n.*, išami, ika, mašawiš.

AURICLE, *n.*, akulii, apa.

AURORA BOREALIS, *n.*, apaliiadalia, amašitakoa-amaliati.

AUTUMN, *n.*, mata. NEXT —, mataduk.

AUTUMNAL, *adj.*, matadu.

AWAKE, *adj.*, itsi, hídamitats.

AWL, *n.*, matsito, matsitoictia.

AXE, *n.*, maiptsa, miiptsa.

B.

BABY, *n.*, makadišta, makidakši.

BACK, *n.*, išita. — *adv.*, ipita, ipitadu. — AND FORTH, dumaliita.

BACKBONE, *n.*, išítahidu.

BACKWARD, *adv.*, ipitakoa, ipitalia, išitakoa, išitalia.

BACON, *n.*, mašiitadalipitsišui, šui.

BAD, *adj.*, išia.

BAD-LANDS, *n.*, amušia, amašipe, *etc.*

BADGER, *n.*, amaka.

BAG, *n.*, iši.

BAKER, *n.*, madáliapi-akuhídi.

BALD, *adj.*, ada deša.

BALL, *n.*, mautąpi.

BAND, *n.*, icke, daki.

BANK, *n.*, amadeta, mídideta.

BANNER, *n.*, madakapilii.

BARGE, *n.*, midamati.

BARK, *n.*, midaiši, midiši [bidiši]. — *v. i.*, muadaki. — *r. t.*, daliąpi.

BARREL, *n.*, midiope-kakilii.

BARTER, *v. t.*, maihu [baihu, waihu].

BASE, *n.*, uti, aduúti. — *adj.*, išia.

BASIN, *n.*, matsamidi.

BASKET, *n.*, midąliasi [bidąliaši].

BAT, *n.*, išuatišia.

BATHE, *v.*, midipi, midipike [bidipi], dipi dipike.

BATTLE, *n.*, makimąkia.

BAY, *adj.*, tsidišipi.

BEADS, *n.*, akutohi, maaliidulia.

BEAK, *n.*, tsakaka apa.

BEAN, *n.*, amazi.

BEAR, *n.*, dalipitsi. — SKIN, dalipitsiodalipi. BEAR'S CLAW, dali pitsiicpu. — CUB, dalipitsidaka. — TRACK, dalipitsiti.

BEAR.

BEAR, v. t., ki ; edede.

BEARD, n., iki.

BEAT, v. t., diki.

BEAUTIFUL, adj., tsąki [sąkits], ite-tsąki.

BEAVER, n., midapá [bidapá, mira-pá].

BED, n., aduliąpi, itaduliąpi, maa-duliąpi. BEDDING, uaki.

BEEF, n., mité-iduksiti.

BEETLE, n., pedaknpa'te.

BEFOOL, v. t., kimadulitake, ma-dulitake.

BEFORE, prep., adv., itekoa, itsika.

BEG, v. t., kadi.

BEGGAR, n., aknkádiksa.

BEHIND, adv., ipitadu, ipitakoa.

BEHOLD, v. t., ika, ikada', ikaka.

BELCH, v. i., kipsuki, psuki.

BELIEVE, v. t., idie.

BELL, n., maitamna.

BELOW, prep., adv., miktata, mik-takoa, utikoa.

BELT, n., maipąsaki, maikipasaki.

BEND, v. t., dutskupi, kipatskupi, kipatskupike, patskupi, saku-pike.

BENT, part., kipątskupike.

BENUMB, v. t., otsliamike.

BERDACHE, n., miati.

BESIDE, adv., utikoa.

BESPATTER, v. t., opape.

BEWITCH, v. t., duskn.

BEYOND, prep., itaokadu, itaoka-koa, oka, okadu, okakoa.

BID, v. t., iske.

BIG, adj., ictia.

BIGGER, adj., ictia itaokakoa.

BIG-HORN, n., azietia.

BILLOW, n., mididąllisi.

BIND, v. t., duti.

BIRD, n., tsakaka.

BISECT, v. t., dopahe, dopaheke.

BISON, n., mite, kedapi.

BIT, n., kausta alipi, uetsa iduti.

BONE.

BITE, n., adudátsa. — v. t., dat-sa, datąpi [latąpi].

BITTER, adj., adui [elui].

BLACK, adj., sipi, sipisa. — PAINT, amasipisa.

BLACK-BIRD, n., tsakaka sipisa.

BLACK-DYE-STUFF, n., isipisake.

BLACKEN, v. t., sipihe, sipisake.

BLACKENING, part., sipisadui, ki-sipisadui.

BLACKFEET INDIANS, n., itsisibi-sa.

BLACKING, n., midahupa-ikitsatike.

BLACKISH, adj., sipisadsi.

BLADDER, n., úsikadąlii.

BLANKET, n., itasi, masi, uąki.

BLEACH, v. t., iliotakike, kiatąkike.

BLEACHING, part., atahadui, ilio-takadui.

BLEED, v. i., idihu.

BLIND, adj., ista desa.

BLOOD, n., idi.

BLOODY, adj., iditsaki.

BLOSSOM, n., odakapąki. — v. i., dakapąki, kidakapąki.

BLOTCHED, adj., pulii.

BLOW, v. t., kadse, katsi.

BLUE, adj., tohi. — DYE-STUFF, n., itohike, ikitohike.

BLUISH, adj., tohadsi, tohisa.

BLUFF, n., amadeta, amadetaku-maku, amadetakulialii.

BLUNT, adj., sasuki.

BOAR, n., masiitadalipítsi-kédapi.

BOARD, n., midatsnka.

BOAT, n., mati. SAIL-BOAT, hut-simati.

BODKIN, n., matsitoka.

BODY, n., ilio (lio, dilio, malio).

BOIL, n., aduitúdi, adupua.

BOIL, v. i., midue [bidue]. — v. t., miduehe, midueke, kimidueke.

BOLD, adj., kiadetsi.

BOLT, n., ikipatąki, maíkipatąki.

BONE, n., hidu.

BONNET.

BONNET, *n.*, apoka, mía-apoka.

BOOK, *n.*, mamadaki.

BOOT, *n.*, midahupa [bidahupa].

BORDER, *n.*, deta, adudeta.

BOSOM, *n.*, imąki.

BOTTLE, *n.*, midiaduiiśi [bidielui–].

BOTTOM, *n.*, mikta, uti; tsuka, tsuitaokadu, tsuitadotadu, *etc.*

BOW, *n.*, itadulia, midulia.

BOWELS, *n.*, śipa.

BOWL, *n.*, matsamidikaza.

BOX, *n.*, iope, maiope, midaiope, midiope [bidiope].

BOX-ELDER, *n.*, miteatadike.

BOY, *n.*, makadiśtamatse.

BRAID, *n.*, adaiduti. — *v. t.*, dak-tsuti.

BRAIN, *n.*, tsuąta.

BRANCH, *n.*, aduśaśa.

BRASS, *n.*, uetsaśidi.

BRAVE, *n.*, maadukiadetsi.

BRAVE, *adj.*, kiadetsi.

BREAD, *n.*, madąhapi, madąliapi-hopi, madąliapitsoki.

BREAK, *v. t.*, adaliolii, daliolii, da-kaliolii, liolii, duliolii, paliolii [na-kaliolii, ruliolii], kiadaliolii, kída-kaliolii, kiduliolii, kidulioliike, dakata [nakata], dupi.

BREAST, *n.*, imąki, a'tsi.

BREECH-CLOTH, *n.*, idiipśaki.

BRETHREN, *n.*, itametsa.

BRIDLE, *n.*, iduti.

BRIGHT, *adj.*, itsitsi, kaditska, ataiśe.

BRIGHTEN, *v.*, itsitsike, kadítskake, kiitsitsike, kikaditskake.

BRING, *v. t.*, akhu, kiakhu, aki-kahe.

BRISTLE, *n.*, hi.

BRITTLE, *adj.*, tapa, tapai.

BROAD, *adj.*, śoki, śaśukl.

BROOK, *n.*, azikaza.

BROOM, *n.*, maśiailia.

BROTH, *n.*, hupa.

CANDLESTICK.

BROTHER, *n.*, iaka (miaka, diaka), itadu (matadu, ditadu), itametsa (matametsa, ditametsa), itsuka (matsuka, ditsuka). — IN-LAW, ida'ti, iśikiśi.

BRUISE, *n.*, odakśąki. — *v. t.*, dak-śąki, kidakśąki.

BUCK, *n.*, tsitatąki kedapi.

BUCKET, *n.*, midąlia.

BUCKSKIN, *n.*, tsítatąki-odálipi, a-tiśia.

BUFFALO, *n.*   *See* BISON.

BUFFALO-BERRY, *n.,* mahiśi. — TREE, mahiśia.

BUFFALO-ROBE, *n.*, dalipi, itaśi, maśi, mite-odalipi [bite-oralipi].

BULKY, *adj.*, titsi.

BULL, *n.*, kedapi.

BULLET, *n.*, adupoadui.

BUNDLE, *n.*, makidakśi. — *v. t.* ki-dakśi.

BURN, *v. t.*, adalia, adakiti, ada-papi.

BURST, *v. i.*, kiduta.

BUTCHER, *n.*, akukitahe, — *v.*, hakątsi, kihakątsi.

BUTTER, *n.*, á'tsimidi-tsáda.

BUTTON, *n.*, ikatipe, imąkikatipe, maikatipe. — *v. t.*, katipe.

BUY, *v. t.*, maihu.

C.

CACHE, *n.*, amaiśi, kohatiiśi.

CACTUS, *n.*, pątskidia, pątskidiaoka.

CAKE, *n*, madáliapi-tsikóa.

CALF, *n.*, daktsidi [naktsidi], mite-idaka, mitekaza.

CALICO, *n.*, akupuzi, maśiiliipuzi.

CAMBRIC, *n.*, maśiiliiliapi.

CAMP, *n.*, ati, adati.

CANDLE, *n.*, midaiamaliati.

CANDLESTICK, *n.*, midaiamaliati-ioki, midaimaliatiioptsati.

CANDY.

CANDY, *n.*, **matsikoa-hatski, matsikoa-puzi.**

CANNON, *n.*, midália-aduhópi-ietia.

CANOE, *n.*, midaduetsa [bidaluetsa].

CAP, *n.*, apoka.

CAPTIVE, *n.*, da'ki.

CAPTURE, *v. t.*, **akikabe, kiakikabe,** dutse, kidutse.

CARESS, *v. t.*, **kidąlipa.**

CARRY, *v. a.*, **ki.**

CART, *n.*, lialiátua-midiíkaki.

CAT, *n.*, puzike, itupa.

CATERPILLAR, *n.*, midakuduti.

CATKIN, *n.*, mašuakaza.

CAVE, *n.*, ama-aduhópi.

CEASE, *v.*, haka'ta, kihaka'take.

CEDAR, *n.*, midahopa.

CEMETERY, *n.*, dokteoduša.

CENTRAL, *adj.*, dumatakoa.

CENTRE, *n.*, dumata ka'ti.

CEREMONY, *n.*, dalipike, paduididi.

CERTAIN, *adj.*, ka'ti, ka'timats.

CHAIR, *n.*, midaiakaki.

CHANGE, *v. t.*, **ihake, kiihake, katika.**

CHANNEL, *n.*, odamu [onawu].

CHAP, *v.*, adapapihe kiadapapike.

CHARM, *n.*, hopa, mahopa.

CHEAP, *adj.*, imaši-kaušta.

CHECK, *v. t.*, kiliaka'take.

CHECKER, *v. t.*, mąkiapeke.

CHECKERED, *adj.*, mąkiape.

CHEEK, *n.*, dodopa.

CHERRY, *n.*, matsu. — TREE, matsua.

CHEW, *v. t.*, daša, duti [ruti].

CHEYENNE INDIANS, *n.*, itašupuzi.

CHICKEN, *n.*, tsitska, mašiitatsakáka-idaka.

CHIEF, *n.*, matseetsi.

CHILD, *n.*, daka, idaka, makadišta.

CHILL, *v. t.*, hapake, kihapake.

CHIMNEY, *n.*, atisi, **aduue.**

CHIN, *n.*, ika.

CHIPPEWAY INDIANS, *n.*, lialiatua.

COMPANION.

CHIRP, *v. i.*, odaki.

CHOKE, *v. t.*, dota dutskiti, **dutąpi.**

CHOP, *v. t.*, daktsąki [naktsąki], dakamitsi, kidaktsąki.

CIRCLE, *n.*, adukakilii.

CIRCULAR, *adj.*, kakilii.

CLAM, *n.*, matoke.

CLAN, *n.*, daki.

CLARIFY, *v. t.*, dehike, kidellike.

CLAW, *n.*, tsakaka itsi.

CLAY, *n.*, ama, uki.

CLEAN, *v. t.*, dušuki, **dutskiši,** hatsu, ilia kidešake.

CLEAR, *adj.*, delii, oliati.

CLIFF, *n.*, ama daliąpeši.

CLIP, *v. t.*, datskiti.

CLOCK, *n.*, midiikikiški ietia.

CLOSE, *v. t.*, mąkipatąki.

CLOSE, *adj.*, atse.

CLOTH, *n.*, mašiilitątsi.

CLOTHE, *v. t.*, **okąta, ituli okąta.**

CLOTHES, *n.*, **ilioiši.**

CLOTHES-PIN, *n.*, maidutskąpi, maituliñ-dutskąpi.

CLOUD, *n.*, apalii, apalii-adušipiša.

CLOYED, *adj.*, liapąti, liapatikša.

CLUB, *n.*, midakaza-títsi.

COAL, *n.*, amaadalia.

COAT, *n.*, itulii, matsé-itulii.

COB, *n.*, hupa, kóhati-hupa.

COCHINEAL, *n.*, ihišike.

COCK, *n.*, maštiitatsakaka.

COFFEE, *n.*, amazišipiša, maadaha; midišipia [minišipiša], matsikoa.

COHERE, *v. i.*, mąkikaditskapa.

COLD, *adj.*, akhapa, hapa, tsidia.

COMB, *n.*, ikidulioki, maadaikidulioki, maikidulioki. — *v. t.*, dulioki, kidulioki.

COMBAT, *n.*, makimąkia.

COME, *v. i.*, hu, ate.

COMMAND, *v. t.*, iske, ške.

COMPANION, *n.*, idakoe (madakoe, didakoe), iko'pa (mako'pa, diko'pa).

COMPLETE.

COMPLETE, v. t., kikomihe, kikomike.

COMPLETED, part., komi, kowits.

COMRADE, n.   See COMPANION.

CONFINE, n., adudeta, deta. —
v. t., duti.

CONICAL, adj., tsohi, tsuahe.

CONSUME, v. t., kiadaliake, kiada-
kiti, pe.

CONSUMED, part., kiadalia.

CONTAIN, v. t., itski, matu.

CONTEST, v., mąkia, mąkieke.

CONTINUE, v. i., daka, hidakatsa.

CONTRACT, v. t., kikadištake, kikauštake.

CONVERSE, v. t., ikúpa-ide, ma-
kiide.

CONVEX, adj., poaduadsi.

COOK, n., akumadihe, maakuma-
dihe. — v. t., madihe, otihe,
otike.

COOKED, part., oti.

COOL, v. t., kątsihe, tsidiake, etc.

COPPER. n., netsahišiši. ·

COPSE, n., mida-šikía, mida-šípa.

COPY, v. t., kutski.

CORAL-BERRY, n., mašukaakšu.
— BUSH, mašukaákšua.

CORD, n., ašu, matąlipi.

CORN, n., hopati, kohati, madąskihe,
matua. — COB, hupa. — HUSK,
hopatiši. — STALK, kohatia. —
MEAL, kohatipi.

CORPSE, n., dokte [nokte].

CORPULENT, adj., idipi.

COST, n., imaši.

COSTLY, adj., ímaši-ahú.

COTTONWOOD, n., maku, maku-
kazi.

COUGH, v. i., hua, huakša.

COUNT, v. t., kidumi.

COUNTRY, n., ama, itama.

COURT, v. t., akape, mia ákape.

COVER, n., iitipe, iši, maiši.

COW, n., mite, mašiitamite.

DAMAGE.

COWARDLY, adj., kíadetsitats.

COYOTE, n., motsa [lootsa].

CRACK, v. i., duta.

CRACKERS, n., madąliapitsoki.

CRADLE, n., maidakudsi, maikidakudsi, makadistaidakudsi.

CRANE, n., apitsa.

CRAZE, v. t., kimadaliąpake, mada-
liąpake.

CRAZY, adj., madaliąpa.

CREASE, n., aduliakupi, maadulia-
kupi.

CREEK, n., azikaza.

CREEP, v. i., miti.

CREE INDIANS, n., šahe.

CRESCENT, n., midikidahe.

CRIMSON, adj., hišadsi. — DYE-
STUFF, n., ihišadsike.

CROOKED, adj., šikupi.

CROOKEN, v. t., kišakupike, šaku-
pihe, šakupike.

CROP, n., ilii.

CROSS, adj., atska.   — v. t., akąlipi,
tadi.

CROW, n., pedetska.

CROWD, v. t., lialiuake, kilialiuake.

CROW INDIANS, n., kiliatsa.

CRY, v. i., imia.   To CAUSE TO —,
imiake, kiimiake.

CUB, n., idaka.

CUP, n., midiihike.

CUPBOARD, n., matąkiadukiduša.

CURE, v. t., dešake, kidešake, kit-
sąkike, tsąkike.

CURLY, adj., šikia.

CURRANT, n., mitektsatsa.

CUT, v. t., daktsąki, datskiti, idalipi, pamitsi, patsąki, kidaktsąki,
kidatskiti, etc.

D.

DAKOTA INDIANS, n., itabatski.

DAMAGE, v. t., išiake, kiišiake.

DAMP.

DAMP, *adj.*, adatskui.

DANCE, *n.*, makidiši, paduididi. — *v. i.*, kidiši.

DARK, *adj.*, ha'peša, šipišadsi.

DARKEN, *v. t.*, ha'pešeke, kiha'pe-seke, aduoktsihe, šipišadsihe.

DARKENING, *part*, ha'pešadui, ki-ha'pešadui.

DARKNESS, *n.*, aduoktsi.

DAUB, *v. t.*, ipkiti, opape.

DAUGHTER, *n.*, ika (ka, maka, di-ka).

DAWN, *n.*, ata, atade, kiduha-kute.

DAY, *n.*, mape. BY DAY, mape-du.

DEAD, *adj.*, te, tets.

DEAF, *adj.*, akulii deša.

DEBASE, *v. t.*, kiišiake.

DECEITFUL, *adj.*, mitapakša.

DECEIVE, *v. t.*, mitapa [witapa], mitapadsi.

DECREASE, *v. t.*, kadištake, kau-štake, kikadištake, kikauštake.

DECREASING, *part.*, kadištadui, kauštadui, kikadištadui, kikau-štadui.

DEEP, *adj.*, damu [nawuts].

DEEPEN, *v. t.*, damuke, kidamuke.

DEER, *n.*, tsitašipiša, tsitataki.

DEGENERATING, *part.*, išiadui, kii-šiadui.

DEITY, *n.*, itakatetaš, itsikamahi-diš.

DELIRIOUS, *adj.*, madaliapa.

DENUDE, *v. t.*, adaliape.

DEPOSIT, *v. t.*, duše, kiduša.

DERIDE, *v. t.*, uati.

DESCEND, *v. i.*, miktata de.

DESERT, *n.*, amaišia.

DESTROY, *v. t.*, kidešake, kitahe.

DETER, *v. t.*, kihaka'take.

DEVOUR, *v. t.*, kiduti [kiruti].

DIE, *v. i.*, te, ta, tehe.

DIFFERENT, *adj.*, iha.

DOWN.

DIRT, *n.*, ama, ilia.

DIRTY, *adj.*, amatsaki, iliatsaki, tsadatsaki, kiamatsaki, kiiliatsa-ki.

DIRTY, *v. t.*, amatsakike, iliatsaki-ke, tsadatsakike, kiamatsakike, *etc.*

DISCOVER, *v. t.*, odapi, kiodapi.

DISEASE, *n.*, ilioade, mailioade.

DISH, *n.*, mataki.

DISHONEST, *adj.*, ašádikša.

DISLIKE, *v. t.*, ikú'pade, iku'padsi, kidéšitats, kiiku'pade.

DISLOCATE, *v. t.*, kipšuti, pšuti.

DISPLEASE, *v. t.*, da'taišiake [na'-taišiake].

DISREGARD, *v. t.*, íkatats.

DISSIPATED, *v. t.*, maduliápakša.

DISTANT, *adj.*, tiša.

DISTEND, *v. t.*, dakapuši, kidaka-puši.

DISTRESS, *v. t.*, kida'taišiake.

DIVIDE, *v. t.* — IN TWO, dopake [nopake]. — IN THREE, damike [nawike]. — IN FOUR, topake, kitopaheke, kitopake. —, *v. i.*, sasa.

DIVERGE, *v. i.*, liami [liawi].

DIVORCE, *v. t.*, haheta, hahetake.

DIZZY, *adj.*, tsahidumidi.

DO, *v.*, ha, he.

DOE, *n.*, tsitataki mika.

DOG, *n.*, mašuka, pedakuduti.

DOG BAND, *n.*, mašuka icke.

DOGWOOD, *n.*, matsuotaka.

DOLL, *n.*, makadištake.

DOLLAR, *n.*, uetsa-duetsa [luetsa].

DOMINOES, *n.*, hidnimakia.

DONE, *part.*, komi [kowi, kowits].

DOOR, *n.*, mide [bide].

DOUBLE, *v. t.*, patskupi.

DOUGH, *n.*, madáliapi-tsa″.

DOVE, *n.*, mádaitakupeic″ki.

DOWN, *adv.*, miktádu [wiktaru], miktakoa [wiktakoa], utikoa.

DOWNWARD.

DOWNWARD, *adv.*, **wiktata** [wikta-ta], utilia.

DOZE, *v. i.*, hamide, hidamide.

DRAG, *v. t.*, **duliade.**

DRAIN, *v. t.*, daliupi, kidaliupi.

DREAM, *v. i.*, mašiade.

DREDGE, *v.*, duto'ti. .

DREGS, *n.*, **pedi.**

DRESS, *n.*, **ilioiši.** — *v. t.*, **okata.**

DRIED, *part.*, kiudsike.

DRINK, *n.*, **oze.** — *v. t.*, hi, midihi.

DROP, *v. i.*, **pati,** kipati. — *v. t.*, patihe, patike, kipatike.

DROWNED, *part.*, tsipak tets. *See* tsipi.

DROWSY, *adj.*, hamicti, **hidamicti.**

DRUM, *n.*, midalia. — **STICK,** midaliadiki.

DRUNK, *adj.*, madaliapa.

DRY, *adj.*, **udsi.** — *v. i.*, **udsike, kiudsike.** — ING, *part.*, **udsadui.**

DUCK, *n.*, miliaka.

DULL, *adj.*, šašuki, šoki. — *v. t.*, kišokike.

DUNG, *n.*, **aduedi, pedi.**

DURING, *adv.*, **du, šedu.** — **THE AUTUMN, matadu.** — **THE COMING AUTUMN, mataduk.** — **THE DAY, mapedu.** — **THE NIGHT,** makudu, oktsiadu. — THE SEASON, kadudu. — **THE SUMMER,** adedu. — **THE WINTER,** madadu.

DUSK, *n.*, **oktsiade.**

DUST, *n.*, **midatsapi.**

DWELL, *v. i.*, amaki, amakadaki.

DYE, *v. t.* — BLACK, sipišake. — BLACKISH, sipišadsike, kisipišadsike. — BLUE, tohike, kitohike. — BLUISH, kitohadsike, kitohišike. — RED, hišike, kihišike. — **YELLOW, tsidike,** kitsidike.

DYE-STUFF, *n.* *See names of different colors.*

DYING, *part.*, **tade, tadets.**

ENCIRCLE.

E.

EAGLE, *n.*, **iplioki,** maišu, tsatsi.

EAR, *n.*, **akulii, apa.** — OF CORN, hopati.

EARLY, *adv.*, itsikakoa, kiduhakutedu.

EARTH, *n.*, **ama.**

EARTHWARD, *adv.*, **amakoa,** amata.

EAST, *n.*, **ušati.** — ERN, *adv.*, ušatikoa. — WARD, ušatilia, ušatita.

EAT, *v. t.*, **duti, kiduti,** pe.

EATER, *n.*, akudúti.

EBB, *v. i.*, kidamoki, **kiduliemi.**

EDGE, *n.*, **aduaptsa,** adudeta, deta.

EGG, *n.*, **tsakakadaka.**

EIGHT, *adj.*, **dopapi** [nopapi].

EIGHTH, *adj.*, **idopapi.**

EIGHTHLY, *adv.*, **idopapidu.**

EIGHTEEN, *adj.*, alipidopa.

EIGHTY, *adj.*, dopapitika.

ELASTIC, *adj.*, dupupi. — GUM, *n.*, idupupi.

ELBOW, *n.*, **išpalii,** (mišpalii, dišpalii).

ELEVEN, *adj.*, alipiduetsa [alipiluetsa].

ELK, *n.*, **madoka** [maroka].

ELM, *n.*, midai.

ELSEWHERE, *adv.*, ihadu, ihakoa.

EMACIATED, *adj.*, liadaliikša.

EMBERS, *n.*, midahapokša.

EMBRACE, *v. t.*, **kidalipa.**

EMBROIDERY, *n.*, adupúdsike, mašiiptse.

EMERGE, *v. i.*, **ate, atehe.**

EMETIC, *n.*, **maikadé.**

EMPTY, *v. t.*, **kidaliupi,** kipaliue.

ENCAMP, *v. i.*, **atihe.**

ENCHANT, *v. t.*, **dušku.**

ENCIRCLE, *v. t.*, **dutskiti, ialialia.**

END.

END, *n.*, ataka, iepu. At END, a-takakoa.

ENEMY, *n.*, maiha.

ENEMY-WOMAN BAND, *n.*, maiha-miaicke.

ENLARGE, *v. t.*, ictiake, kiictiake.

ENOUGH, *adv.*, ahu, komi.

ENRAGE, *v. t.*, kiadeheke.

ENTER, *v. t.*, mididi [bidedi], pi.

ENTIRE, *adj.*, liakaheta.

ENVY, *v. t.*, uá, uakśa, kiná.

EQUAL, *adj.*, makśia, makśiaka, śeka. — NEARLY, makśiade, makśiakadsi. *See* ALIKE.

EQUALIZE, *v. t.*, kimakśeśeke, makśeśeke, makśiakake, *etc.*

ERASE, *v. t.*, adaśuki, duśuki, kiadaśuke.

ERMINE, *n.*, utsitsa.

EVENING, *n.*, oktsiade, o'pa. NEXT —, o'paduk.

EXAMINE, *v. t.*, kikiśki.

EXCAVATE, *v. t.*, ho'pike, kiho'pike.

EXHAUST, *v. t.*, kidaliupi, kikomike.

EXHIBIT, *v. t.*, ‍ atehe, ateheke.

EXPOSE, *v. t.* ‍} kiatehe, kiateheke.

EXTEND, *v. t.*, kidakahe.

EXTERMINATE, *v. t.*, kideśake, etsa kideśake.

EXTERNAL, *adj.*, ataśikoa.

EXTINGUISH, *v. t.*, katsi.

EXTRACT, *v. t.*, daśku, duśka, paśku.

EYE, *n.*, iśta. — LASH, iśtapi. — LID, iśtadalipi. — WASH, iśtaoze. —, WHITE OF, iśtaduiliotaki.

⁕

F.

FACE, *n.*, ite.

FACING, *adv.*, ta. *See* iteakata *and* iteamata.

FAIR, *adj.*, delii, oliati.

FINE.

FALL, *n. See* AUTUMN. — *v. i.*, liue, pati, kipati.

FAN, *n.*, maikidakudi. — *v. t.*, dakudi, kidakudi.

FAR, *adv.*, tiśa, oka tiśa.

FARM, *n.*, adukati. — *v. t.*, amaoze.

FARMER, *n.*, akuamaoze.

FAST, *adj.*, hita, tsoki.

FASTEN, *v. t.*, duti, kitsokike.

FAT, *n.*, śui, tsada. — *adj.*, idipi.

FATHER, *n.*, ate, tatiś.

FATIGUE, *v. t.*, daheka'tike, kidaheka'tike.

FATIGUED, *adj.*, daheka'ti.

EATTEN, *v. t.*, idipike, kiidipike.

FATTENING, *part.*, idipadui, kiidipadui.

FAWN, *n.*, tsitataki idaka.

FEAR, *v. t.*, kie.

FEAST, *n.*, maihadi.

FEATHER, *n.*, hi, tsakakahi. *See* QUILLS.

FEED, *v. t.*, kidutike, madutiku.

FEMALE, *n.*, adumika, mia, mika, mikats.

FEMUR, *n.*, idikihidu.

FEW, *adj.*, kauśta.

FIBROUS TISSUE, *n.*, matsua, matsuapakiśi.

FIELD, *n.*, adukati.

FIERCE, *adj.*, atska, atskakśa.

FIFTEEN, *adj.*, alipikiliu.

FIFTEENTH, *adj.*, ialipikiliu.

FIFTH, *adj.*, ikiliu.

FIFTHLY, *adv.*, ikiliudu.

FIFTY, *adj.*, kiliuapitika.

FIGHT, *n. See* BATTLE. — *v. t.*, kiamakia [kiwakia].

FIGURED, *adj.*, puzi.

FILL, *v. t.*, kimaazike, maazihe, oze.

FIND, *v. t.*, odapi, okipapi.

FINE, *adj.*, tamulii [tawulii], tamuliidi.⁕

FINGER.

FINGER, *n.*, šakiadutsamihe, išąki-adutsamihe. — NAIL, šakiicpu, išąkiicpu. — RING, šakioptsati. LITTLE —, šakikazi. MIDDLE —, šakidumatadu. RING, — šakikazi-utidu.

FINISH, *v. t.*, komihe [kowihe], ki-komihe.

FIRE, *n.*, midaha. — PLACE, aduue.

FIRST, *adj.*, itsika.

FIRSTLY, *adv.*, itsikadu.

FISH, *n.*, mua. — *v. See* ANGLE. — HOOK, maidutskupi, muaiduts-kupi. — LINE, muaidutsi.

FIT, *v. t.*, itski.

FIVE, *num. adj.*, kiliu.

FIX, *v. t.*, kikše. — ER., *n.*, akuki-kše.

FLAG, *n.*, madakapilii.

FLAP, *n.*, odakapilii, etadsiodaka-pilii.

FLAT, *n.*, amatsuka. — *adj.*, tsuka.

FLAY, *v. t.*, daliipi.

FLEE, *v. i.*, kada [kara].

FLEET, *adj.*, hita, hítąts.

FLEETLY, *adv.*, hita, hitaha.

FLESH, *n.*, idukšiti.

FLOAT, *v. t.*, dakapiliike, kidaka-pihike. — *v. i.*, dakapilii, kida-kapilii.

FLOOR, *n.*, midatsuka.

FLOUR, *n.*, kohatitąpa.

FLOWER, *n. and v. i. See* BLOS-SOM.

FLY, *n.*, maapokša, maapuzi.

FLY, *v. i.*, kada, kide, kideakde.

FOAM, *n.*, pulii. TO CAUSE TO —, puliike, kipuliike.

FOG, *n.*, pue.

FOGGY, *adj.*, pue, puekša.

FOLD, *v. t.*, kipamudsi, pamudsi, patskupi, kidutskupi.

FOND, *adj.*, ohi.

FONTANEL, *n.*, ikidutata, maikidu-táta.

FUTURE.

FOOD, *n.*, maduti.

FOOL, *n.*, madulita.

FOOT, *n.*, itsi. — PRINT, itsiti.

FOREHEAD, *n.*, ilii.

FORENOON, *n.*, midimapedupahide.

FOREST, *n.*, mida.

FORGET, *v. t.*, kidaliiše.

FORK, *n.*, adušaša, aziicpušaša, maipatsati, mika'idutsi, maipa-kade.

FORKED, *adj.*, šaša.

FORMERLY, *adv.*, itsikadu.

FORT, *n.*, akumakikua ati.

FORTY, *adj.*, topapitika.

FORWARD, *adj.*, *adv.*, itelia, itekoa.

FOUR, *num. adj.*, topa.

FOURTH, *num. adj.*, itopa.

FOURTEEN, *num. adj.*, alipitopa.

FOX, *n.*, ilioka. — BAND, *n.*, ilioka-icke. — CUB, iliokadaka. — TRAP, iliokaitipe.

FRAGILE, *adj.*, pidalipa, tapati.

FRAGRANT, *adj.*, iditsitsąki. — GRASS, matsuątsa.

FRECKLED, *adj.*, pulii.

FRENCHMAN, *n.*, maši, maši-ka'li.

FRESH, *adj.*, tsa.

FRIEND, *n., See* COMRADE.

FRILL, *v. t.*, pidieke, kipidieke.

FRILLED, *adj.*, pidie.

FRINGED, *adj.*, dąliami.

FROG, *n.*, šaaka, šaka.

FRUIT, *n.*, makata, matsu.

FRY, *v. t.*, miditi.

FRYING-PAN, *n.*, maimiditi, idukši-tiomiditi.

FULL, *adj.*, maazi, kimaazi.

FUR, *n.*, aduhi, hi, i.

FURROW, *n.*, aduliakupi. — *v. t.*, liakupihe, kiliakupike.

FURROWED, *adj.*, liakupi.

FURTHER, *adv.*, itaokadu, okadu, okakoa.

FUTURE. *See* duk, itakuahiduk, tieduk.

GAIT.

G.

GAIT, *n.*, odidi.
GANDER, *n.*, mida-kédapi.
GARLIC, *n.*, mika'uti.
GARMENT, *n*, itulli.
GARNISH, *v. t.*, iptsi.
GAR-PIKE, *n.*, muapahatski.
GARRULOUS, *adj.*, idekša.
GATHER, *v. t.*, hake.
GARTER, *n.*, idikedikša, maidike-dikša.
GAZE, *v. i.*, ika ka'ti.
GET, *v. t.*, dutsi.
GHOST, *n.*, dokidalii [uokidalii], idalii.
GIANT, *n.*, akuhatski.
GIRDLE, *n.*, maipašaki. — *v.*, kipašaki, pašaki.
GIRL, *n.*, makadištamia, miakaza.
GIVE, *v. t.*, ku, muk. — BACK, kiku.
GLAD, *adj.*, da'tatsaki. — *v. t.*, kida'tatsakike.
GLASS, *n.*, maikika.
GLEAM, *v. i.*, itsitsi. — TO CAUSE TO, *v. t.*, itsitsike, kiitsitsike.
GLISTEN, *v. i.*, kaditska.
GLOBULAR, *adj.*, poaduadsi, poadui.
GLOOMY, *adj.*, apalitatsi.
GLOVE, *n.*, huki.
GLUE, *n.*, maikaditškapa. — *v.*, kikaditskapake.
GLUTTON, *n.*, akudútikša.
GO, *v.*, dakoa, de, koe, kada. — OUT, atadi, kiatadi.
GOITRE, *n.*, dotictia [lotictia].
GOLD, *n.*, uetsa, uetsaka'ti.
GONE, *part.*, dets.
GOOD, *adj.*, tsaki, tsakicti, tsakits [sakits].
GOODISH, *adj.*, tsakadsi.
15

HALT.

GOOSE, *n.*, mida. — BAND, mida-icke.
GOSLING, mídaidaka.
GRANDCHILD, *n.*, itamapiša (mata-mapiša, dítamapiša).
GRANDFATHER, *n.*, adutaka.
GRANDMOTHER, *n.*, iku.
GRAPE, *n.*, mašipiša. — VINE, ma-šipišaa.
GRASP, *n.*, adalielii.
GRASS, *n.*, mika' [bika'], matsuatsa.
GRATIS, *adv.*, išatsa.
GRAVE, *n.*, dokteoduša amakoa.
GRAVEL, *n.*, mi'kaza.
GRAY, *adj.*, liota. — ISH, liotiša. — BLANKET, *n.*, tšeša-maši. — HORSE, aku-hotaiše.
GREASE, *n.*, tsuda. — *v.*, kitsa-datsakike.
GREASY, *adj.*, tsadatsaki.
GREEN, *adj.*, mika'tohiša.
GRIND, *v. t.*, pa, pi, kipa.
GROOVE, *n.*, aduliakupi.
GROUND, *n.*, ama.
GROUSE, *n.*, tsitska [sitska].
GROW, *v. i.*, apadi. — *v. t.*, apadike, kiapadike, okipadi.
GROWN, *part.*, apadike.
GULLY, *n.*, amadaktsaki.
GUM, *n.*, mašika, oduškaškapka.
GUN, *n.*, midulia [bidulia]. — POWDER, midatsapi [bidatsapi].
GYPSUM, *n.*, madolia.

H.

HACK, *v. t.*, dakaptsi.
HAIL, *n.*, ma'kalipitami.
HAIR, *n.*, ada, hi, i. — OIL, atui-tsati.
HALF, *n., adj.*, itatsu, itatsuhe, tsu, tsuta.
HALT, *v. i.*, haka'ti. — *imper.*, liaka'ta. — *v. t.*, kiliaka'tike.

HALVE.

HALVE, *v. i.*, kidopake, tsutahe.
HAMMER, *n.*, **makidiki.**
HAND, *n.*, iṣaki, śaki.
HANDKERCHIEF, *n.*, plietaiśi.
HANDLE, *n.*, hupa.
HANG, *v. t.*, ikoki, kiikoki.
HAPPY, *adj.*, da'ta-tṣaki.
HARD, *adj.*, tsatsuki, tsoki.
HARDEN, *v. t.*, tsatsukihe, tsatsu-
    kike, tsokike, kitsokike.
HARDENING, *part.*, tsokadui, kitso-
    kadui.
HARE, *n.*, itaki, itaksipiśa.
HAS, *v.*, matu.
HASTEN, *v. i.*, śidiśi. — *v. t.*, śidiśi-
    ke, kiśidiśike.
HAT, *n.*, apoka.
HATCHET, *n.*, **maiptsadaka.**
HATE, *v. t.*, iku'pa.
HAW, *n.*, mamua [mabua]. — TREE,
    mamuaa.
HAY, *n.*, mika'udsi.
HE, *pron.*, i, śe.
HEAD, *n.*, atu. — ACHE, atuade.
    — DRESS, apoka.
HEAL, *v. t.*, kitsakike.
HEAR, *v. t.*, kikua.
HEART, *n.*, da'ta [na'ta].
HEAT, *n.*, maade, tsamak. — *v. t.*,
    tsamehe [tsawehe], kitsameke,
    etc.
HEAVENS, *n.*, apalii.
HEAVY, *adj.*, daktsia [naktsiats].
HEIGHTEN, *v. t.*, makuke, kima-
    kuke.
HER, *pron.*, i, ita. HERS, itamae.
HERON, *n.*, apitsatohi.
HICCOUGH, *v. i.*, hatsakeki.
HIDE, *v. t.*, alioa, ialioe. — *n.*, oda-
    lipi.
HIGH, *adj.*, maku.
HILL, *n.*, amadia, amadeta, ama-
    maku.
HIM, *pron.*, i. — SELF, icki.
HIS, *pron.*, ita, ita-mae.

INCLOSE.

HIT, *v. t.*, diki; aate, kiaate.
HOE, *n.*, amae. — OF BONE, hidúa-
    mae. — OF IRON, úetsa-amae.
HOG, *n.*, maśiitadalipitsi.
HOLD, *v. t.*, adalielii, akśi, kiakśie,
    optsati, oki.
HOLE, *n.*, aduhopi, maaduhopi.
HOLLOW, *adj.*, hopi, ho'pits.
HOMINY, *n.*, makipa.
HORN, *n.*, azi, aziliami.
HORSE, *n.*, itsuaśuka, itaśuka.
HOT, *adj.*, tsame [tsawets], tsame-
    kśa.
HOUSE, *n.*, ati.
HOW, *adv.*, tośe. — LONG AGO,
    tuakiśedu. — LONG HENCE, tua-
    kaduk. — MANY, tuami. —
    MUCH, tuaka.
HOWL, *v. i.*, muadaki.
HUM, *v. i.*, hoike.
HUNDRED, *adj.*, pitikietia.
HUNGRY, *adj.*, adiiti.
HUNT, *v. t.*, kidi, kikidi.
HURRY, *v. i.*, śidiśi.
HURT, *v.*, dataki.
HUSBAND, *n.*, kida, kidaś.
HUSK, *n.*, hopatiiśi, maiśi.

I.

I, *pron.*, ma, mi [wa, ba, wi, bi].
ICE, *n.*, madulii.
ICICLE, *n.*, madulii-icpu.
IGNORANT, *adj.*, *v. i.*, adaliiśe.
ILLUMINATE, *v. t.*, kiamaliatike.
IMITATE, *v. t.*, kutski, ikutski.
IMITATOR, *n.*, maikutskiśa.
IMPORTUNE, *v. t.*, kadikśa, kikadi.
IMPOVERISH, *v. t.*, kiadiaśadsike.
IMPROVE, *v. t.*, kitsakike, tsakike.
IN, *prep.*, amahoka, ka.
INCISE, *v. t.*, idalipi.
INCISION, *n.*, aduidalipi.
INCLOSE, *v. t.*, kiamahókake.

INCREASE.

INCREASE, v. t., kiahuke, kiictiake.
INDENT, v. t., datapi [latapi].
INDIAN, n., amakadolipaka [ama-kanolipaka].
INFERIOR, adj., išia itaokadu.
INFIRM, adj., itsiitats.
INFLATE, v. t., dakapušike [naka-pušike], kidakapušike. — ED, dakapuše.
INGENIOUS, adj., kiadetsi.
INHALE, v. t., hi.
INK, n., amašipiša.
INSECT, n., mapokša.
INSIDE, n., amaho. — adj., ama-hoka.
INTERSECT, v. t., dumatitski.
INTOXICATE, v. t., maduliapake.
INVITE, v. t., kikuha.
IRON, n., uetsa, uetsašipiša.
IT, pron., i, še.
ITCHY, adj., liaka, liidia. — TO MAKE, v. t., liakake, kiliakake, kiliidiake.
ITSELF, pron., icki.

J.

JAR, v. t., opšaša.
JEALOUS, adj., idikoamatu, miali-tekša [wialitekša].
JEWEL, n., apokša.
JINGLE, v. i., tsimua. — v. t., kit-simuake.
JOG, v. t., dapšuti [napšuti].
JOINT, n., adušuka.
JOURNEY, n., didi.
JUICE, n., adumidi.

K.

KEEP, v. t., e. I WILL —, mé-wits.
KETTLE, n., midalia.

LATELY.

KEY, n., midéiduška, midiópeidu-ška.
KICK, v. t., adaliape, adape, kiada-liape.
KIDNEY, n., alioka.
KILL, v. t., ta, tahe, kitahe.
KIND, n., aku. WHAT —? aku-to?
KINDLE, v. t., kadalia.
KINDRED, n., itadolipaka.
KISS, n., ikidatsope, maikidatso-pe. — v. t., ikidatsope, kidatso-pe.
KITCHEN., n., akumadiheati.
KITTEN, n., puzikedaka.
KNEAD, v. t., dutsuki, kidutsuki.
KNEE, n., liualia, iliualia.
KNIFE, n., maetsi [baetsi].
KNIFE-CASE, n., maetsiiši.
KNOCK, v. t., daktsuti.
KNOW, v. t., eke. See ¶ 198.
KNUCKLE, n., šakadušuki.

L.

LACERATE, v. t., adakape, dukapi, kiadakape.
LADLE, n., azi, azidelie.
LAKE, n., midiictia.
LAME, adj., odidi išia.
LAND, n., ama.
LAND-SLIDE, n., amadéta-tsipíti, áma-tsipíti.
LANGUAGE, n., aduide, ide.
LAP, n., išuti.
LARDER, n., madúti-adukidušá.
LARGE, adj., ictia,
LARIAT, n., iduti, matalipi.
LARK, n., imakšidi [iwakšidi].
LAST, adj., ipita, ipitadu. — FALL, n., matášedu. — NIGHT, oktsi-šedu. — SUMMER, adešedu. — WINTER, madašedu.
LATELY, adv., tata, tatakoa.

LATHER.

LATHER, *n.* *See* FOAM.

LAUGH, *v. i.*, ka', ka'kša.

LAY, *v. t.*, duša, edede, liapihe.

LAZY, *adj.*, da'taliepi [na'taliepi].

LEAF, *n.*, midaapa, midápa [bidapa].

LEAK, *v. i.*, datskati [latskati].

LEAN, *adj.*, liadalii. — *v. i.*, ikalie, ipataki.

LEFT, *adj.*, idakiša. — SIDE, *n.*, aduidakiša.

LEFT-HANDED PERSON, *n.*, maadu idakiša.

LEG, *n.*, idiki. FORE-LEG, ada.

LEGEND, *n.*, mazi.

LEGGINGS, *n.*, itadsi.

LENGTHEN, *v. t.*, hatskike, kihatskike, kimakuke. — ING, *part.*, hatskadui, kihatskadui.

LESS, *adv.*, itadotadu.

LEVEL, *adj.*, tsuka.

LIAR, *n.*, akumítapakša.

LIBERATE, *v. t.*, kabe.

LICK, *v. t.*, datšipi [latsipi].

LID, *n.*, iitipe.

LIE, *v. i.*, *See* DECEIVE. — DOWN, liapi.

LIFT, *v. t.*, duhi.

LIGHT, *n.*, amaliati. — *adj.*, dakuliti, pidalipa.

LIGHTEN, *v. t.*, dakulitike [nakuhtike], kidakulitike.

LIGHTNING, *n.*, kadicka [karicka].

LIGNITE, *n.*, amaadalia.

LIKE, *v. t.*, ite, kideta, kidešadsi.

LIKE, *adj.*, *adv.*, kuiša, kuišadsi, kupi, inakšeše, šese. To MAKE —, *v. t.*, kimakšešeke, kuišake, *etc.*

LIP, *n.*, aputi, ideta.

LIQUEFY, *v. t.*, midike, kimidike.

LIQUID, *adj.*, miditsi [biditsi].

LIQUOR AMNII, *n.*, dakaadumidi.

LITTLE, *adj.*, kadišta [karišta], kadištadi, kaušta, kauštaalipi.

MARRY.

LIVER, *n.*, apiša.

LO, *int.*, ika, ikaka.

LOCK, *n.*, mataliiši. — *v. t.*, kitsokike.

LODGE, *n.*, amate', ati, atitsunhe.

LONESOME, *adj.*, liemi [liewi], liemikša.

LONG, *adj.*, hatski. — AGO, itsikakoa, mate, matekoa. — TIME, tia, tie.

LOOK, *v. t.*, ika. — BEHIND, ikipamidi. — THROUGH, aktseša, kiaktsiša.

LOOKING-GLASS, *n.*, maikika.

LOOSEN, *v. t.*, datsipi [latsipi], dušipi.

LOSE, *v. t.*, liapihe, liapihekša.

LOST, *part.*, liapi, liapits.

LOVE, *v. t.*, kideši, kideta, ohi, ite.

LOW, *adj.*, padopi, padopidi.

LUKEWARM, *adj.*, šakapi.

LUNGS, *n.*, dalio [ualio].

LYNX, *n.*, itupa, itupapuzi.

M.

MAGIC, *n.* *See* MYSTERY.

MAGPIE, *n.*, icpe.

MAIDEN, *n.*, adukidadeša.

MAIZE, *n.*, kohati.

MAKE, *v. t.*, he, hidi, kikša.

MAKER, *n.*, akuhidi.

MALE, *adj.*, adumatsé, adukedapi.

MALLET, *n.*, maupaki, mi'maupaki.

MAMMARY GLAND, *n.*, a'tsi, antsi.

MAN, *n.*, matse, itaka, šikaka.

MANDAN INDIANS, *n.*, adalipakoa.

MANKIND, *n.*, dolipaka [nolipaka].

MANY, *adj.*, ahu.

MARE, *n.*, mika, mikats.

MARRY, *v. t.*, uahe, uaheke, kidahe.

MARSH.

MARSH, *n.*, maha.

MASSACRE, *n.*, ditsi [nitsi].

MATCH, *n.*, midahaidukapi.

MATTRESS, *n.*, uakitatsi.

ME, *pron.*, mi [bi, wi].

MEAL, *n.* *See* FEAST. CORN-MEAL, holiatipi.

MEASURE, *n.*, maikikiski, maikut-ski. — *v. t.*, kikiski, kutski.

MEAT, *n.*, iduka [iruka], iduksiti, mahakakiski.

MEDICINE, *n.*, hopadi.

MEET, *v. t.*, itsauzie, uzia.

MELANCHOLY, *adj.*, liemiksa [hewiksa].

MELT, *v. t.*, kimidike, midike.

MEND, *v. t.*, kiksa, kitsakike.

MENDER, *n.*, akukikse.

METAL, *n.*, netsa.

METEOR, *n.*, icka-pati.

MIDDLE, *n.*, dumata. — *adj., adv.*, dumatadu. TOWARD THE —, dumatakoa, dumatalia, dumatata.

MILK, *n.*, a'tsimidi [a'tsibidi]. — *v. t.*, dutskipi.

MIMIC, *n.*, maikutskiksa.

MINCE, *v. t.*, dakamitsi, kidakamitsi, kipamitsi, pamitsi.

MINE, *n.*, odutsi. — *pron.*, matamae.

MINK, *n.*, daktsua [naktsua].

MINNECONJOU INDIANS, *n.*, midikaoze.

MINT, *n.*, hisua.

MINUTE, *adj.*, tamulii [tawulii], tamuliidi.

MISS, *v. t.*, akitsa, kiakitsa.

MITTEN, *n.*, liuti.

MOCCASIN, *n.*, hupa, itapa.

MODEL, *n.*, ikutski, maikutski.

MOIST, *adj.*, adatskui, adatskuide.

MOLASSES, *n.*, matsikóa-akutídue.

MONEY, *n.*, netsa.

MOON, *n.*, midi [bidi], makumidi, óktsimidi. — FULL, midikakilii.

NECK.

— GIBBOUS, midikakiliide. — HALF, midiitatsu. *See* CRESCENT.

MOOSE, *n.*, ápätapá (*soft-nose.*)

MOP, *n.*, midatsuka idusuki.

MORNING, *n.*, ata, kiduhakute.

MORROW, *n.*, ataduk.

MORTAR, *n.*, maepe, mepi.

MOSQUITO, *n.*, apaka.

MOTHER, *n.*, hidu, hu, huś, ikaś.

MOUNTAIN, *n.*, amaliami.

MOURN, *v. i.*, imiaksa, kiimia.

MOUSE, *n.*, itahu.

MOUTH, *n.*, i. — OF RIVER, aziuti.

MOW, *v. t.*, itskiti.

MUCH, *adj.*, ahu. So —, hidika.

MUCUS, *n.*, plieta.

MUD, *n.*, tipia.

MUDDY, *a.*, tipiatsaki.

MULE, *n.*, apietia.

MULTIPLY, *v. t.*, ahuke, kiahuke.

MUSLIN, *n.*, masiiliiliapi.

MY, *pron.*, ina, mata.

MYSELF, *pron.*, micki.

MYSTERIOUS, *adj.*, hopa.

MYSTERY, *n.*, hopadi, mahopa.

N.

NAIL, *n.*, uetsa-maietade, iśakicpu, śakiicpu, itsiicpu. — *v. t.*, daktade.

NAME, *n.*, dazi [nazi], odaśa'ti.

NARROW, *adj.*, tsua, tsuadsi. — *v. t.*, kitsuake, tsuake.

NAUSEATE, *v. t.*, kikadéke.

NAUSEATED, *adj.*, kade, kadeti.

NAVEL, *n.*, itadelipa.

NEAR, *adv.*, atsa, dota, utikoa.

NEARER, *adv.*, dotadu [lotaru], ita-dotadu, itadotakoa.

NEARLY, *adv.* (*suffix*), de.

NECK, *n.*, ampa. — LACE, maapi, maaliidulia.

NEEDLE.

NEEDLE, *n.*, matsito, adupątskada-
mi.

NEGRO, *n.*, mašišipiša.

NEST, *n.*, ikiši, tsakakaikiši.

NEW, *adj.*, hida. A — THING, *n.*,
aduhida, maaduhida.

NEXT, *adj.* — SUMMER, *n.*, ade-
duk. — WINTER, madaduk.

NIBBLE, *v. t.*, datskąpi [latskąpi].

NICK, *n.*, adudakąptsi. — *v. t.*,
dakąptsi.

NIGHT, *n.*, maku, oktsi.

NIGHTLY, *adv.*, makudu, oktsiadu.

NINE, *num. adj.*, duetsapi.

NINTH, *num. adj.*, iduetsapi.

NINETEEN, *num. adj.*, alipidnetsa-
pi [alipilnetsapi].

NINETY, *num. adj.*, duetsapiapiti-
ka.

NIPPLE, *n.*, a'tsiicpu.

No, *adv.*, deša [nešąts].

NOON, *n.*, midimapedupahi.

NORTH, *n.*, *adj.*, *adv.*, amašita, ama-
šitakoa.

NORTHERN-LIGHT, *n.*, apaliiadalia.

NOSE, *n.*, apa. — BRIDGE OF, apa-
aduśuka. — ROOT OF, apaheda-
pi. — WING OF, apadaka.

NOSTRIL, *n.;* apaaduhopi.

NOT, *adv.*, ta, tats.

NOTCH, *n.*, *v. See* NICK.

NOTHING, *n.*, deša, maodeša.

NUMB, *adj.*, otsliami.

NUMERAL, *n.*, makidumi.

NUMERALS. *See page* —.

NURSE, *v. i. and t.*, a'tsihi, a'tsi-
hike.

O.

O, *int.*, u.

OAK, *n.*, midakamicka [bidaka-
wicka].

OWN.

OAR, *n.*, ilioki.

OBESE, *adj.*, idipikša.

OBLIQUELY, *adv.*, dumilia.

OBTAIN, *v. t.*, dutse [rutse], dutsi.

OCHRE, *n.*, amatsidi.

ODOR, *n.*, aduiditsi, maaduiditsi,
maiditsi.

ODORATE, *v. t.*, iditsike, kiiditsike.

ODOROUS, *adj.*, iditsi, iditsi matu.

OFFICER, *n.*, akumakikúa-matse-
ótsi.

OIL, *n.*, tsada. — *v. t.*, kiitsatike.

OLD, *adj.*, lie, liie. — MAN, *n.*, itakalie.

ON, *prep.*, *adv.*, aka.

ONCE, *adv.*, iduétsadu.

ONE, *n.*, *adj.*, duetsa [luetsa].

ONION, *n.*, mika'uti [bika'uti].

ONLY, *adv.*, ta, tats.

OPEN, *v. t.*, dušipi, duške, kiduši-
pi.

OPPOSE, *v. t.*, mąkia, kimąkia.

OPPOSITE, *adv.*, kuplieda.

ORANGE-COLORED, *adj.*, tsidadsi.

ORDER, *v. t.*, iske.

ORDURE, *n.*, aduedi, pedi.

ORION, *n.*, ickadami.

ORNAMENT, *v. t.*, kipudsi, kipud-
sike, kipuzike, mamadaki, pudsi,
pudsike.

OTHER, *adj.*, iha, ihats.

OTTER, *n.*, midapóka [bidapoka].

OUR, *pron.*, mata. OURS, matamae.

OURSELVES, *pron.*, midoki [wiro-
ki].

OUT, *adv.*, atazikoa. TO GO —,
v., atadi.

OUTSIDE, *n.*, atazi.

OUTWARD, *adv.*, atazilia.

OVER, *prep.*, *adv.*, akoka, hakoka.

OVERTURN, *v. t.*, kipa'te, pa'te.

OWL, *n.*, hute, itákupe.

OWN, *adj.*, mae, itamae.

PADLOCK.

POKE.

P.

PADLOCK, n., matạliiisa.

PAD-SADDLE, n., matạtsidalioke.

PAIN, v. i., ade. — v. t., adeke, kiadeke.

PAINT, n., **ui.** — v. t., madaki.

PAINTING, n., mamadaki.

PALATE, n., akata.

PALE, adj., iliotaki, oliati.

PALISADE, n., midạkśi.

PAN, n., midạkśi. See **FRYING-PAN.**

PANTALOONS, n., itadsi, maśiitad-si.

PARCH, v. t., adaliake, kiadaliake, kiadapapike.

PARCHED, part., adalia.

PARE, v. t., datskipi [latskipi].

PARFLÉCHE, n., dalipitsoki.

PARFLÉCHE-CASE, n., mạkiiśi.

PART, n., adạlipi, kaustaalipi, maa-dạlipi, tsu, tsuta, tsutaka.

PASS, v. t., itsauzie, mạkiniakada-ha, mạkimakadabatidie, oda.

PASTE, n., maikaditskapa. — v. t., kikaditskapake.

PATH, n., adi [ari].

PAUNCH, n., kilia.

PAWNEE INDIANS, n., tśeśadolipa-ka.

PEA, n., amazi.

PEBBLE, n., mi'kaza.

PEG, n., maictade.

PELICAN, n., apaśaki.

PELT, n., dalipi, odalipi.

PEN, n., úetsa-maíakakạśi.

PENCIL, n., maiakakaśi, **maimada-ki.**

PENDANT, n., maitsimua.

PEOPLE, n., dolipaka.

PERFORATE, v. t., hopike, kiho-pike.

PERFORATED, adj., ho'pi, hopits.

PERFUME, n., aduiditsitsạki, maa-duiditsitsạki.

PERSPIRE, v. i., tsameate (tsawea-**tels.**)

PERSUADE, v. t., kadạtsike (karạ-tsike), kikadatsike.

PESTLE, n., maepaka, mepaka.

PETRIFY, v. t., kinn'ke.

PHLOX, n., pedetskaitaạipiśa.

PHYSICIAN, n., **maśi-hopa,** matse-hopa.

PICK, v. t., kidakapi.

PICTURE, n., mamadaki [mawa-daki.]

PIECE, n., adạlipi.

PILLOW, n., dalikiśi, ódakśisi.

PILLOW-CASE, n., dalikiśisi [naliki-śisi].

PIN, n., matsito-utipoadui.

PINCERS, n., maidutskapi.

PINCH, v. t., datskạpi, dutskạpi.

PINE, n., maatsi, matsi.

PINK, adj., biśi-ámabu-liota.

PIPE, n., ikipi. — STEM, ikipihu-pa.

PITCHFORK, n., mika'idutsi.

PLACE, n., kuadu, śedu (¶ ¶ 47, 50). — v. t., kiamabokake, ki-duśa, patạki.

PLAIN, n., teduti [terútiś].

PLANT, v. t., amaoze. — n., a, maa.

PLATE, n., **matạki.**

PLAY, v. i., mạkia, midaliaticke.

PLAYING-CARDS, n., maimạkieke, maśiitaimạkieke.

PLEIADES, n., ickalialiua.

PLUCK, v. t., dukiti, kidukiti.

PLUM, n., makata. — TREE, **ma-kataa.**

PLUME, n., matslioki, **oki.**

POINT, n., icpu.

POISON-VINE, n., mailiaka.

POKE, v. t., dutati.

POLISH.

POLISH, v. t., kitsatike, tsatike. — n., maikitsatike.

POMME-BLANCHE, n., ahi'.

POOR, adj., adiašadsi, liadalii.

POPGUN, n., miduliake.

POPLAR, n., midahádsi-pakpąkši.

POPLITEAL SPACE, n., idikalia.

PORCUPINE, n., apadi. — QUILLS, apadihi.

POST, n., atutikoaiptsa, aduiptsi, iptsa, iptsi.

POT, n., midąlia [bidalia].

POTATO, n., kakša, maíitakakša.

POUCH, n., iši, opeiši.

POUR, v. t., paliue, katike.

POWDER, n., midątsapi. — HORN, midątsapiiši.

PRAIRIE, n., amaadatsa, teduti.

PRAIRIE-HEN, n., tsitska [sitska].

PREGNANT, adj., edi-ictía.

PRESENTLY, adv., itekoahi, itekoahiduk.

PRESS, v. t., datati, dutąpi, dutskąpi.

PRETTY, adj., ite, tsąki.

PRICE, n., imaši.

PRICKLY, adj., lialia.

PRICKLY PEAR, n., pątskidia.

PROTRUDE, v. t., kiptsuti, ptsuti.

PSORALEA, n., ahi', ahi'mika.

PULL, v. t., dukidi.

PUMA, n., itupaietia.

PUMPKIN, n., kakui-ictía.

PUNCH, v. t., patskąpi.

PUNCTURE, v. t., kipąkade, pakade.

PUPIL, n., išta-adušipiša.

PUP, n., mašuakaza.

PURULENT, adj., itudi.

PUSH, v. t., adakide, pąkide, kiadakide.

Q.

QUADRANGLE, n., adupąlii-topa.

REED.

QUARTER, n., adukitopake. — v. t., kitopaheke, topaheke, topake.

QUENCH, v. t., kątsi.

QUICK, adj., liatatąki, šidiši.

QUICKEN, v. t., šidišike.

QUIET, v., tsąkihamak.

QUILL, n., apadi, apadihi, išu, kamickišu, matslioki, oki.

QUIVER, n., maitaiši.

R.

RABBIT, n., itąki, itąkšipiša.

RACE, v. t., tidieke, mąkiatidieke.

RAIN, n., v., liade, liadets.

RAINBOW, n., midiapoka.

RAISE, v. t., duhi, kidubi.

RAISIN, n., mašipiša.

RAKE, n., maikiduliadi. — v. t., kiduliade.

RANCID, adj., puade.

RAPID, adj., liatatąki.

RAPIDLY, adv., liatatąka, liatatąkaba.

RAT, n., itahuietia.

RATTLE, v. i., liamua [habua]. — v. t., liamuake, kiliamuake.

RATTLESNAKE, n., adutsidiamatu.

RAVEN, n., adiša, pedetska.

RAVINE, n., amadaktsąki, amaaduliakupi, datipi.

RAW, adj., tsa. — HIDE, n. See PARFLÊCHE.

RAZE, v. t., dutsiti [rutsiti], kidutsiti.

RAZOR, n., maídakakiti.

RECEPTACLE, n., ioki, iope iši, maioki, maiope, maiši.

RED, adj., hiši.

REDDISH, adj., hišadsi, hišiši.

REDDEN, v. t., hišike, kihišike.

REDDENING, part., kihišišadui.

REED, n., pupu.

REFLECTION.

REFLECTION, *n.*, idaliilii.

REFUSE, *v. t.*, itsa.

RELATION, *n.*, itadolipaka.

RELEASE, *v. t.*, duśa, duśe, kahe.

REMEMBER, *v. i.*, kądami, kikąda-mi.

REMIND, *v. t.*, kądamike, kikąda-mike.

REPTILE, *n.*, mapokśa.

RESEMBLE, *v. t.*, kike. *See* ALIKE.

RESOLUTE, *adj.*, da'tatsoki (ua'tatsoki).

RETURN, *v. t.*, kiku.

RIB, *n.*, duta.

RIBBON, *n.*, mapidalipa.

RIDDLE, *v. t.*, kiho'pike.

RIDE, *v. t.*, kidie, kidumahitatidie.

RIDICULE, *v. t.*, nati, natikśa.

RIGHT, *n.*, idapa. — *adv.*, idapalia, idapakoa.

RIND, *n.*, aduaka, aduiśi.

RING, *n. See* FINGER-RING. — *v. i.*, tamua.

RIPE, *adj.*, oti. — *v. t.*, kiotike, otibe, otike.

RISE, *v. i.*, ate, iduhi.

RIVER, *n.*, azi. *See* MOUTH *and* SOURCE.

ROAD, *n.*, adi.

ROAST, *v. t.*, hatsite.

ROBE, *n.*, dalipi, itaśi, maśi, miteo-dalipi.

ROCK, *n.*, mi'.

ROCK, *v. t.*, dakudsi, liakahe, kida-kudsi.

ROIL, *v. t.*, midiśake.

ROLL, *v. t.*, dumudsi, pamudsi; ka-·ki; ukaki.

ROOF, *n.*, atidutidu.

ROOT, *n.*, uti.

ROPE, *n.*, aśu, matąlipi.

ROSE, *n.*, mitskapa. — BUSH, mi-tskapaa. — FLOWER, mitska-paodakapąki.

ROTTEN, *adj.*, pua, puats.

SCORCH.

ROUGE, *n.*, iteui.

ROUND, *adj.*, kakilii. — NEARLY, kakiliide. — TO MAKE, *v.*, ka-kiliike, kikakiliike.

ROUSE, *v. t.*, itsihe.

ROW, *v. i.*, lioki (malioki, dalioki).

ROW, *n.* IN A —, daktsike, ki-daktsike.

RUB, *v. t.*, kipąkiśi, kipalitue.

RUFFLE, *n.*, adupidie. — *adj.*, pi-die. — *v. t.*, pidieke, kipidieke.

RUMEN, *n.*, kiliaadupidalipa.

RUN, *v. i.*, tidie, mąkiatidie.

S.

SACRED, *adj.*, hopa, hopáts.

SAD, *adj.*, liemikśa.

SADDLE, *n.*, dalioke.

SAGE, *n.*, iliokatąki, uliimaduti.

SAGE-HEN, *n.*, tsitskaictia.

SALERATUS, *n.*, madąliapiikida kapuśi.

SALT, *n.*, amaliota.

SAND, *n.*, puliaki. — BAR, puliąki-ate.

SAPLING, *n.*, aduokipadi.

SATIATE, *v. t.*,) liąpatike, kiliąpa-

SATISFY, *v. t.*,) tike.

SATIATED, *liąpąti, liąpątikśa*.

SATURATE, *v. t.*, kiadątskuike.

SAW, *n.*, midiíapąti.

SAW, *v. t.*, ide, heduts, heidekime.

SCABBARD, *n.*, midiisiśi.

SCALD, *v. t.*, otihe.

SCALDED, *part.*, oti, otits.

SCAR, *n.*, adueta [erueta].

SCARED, *adj.*, liopąśi.

SCARLET, *adj.*, hiśi, hiśi-ká'ti.

SCENT, *n.*, aduiditsi, aduiditsitsąki, akuiditsitsąki. — *v. t.*, iditsike, iditsitsąkike, kiiditsitsąkike.

SCISSORS, *n.*, maitskiti.

SCORCH, *v. t.*, adapapi, adapapike.

SCRAPE.

SCRAPE, *v. t.*, hatsa, kidakakiti.
SCRATCH, *v. t.*, kae, ke, kike ; adakąpi.
SEAM, *n.*, adukikaki.
SEASON, *n.*, kadu. IN A —, *adv.*, kadudu.
SEAT, *v. t.*, amakike, kiamakike.
SECOND, *adj.*, idopa.
SECONDLY, *adv.*, idopadu.
SEE, *v. t.*, ika (¶ 201), ąktsiśa·.
SEED, *n.*, adutsua.
SEEK, *v. t.*, kidi, kikidi.
SEIZE, *v. t.*, adalielii.
SERVICE-BERRY, *n.*, matsutąpa.
SET, *v. i.*, imalipi.
SEVEN, *adj.*, śapua. — TH, iśapua.
SEVENTEEN, *adj.*, alipiśapua.
SEVENTY, *adj.*, śapuapitika.
SEVER, *v. t.*, adatsąki, dutsąki.
SEW, *v. t.*, kikaki.
SHABBY, *adj.*, kuti.
SHAD-BUSH, *n.*, matsutąpaa.
SHADE, *n.*, dalii, daliilii. — *v.*, aduoktsibe.
SHADOW, *n.*, aduoktsi.
SHAKE, *v. t.*, liakahe; adato'ti, dakato'ti, 'kiadato'ti, kipato'ti, *etc.*
SHALLOW, *adj.*, liepi, liepikśa.
SHAME, *v. t.*, itądike, kiitodike.
SHARP, *adj.*, śptse.
SHAVE, *v. t.*, dakakiti, kidakakiti.
SHAWL, *n.*, maśidąliami.
SHE, *pron.*, i, śe.
SHEAR, *v. t.*, datskiti.
SHELL, *v. t.*, daśie, daliade.
SHEEP, *n.* *See* BIGHORN.
SHIELD, *n.*, midaki.
SHINE, *v. i.*, amaliati, kaditska.
SHIRT, *n.*, matsó-itulii.
SHIVER, *v. i.*, dada.
SHOAL, *n.*, aduliepi, maaduliepi.
SHOE, *n.*, hupa, itapa.
SHOOT, *v.*, di, tadatodi, ualipi.
SHORE, *n.*, midideta.

SLOW.

SHORT, *adj.*, padui, padopi, padopidi.
SHORTEN, *v. t.*, paduike, kipaduike.
SHORTENING, *part.*, padnadui, kipadopadui.
SHOT, *n.*, adupóadni·kadiśta.
SHOULDER, *n.*, idąśpa.
SHOULDER, *v. i.*, idaśpakipe.
SHOVE, *v. t.*, kipkidi, kiptsuti, pakidi.
SHOVEL, *n.*, amaidąliiśe.
SHOW, *v. t.*, atehe, ateheke.
SHUT, *v. t.*, kipatąki, mąkipatąki.
SICK, *adj.*, ilioade.
SIDE, *n.*, adupątska, tsu, tsuta.
SIGH, *v. i.*, idialii, kiidialii.
SILVER, *n.*, uetsailiótaki.
SINEW, *n.*, matsua, matsuapąkisi.
SING, *v. i.*, pahi, kipahi.
SINK, *v. i.*, tsipi. — *v. t.*, tsipike, kitsipike.
SIRIUS, *n.*, iekadehi.
SISTER, *n.*, idu, iku, itakisa, itaku, itamia. — IN-LAW, uaka.
SIT, *v. i.*, amaki, kiamaki.
SIX, *num. adj.*, akama.
SIXTH, iakama.
SIXTEEN, *adj.*, alipiakama.
SIXTY, *adj.*, akamaapitika.
SKATE, *n.*, maidaktsadake. — *v. i.*, daktsadake.
SKEWER, *n.*, maipatsa'ti.
SKIFF, *n.*, midamati.
SKIN, *n.* *See* PELT *and* ROBE.
SKULL, *n.*, atúhidu.
SKUNK, *n.*, lioka.
SKY, *n.*, apalii.
SLED, *n.*, maidutsada, midamaidutsada.
SLEEP, *v. t.*, hami, hamikśa, hidami.
SLEEPY, *adj.*, hamicti, hidamicti, liolioi.
SLIDE, *v. i.*, dutsada, kidutsada.
SLOW, *adj.*, śua.

SLOWLY.

SLOWLY, *adv.*, hopa, šua, šnaha.

SMACK, *v.*, datsope.

SMALL. *See* LITTLE. — POX, maliaka.

SMART, *v. i.*, hašiši, kihašiši.

SMASH, *v. t.*, dakata [nakata], ualipi.

SMELL, *n.*, maaduiditsi, maiditsi. — *v. t.*, mupi. — *v. i.*, iditsi.

SMOKE, *n.*, *v. i.*, pie, piekša. — *v. t.*, opehi.

SMOOTH, *adj.*, tsutsute. — *v. t.*, kipkite, kitsutsutike, pakiti.

SMOOTHING-IRON, *n.*, maikipkiti, maituliikipkiti.

SNAG, *n.*, midaicpati.

SNAIL, *n.*, maišpadumidi.

SNAKE, *n.*, mapokša.

SNAP, *v. i.*, adatalipe.

SNEEZE, *v. i.*, halipi, kihalipi.

SNOW, *n.*, ma'pidetskištapedi. — *v. i.*, ma'pi, ma'pits.

SNOW-BIRD, *n.*, madadaka.

SNUFF, *n.*, maihalipi.

SOAP, *n.*, maitidušuki [maitirušuki.]

SOCKET, *n.*, ioki, maióki.

SOFT, *adj.*, tapa.

SOFTEN, *v. t.*, tapake.

SOIL, *v. t.*, kiawatsakike, kiiliatsakike, kitsadatsakike, *etc.*

SOILED, *adj. See* DIRTY.

SOLDIER, *n.*, akumakikua, masi''-akumakikúa.

SON, *n.*, idiši.

SONG, *n.*, makipahi.

SOON, *adv.*, itekoahiduk.

SORE. *See* SCAR. — *v. i.*, ade, hašiši.

SOUP, *n.*, hupa.

SOUR, *adj.*, adui. — *v. t.*, aduike.

SOURCE, *n.*, aziicpu.

SOUTH, *n.*, *adv.*, umata, umatalia, umatakoa, umatata.

SOW, *v. t.*, amaoze.

STOMACH.

SPAN, *n.*, itakidakahe, šakiitakidakahe.

SPAN, *v. t.*, kidakahe.

SPILL, *v. t.*, adaliu, liu, paliue.

SPIRIT, *n.*, dalii, idalii, dokidalii.

SPIT, *v.*, akšue, kiakšue, sue.

SPOILING, *part.*, išiadui, kiišiadui.

SPONGE, *n.*, midiidaliupi, maimidipike.

SPOOL, *n.*, midaiapi.

SPOON, *n.*, azi, azidelii, azišipiša, aziuetsa.

SPOTTED, *adj.*, puzi.

SPREAD, *v. t.*, dakahe, kidulia.

SPRING, *n.*, maha.

SPRING, *v. i.*, dutsiši, kidutsiši.

SPRINKLE, *v. t.*, duto'ti, kiduto'ti.

SPROUT, *n.*, aduišamike. — *v. i.*, apadi, išamike.

SQUARE, *n.*, adupaliitopa.

SQUAW, *n.*, mia, amakadolipákamia.

SQUEAL, *v. i.*, daki [naki].

SQUEEZE, *v. t.*, datati, datapi, dutskapi, dutskati, kidatati, kidatapi, kidutsati.

SQUINT-EYED, *adj.*, ištaduta.

SQUIRT, *v. t.*, datskati.

STAIN, *v. t. See* SOIL.

STAR, *n.*, icka.

STARVE, *v. t.*, kiadiitike, kiliadaliike, kiliadaliikšake.

STEAL, *v. t.*, ašadi.

STEAM, *v. i.*, pue. — BOAT, matišiša.

STEEP, *adj.*, daliapeši.

STEM, *n.*, aduhúpa, hupa.

STENCH, *n.*, aduiditsiišia.

STERNUM, *n.*, imakidu.

STICK, *n.*, midakuza. — *v. t.*, datsa'ti, kidatsa'ti, kipakade, pakade, patsa'ti. *See* ADHERE.

STING, *v. t.*, hašišike, kihašišike.

STINK, *v. i.*, iditsiišia.

STOMACH, *n.*, kilia.

STONE.

STONE, *n.*, mi', mi'kaza.

STOP, *v.*, baka'ta, liaka'tibe, kilia-ka'tike, opšaša.

STOPPLE, *n.*, iapạti, maiapạti.

STOVE, *n.*, úetsa-aduua.

STORE, *v. t.*, kiduša.

STORE-ROOM, *n.*, adukiduša, ma-adukiduša.

STRAIGHT, *adj.*, tsamutsi [tsawu-tsi].

STRAIGHTEN, *v. t.*, tsamutsike, tsa-mutsibe, kitsamutsike. — ING, *part.*, tsamutsadui.

STRANGLE, *v. t.*, dutskiti.

STRAWBERRY, *n.*, amaalioka.

STRENGTHEN, *v. t.*, itsiike, kiitsi-ike.

STRIKE, *v. t.*, diki.

STRIPE, *v. t.*, lialiike, kilialiike, ki-puzike, puzike.

STRIPED, *adj.*, puzi.

STRONG, *adj.*, itsii, itsiits.

STROUDING, *n.*, akubiši.

STURGEON, *n.*, muapadelii.

SUBORDINATE, *n.*, maiške.

SUCK, *v. t.*, a'tsibi, datsuki.

SUCKLE, *v. t.*, a'tsibike.

SUGAR, *n.*, matsikoa (*fr.* tsikoa).

SULTRY, *adj.*, adekša.

SUMMER, *n.*, ade, maade.

SUN, *n.*, midi [bidi], mapemidi. — RISE, midiate. — SET, midii-malipi.

SUNDAY, *n.*, mapebopa.

SUNFISH, *n.*, muatsuka.

SUPPORT, *v. t.*, ạkšie, kiạkšie, oki.

SURFEIT, *v. t.*, kiliapạtike, kiliapạ-tikšake.

SURROUND, *v. t.*, ialialia, oki, op-tsati.

SURVEY, *v. t.*, ama kikiški.

SWALLOW, *n.*, amašodiša.

SWALLOW, *v. t.*,, kipe, pe.

SWEEP, *v. t.*, mašialia.

SWEET, *adj.*, tsikoa.

TEN.

SWEETEN, *v. t.*, ketsikoake, tsiko-ake.

SWELL, *v. i.*, kipuake, puadui.

SWELL, TO CAUSE TO, *v. t.*, kipu-ake, puake.

SWELLING, *n.*, adupua. — *part.*, kipuadui, puadui.

SWIM, *v. i.*, midididi [bidiniri].

SWING, *n.*, maikidakudsi. — *v. t.*, dakudsi, kidakudsi.

SWOLLEN, *adj.*, pua, puạts, katsuka.

SWORD, *n.*, midiiši.

SYRINGE, *n.*, maidatskati.

T.

TAIL, *n.*, icpe, tsita.

TAINTED, *adj.*, puade.

TAKE, *v. t.*, dutse, kidutse, kuts. — BACK, kudsi. — DOWN, du-lipi, kidulipi.

TALE, *n.*, mazi.

TALK, *n.*, aduide, ide. — *v. i.*, ide.

TALL, *adj.*, hatski, maku.

TALLY, *v. i.*, dakạptsibe [uakaptsi-de].

TANGLED, *adj.*, šikia, šipe.

TAPERING, *adj.*, tsobi, tshuahe.

TASSEL, *n.*, okiicpu.

TASTE, *v. t.*, kikiški.

TATTOO, *v. t.*, pi, kipi.

TATTOOING, *n.*, pi, adupi.

TAWNY, *adj.*, šidi. — TO MAKE, *v. t.*, šidike, kišidike.

TEA, *n.*, midapa [bidapa].

TEAR, *v. t.*, adalieše, dalieše [la-], dulieše, dukạpi, kiadalieše, kidu-lieše, *etc.*

TEARS, *n.*, ištamida.

TEDIOUSLY, *adv.*, bopa.

TELL, *v. t.*, kime.

TEMPLE, *n.*, atibopá.

TEN, *num. adj.*, pitika. TENTH, ipi-tika.

TENTHLY.

TENTHLY, *adv.*, ipitikadu.

TENDON, *n.*, akazi.

TENT, *n.*, atitsuahe, **mašiili ati.**

TEPID, *adj.*, šakapi. — TO MAKE, **šakapike.**

TERRIFIED, *part.*, hopąši, kihopąši.

TERRIFY, *v. t.*, hopąšike, kihopąšike.

THAT, *pron.*, hido, ku, kua, kutsąki, še, šetsąki.

THEE, *pron.*, di [ni].

THEFT, *n.*, maašadi.

THEIRS, *pron.*, itamae. *See* ¶ 122.

THEMSELVES, *pron.*, hidoki.

THEN, *adv.*, šedu [seru].

THERE, *adv.*, hiduka, kuadu, šedu, šekoa. — ARE, *v.*, matu.

THICK, *adj.*, tątsi, titsi, titsikša.

THICKEN, *v. t.*, tątsike, titsike, kitątsike, kititsike.

THICKENING, *part.*, tątsadui, titsadui, kitątsadui, kititsadui.

THICKISH, *adj.*, tątsadsi.

THIN, *adj.*, liapi; liadalii.

THINK, *v. i.* and *t.*, idie.

THIRD, *num. adj.*, idami [inawi].

THIRSTY, *adj.*, udsi.

THIRTY, *num. adj.*, damiapitika.

THIRTEEN, *num. adj.*, alipidami.

THIS, *pron.*, hidi. — MUCH, *adv.*, hidika, hidikats. — PLACE, hidikoa.

THOU, *pron.*, da, di.

THOUSAND, *num. adj.*, pitikietiaakakodi.

THREAD, *n.*, maikikaki.

THREE, *num. adj.*, dami [nawi].

THROAT, *n.*, doti [loti].

THROUGH, *prep.*, *adv.*, dumatadu.

THROW, *v. t.*, iše, kipątike, pątihe.

THUMB, *n.*, šakita.

THUNDER, *n.*, tahu, **tahuidaka.**

THUS, *adv.*, hidiše, kua.

TICK, *n.*, uąkitątsi.

TICKLE, *v. t.*, šašukihe.

TWENTY.

TIE, *v. t.*, dutskiti.

TIRE, *v. t.*, dahika'tike, kidabika'tike.

TIRED, *adj.*, dabeha'ti.

TO, *prep.*, lia, ka.

TOBACCO, *n.*, ope. — BAG, opeiši.

TO-DAY, *n.*, *adv.*, hidi-mape.

TOE, *n.*, itsiadutsamihe.

TOGETHER, *adv.*, apika, ikupa.

TO-MORROW, *n.*, *adv.*, ataduk [ataruk].

TONGUE, *n.*, dezi.

TO-NIGHT, *n.*, hidi-oktsi, makuduk, oktsiaduk.

TOOTH, *n.*, i, iša, hi.

TOP, *n.*, iepu.

TORN, *part.*, daheši, duliéše, pakąpé.

TOSS, *v. t.*, liamike, kiliamike.

TOTEM, *n.*, daki.

TOUGH, *adj.*, kawicka.

TOWARD, *prep.*, lia, ta, dotalia.

TOWEL, *n.*, maikipąkiši. *See* ¶ 44.

TRADE, *v. i. See* BUY.

TRADER, *n.*, akumaihu.

TRAIL, *n.*, adi.

TRAMP, *v. i.*, dakatąlii.

TRAMPLE, *v. t.*, adatąpi, adatehe.

TRANSPARENT, *adj.*, delii.

TRAP, *n.*, itipe, maitipe, maikiku.

TRAVELLING-PARTY, *n.*, dadi.

TREMBLE, *v. i. See* SHIVER.

TRIANGLE, *n.*, adupąliidami.

TRULY, *adv.*, ka'ti.

TRY, *v. t.*, maihe [waihe].

TUBER, *n.*, kakša.

TUCK, *v. t.*, opaša, opašaku.

TUMOR, *n.*, adupua.

TURBID, *adj.*, midiša.

TURN, *v. t.*, dumidi, dumilia, kątake.

TURNIP, *n.*, ahi'.

TURTLE, *n.*, matąlii.

TWELVE, *num. adj.*, alipidopa.

TWENTY, *num. adj.*, dopapitika.

TWICE.

TWICE, adv., dopa, dopatsakoa.

TWILIGHT, n., ha'pešede.

TWINKLE, v. i., kaditska.

TWIN, n., dakadutska [nakalu-].

TWIST, v. t., adamidi, dumidi, kidumidi, pamidi.

TWO, num. adj., dopa [nópats].

U.

UDDER, n., a'tsi.

UGLY, adj., išia, iteišia.

UNCLE, n., ate, itadu.

UNDER, prep., miktakoa [wikta-].

UNDERSTAND, v. t., eke.

UNFOLD, v. t., dakatihe.

UNITE, v. t., kiikupake, kidué-
tsake.

UNTIE, v. t., dašipi, dušipi, dutšipi,
kidutšipi.

UPLAND, n., amaadatsa.

UPON, prep. adv., akoka.

UPRIGHT, n., aduiptši.

UPSET, v. t., adaline, liue.

URSA MAJOR, n., ickašapua.

Us, pron., mido [miro, wido].

V.

VALLEY, n., amaliakupi.

VALUE, n., imaši.

VAPOR, n., pue.

VARNISH, n., maikitsatike.

VENISON, n., tsitataki idukšiti.

VENUS, n., ickaictia.

VERMILION, n., ui, iteui.

VERY, adv., ka'ti.

VEST, n., mapatópe.

VILLAGE, n., ati, ati ahu.

VINE, n., mašipišaa.

VIOLIN, n., mašiitamakipahi.

VIRGINIA CREEPER, n., mahopa-
miaitamatsua.

VISIT, v. t., uzie, kiuzie, midedi.

WHISKEY.

VOMIT, v. i., kade.

VORACIOUS, adj., adiítikša.

W.

WAGON, n., midaikaki.

WAIST, n., hedapi.

WAIT, v. i., haka'ta.

WAKEN, v. t., itsihe.

WALK, v. i., dide.   See GAIT.

WAR, n., makimakía.

WARM, adj., ade, tsame.

WAR-PARTY, n., matsedidi.

WARPING, part., kišakupadui, ša-
kupadui.

WARRIOR, n., akumakikua.

WASH, v. t., dušuki, dutskiši, kidu-
šuke, kidutskisi.

WASHING, n., makidutskiši.

WASP, n., mapatskakiditi.

WATCH, n., midiikikiški [bidi-].

WATER, n., midi.   — v. t., midihike.

WATERY, adj., miditsi.

WAVE, n., mididáhiši [bididáliiši].

WAVE, v. t., pato'ti.

WE, pron., ma, mi, mido, midoki.

WEARILY, adv., hopa.

WEASEL, n., utsitsa.

WED, v. t., uahe.

WEDGE, n., mitsi.

WEEP, v. i., imia, ištamidi pati.

WEIGH, v. t., kikiški.

WEIGHT, n., maikikiški.

WELL, adv., tsakihe.

WEST, n., adj., adv., patsati, patsatikoa.   — WARD, patsatilia.

WET, adj., adatskui.   — v. t., ada-
tskuike, kiadatskuike.

WHAT, pron., tapa, taka, takada, to.

WHEN, adv., tuakaduk, tuakašedu.

WHERE, adv., to, todu [toru], toka.

WHICH, pron., tapa, tape.

WHIP, n., iki.   — v., diki.

WHISKEY, n., midiadui [bidialui].

WHISPER.

WHISPER, v. i., tsitside.

WHISTLE, n., ikozi. — v. kozi.

WHITE, adj., ataki, ihotaki, oliati. — MAN, n., maši.

WHITEN, v. t., iliotakike, kiataki-ke, etc.

WHITE-WASH, n., atiipkiti.

WHITHER, adv., tapata, toka, tokta, tota.

WHO, pron., tape.

WHOLE, adj., liakaheta.

WHOSE, pron., tapeta, tapeita, ta-péitamae.

WHY, adv., toše.

WIDE, adj., šoki.

WIFE, n., itadamia, ua.

WILD, adj., idapudi.

WILLOW, n., maliuliiša, midahadsi.

WIND, n., hutsi.

WINDOW, n., maikika.

WING, n., icpa.

WINK, v. i., istaliulii.

WINTER, n., mada, tsidie. See LAST and NEXT.

WITH, prep., api, apika, ikupa.

WOLF, n., motsa [botsa], tšeša.

WOLF-BERRY, n., mašukaakšu.

WOMAN, n., mia, miakaza.

WOOD, n., mida [bida].

WORK, v., dahe, kikša.

WORM, n., hupaakuikutski, mapo-kša.

WORMWOOD, n., illokataki-akuši-piša.

YOURSELVES.

WORSE, adj., išia-itaókakoa.

WOUND, n., aduu, aduakšaki, oda-kšake. — v. t., u, dakšaki, duka-pi, idalipi, kidakšaki, kidukapi.

WRAP, v. t., pudsike.

WRINKLE, v. t., liipike, kiliipike.

WRINKLED, adj., liipi, liipits.

WRIST, n., ikuti.

WRITE, v. i., akakaši.

WRITING, n., maakakaši.

Y.

YARDSTICK, n., maikutski.

YAWL, n., midamati.

YAWN, v. i., ida.

YE, pron., dido [niro].

YEAR, n., mada. See WINTER.

YEAST, n., maahapiikidakapuši.

YELLOW, adj., tsi, tsidi. — ISH, tsidadsi. — DYE, n., itsidike. — TO MAKE, v., kitsidike, tsidi-ke. — TURNING TO, tsidadui.

YES, adv., e, hao.

YESTERDAY, n., húdišedu.

YONDER, adv., oka.

YOU, pron., da, di [ua, ni].

YOUNG, n., daka, idaka. — MAN, šikaka. — WOMAN, miakaza.

YOUR, pron., di, dita.

YOURS, pron., ditamae [nitawaets].

YOURSELF, pron., dicki.

YOURSELVES, pron., didoki.

THE END.